Not for ESOL Teachers

*What Every Classroom Teacher Needs to Know
About the Linguistically, Culturally, and
Ethnically Diverse Student*

Second Edition

Eileen N. Whelan Ariza

Florida Atlantic University

Allyn & Bacon

Boston   New York   San Francisco
Mexico City   Montreal   Toronto   London   Madrid   Munich   Paris
Hong Kong   Singapore   Tokyo   Cape Town   Sydney

Executive Editor: *Aurora Martínez Ramos*
Editorial Assistant: *Kara Kikel*
Marketing Manager: *Krista Clark*
Production Editor: *Gregory Erb*
Editorial Production Service: *Walsh & Associates, Inc.*
Composition Buyer: *Linda Cox*
Manufacturing Buyer: *Megan Cochran*
Electronic Composition: *Publishers' Design and Production Services, Inc.*
Interior Design: *Publishers' Design and Production Services, Inc.*
Cover Designer: *Linda Knowles*

For Professional Development resources visit www.allynbaconmerrill.com.

Between the time website information is gathered and then published, it is not unusual for some sites to have closed. Also, the transcription of URLs can result in typographical errors. The publisher would appreciate notification where these errors occur so that they may be corrected in subsequent editions.

Library of Congress Cataloging-in-Publication data unavailable at press time.

Printed in the United States of America

17 16 15 14 13   V069   18 17 16 15 14

Allyn & Bacon
is an imprint of

PEARSON

www.pearsonhighered.com

ISBN-10: 0-13-715455-0
ISBN-13: 978-0-13-715455-5

CONTENTS

FOREWORD

As a classroom teacher, your role has expanded dramatically due to the changes in the current school population. Your students are diverse in many ways: racially, ethnically, and educationally. They speak languages other than English, and some, although born in the United States, speak both English and their own native languages poorly. Many of these students have had limited schooling while others are educationally advanced. All of them come to your classroom door in search of a better life in the future and, more immediately, a teacher who will help them to be successful learners.

You are that teacher. You have chosen a profession that can be rewarding and personally satisfying beyond your expectations. But you have also chosen a profession that is enormously challenging and often frustrating. To become the best teacher you can be, you will need to belong to a collegial group of fellow educators who are willing to share knowledge and skill development with each other. You will require continuing professional development and the information essential to the success of your students.

This book is for you—the teacher of a diverse but eager population of students. It contains the essential concepts needed to educate English language learning students. It is the foundation upon which you will build your expertise through years of experimentation, reflection and hard work.

Dr. Ariza has filled this text with the voices of students and teachers who have faced challenges while engaging with learners from other cultures. Their stories will help you develop the cultural empathy needed to be a successful teacher of English language learners. Reflecting on these voices will enable you to become a cultural mediator—a teacher who is knowledgeable about, comfortable with, and sensitive to the needs of the students in the classroom.

As a result of the information in this book, you will understand how children acquire and learn languages. You will expand your notions of how families interact with school. You will rethink the ways in which the entire school community operates to educate all of the children entrusted to its care. You will redesign your content area lessons in light of language needs, cultural attitudes, and student interest. You will look at testing in a new way and learn how to use assessments that inform both you and your students.

This book is based upon the belief that all children can learn at a high level, and Dr. Ariza is clear that the most important element in student learning is the teacher. It is the day-by-day, minute-by-minute decisions that teachers make in their classrooms that affect the rate of student achievement. A weighty responsibility! Because of this, we teachers must do all that we can to become knowledgeable about our students and the many different ways to construct their learning experiences. Here you will find the specific guidance that you and others in your school need to create positive learning environments for English language learners. The children in your classroom will benefit from your continuing reflection and experimentation. You will benefit from the successes that you will achieve as a result.

Linda New Levine, PhD

PREFACE

In my experiences as a teacher of in-service and preservice teachers who need to know how to teach English language learners in the mainstream classroom, I quickly realized several key issues:

1. Most mainstream teachers in the United States have little familiarity with students from other cultures.
2. It is impossible to fathom the difficulty of learning through a foreign language unless one has experienced the process.
3. Teachers have to look beyond their own cultural lens to understand that their perceptions are not the same as those of students from other countries.
4. Teaching through English to native English speakers has no relation to teaching through English to those who are learning English.
5. We cannot compare English language learners with native English speakers, which is what goes on in our classrooms today.

This book has been a work of love for the student who is learning through a foreign language, as well as tremendous affection, respect, and compassion for the mainstream teacher who is not a trained teacher of English to speakers of other languages (TESOL) yet takes all of the responsibility for the achievement of these very special students.

The biggest gift I can give to mainstream teachers who do not speak another language is to share what I have learned throughout my language-learning and teaching career.

What's New in This Edition

Chapter 1, "Voices from the Classroom," contains new references to make the portrait of today's English learners more complete.

Chapter 3, "Cross-Cultural Understanding in Academic Settings," has been revised and combined with the former Chapter 4. A revised explanation of the iceberg metaphor has been added to this chapter, and a section titled "Nonverbal Communication" has been added to present a concise overview of verbal and nonverbal communication issues that may occur when persons of different cultural backgrounds meet in academic and nonacademic settings. The discussion questions and activities have also been revised.

Chapter 5, "What Teachers Need to Know About Language Acquisition," has been heavily revised to highlight the theoretical approaches to second language learning. The chapter points out the theories that made the most impact on classroom practices, such as Cummins's theory of Common Underlying Proficiency. The revision includes expanded explanations of Krashen's hypotheses and their implications for classroom learning, as well as an original example that illustrates Krashen's refutation of the submersion theory.

Chapter 8, "Differentiated Instruction for English Learners," makes a stronger connection to Chapter 5 on stages of second language acquisition. This chapter also presents a visual that breaks down literacy development into stages.

Chapter 11, "Traditional Assessment: Why It Is Inappropriate," makes use of more recent research and publications to describe and critique current standardized assessment practices. A new vignette illustrates ELLs' experiences during standardized testing, examples of convoluted language on ballots have been revised, and more examples of authentic assessments to evaluate ELLs have been included.

A new Chapter 13, "Beyond the Classroom Walls: Suggestions for Noninstructional Staff," offers guidance to school support personnel for fostering meaningful relationships with ELLs. This chapter also offers suggestions for learning about students' home cultures and prior academic experiences, including useful resources, and offers a table that gives school administrators key advice on helping ELLs by (1) learning about their students' backgrounds, (2) strengthening parent communication, (3) evaluating safety and emergency procedures, and (4) utilizing community resources.

Acknowledgments

I dedicate this book to my bilingual and bicultural children, Stefani and Nico, who belong to the world of individuals who balance their lives with each foot in a different culture. Their patience and adventurousness have been notable, as they trekked along beside me to countries where they got to stand on the equator, to inadvertently experience the effects of tear gas as they passed a disruptive crowd, to blow glass in Venice, to bravely taste *hormigas culonas* (fried ants), to experience the true meaning of spelunking in primitive caves, and to lick the salt on the wall of an underground church made from a salt mine. Their pride and acceptance of their eccentric mother is almost palpable. I also have to thank my own mother, Nancy Whelan, for encouraging me to bring home my culturally distinctive friends, no matter where they were from, what religions they were, what languages they spoke, or the color of their skin. She meant it when she said my friends were always welcome, from any diverse group. She also encouraged me to go back to school, even though I took the seventeen-year undergraduate plan. She suggested I continue with a master's degree in Spanish, which I thought was ludicrous at the time. Thanks, Mom.

I am grateful to Renee Zelden and Janice Zelden, who were a tremendous editorial help for the first edition, and to my dear assistant and colleague Elena Webb, whose editorial and organizational skills are phenomenal. My gratitude also goes to the wonderful colleagues, inservice and preservice teachers Diana Pett, Susanne Lapp, Sally Robison, Diane Talley-Strike, Wilma Diaz, Jini Heller, Diane Chursenoff, Susan Hobson, Dian Holland, Cheryl Quinn, Jennifer Peffer, Honey Smith, Sheila Santiague, Claude Gabriel, Rose Ethel Saint-Claire, and Joey Bautista, who shared their insight, talents, expertise, and personal experiences in teaching students from diverse cultures. I would also like to thank the reviewers who offered helpful feedback during the writing of this edition of this book: Michael Climo, La Mission College; Peggy Laughlin, University of Wyoming, Casper College Center; Clarissa West-White, Florida Agricultural and Mechanical University.

The ideas in this book are based on our personal and anecdotal experiences, as well as from research in the field. I must continually advise the reader not to make the mistake of stereotyping individuals of the portrayed ethnic groups. Individual differences exist within all cultures. I also must apologize to anyone who is offended by my experiences and opinions. I beg of you to keep an open mind. All of the scenarios are true.

Eileen N. Whelan Ariza, EdD
Professor of TESOL
Florida Atlantic University

NOTE: Diana Pett, English as a second language teacher (K–12), Ilion Central School District, Ilion, New York, contributed to Chapter 13 and would like to dedicate it to Jean L. Smith, the longtime and much loved retiring secretary of Ilion Central School's Remington Elementary School, Ilion, New York. Her knowledge of the school, the district, the community, and—most of all—of the students made her a fount of incredible information. Her attentiveness and care for all students allowed Diana to more effectively deal with the changing needs of the English language learners. Thank you, Jean!

Dian Holland, an experienced teacher who is participating in an ESOL professional development course, writes in her journal:

I'm writing this with a mixture of embarrassment and excitement. As a teacher stumbling through lessons with my ESOL kids, I'm beginning to get a sense that they may not think that I'm too bright. So many times I've been guilty of underestimating their intelligence and speaking to them as though they belonged in kindergarten. I feel sorry for these poor kids who have so far been subjected to my patronizing questions. Thank God teacher education is preparing beginning teachers to teach ESOL kids.

I have always been under the assumption that if a kid is ESOL, there is no way I can use a higher level of questioning. So I've subjected my kids to lower level questions and have ALWAYS been so grateful when they answered correctly! After all, I MUST surely be an effective teacher if my ESOL charges can answer accurately. How wrong and misguided I've been! I feel so foolish.

Coming out of the dark . . .

Many excellent books are written for teachers of ESOL (English for speakers of other languages), language teachers, linguists, and so forth. This book, however, is written for classroom teachers who have English learners in their classrooms. As opposed to bilingual education, where the students receive instruction in their native languages, **ESOL** is teaching English to students who are not native English speakers. The popular acronym ESL, for **English as a second language**, is losing popularity because English may be the student's second, third, or fourth language. Therefore, I will refer to English language learners as ELLs.

The classroom teacher who has English language learners in the classroom is expected to teach the same content and curriculum to those students who are not yet proficient in English. Classroom teachers are de facto ESOL teachers because they are teaching English as a new language. K-12 teachers are held responsible for teaching all students, regardless of English language proficiency. Any logical person would agree that it is ludicrous that the teacher should be held accountable for the academic success of a student who does not speak English. Yet every day, in classrooms all over the country, newcomers to English are immersed in mainstream classes, not bilingual classes, and teachers must modify and adapt the school's curriculum with instructional strategies that will promote learning and ensure academic success. This may be called **"Sheltered English"** or SDAIE (specially designed academic instruction in English). How can this be done if the teacher does not speak the student's language? What must teachers do to instruct students who do not speak English? I believe that the teacher must know certain essential details to accomplish this feat. Although this task is comprehensive and extremely complex, it can and must be done. Although I recognize the difficulties encountered in the process of learning English as a new language through content, I believe if a teacher knows basic concepts of teaching this special population, this objective can be achieved. To that end, this book offers the subsequent formula as a foundation or framework to guide K-12 teachers of English language learners. It also serves as a resource for classroom practitioners who need to know just enough for successful teaching of their ELLs in mainstream settings.

Students from other countries may be rich, poor, middle class, well educated, undereducated, literate or illiterate, monolingual, bilingual, or multilingual. There is not one typical profile of the English learner in today's classroom. You can find an American citizen, an immigrant, a refugee, a temporary resident, a migrant worker, a vacationer, or an international student studying abroad. As a result, the mainstream teacher must be prepared for both cultural and instructional situations. Some of the most salient points that teachers should consider are the following:

1. The teacher must understand the culture of the students. Where do they come from? What are their cultural values, their beliefs about life, their family structures, and the role education plays in their overall belief systems?
2. By having a truer idea of what to expect as a result of cultural values, the teacher will be more likely to make accurate cultural distinctions when interpreting behaviors. Instead of perceiving actions through their own "American" cultural

lens, teachers will be more inclined to construe accurate understanding and meaning of behaviors they might ordinarily misinterpret. For example, the student who does not look the teacher in the eye might be seen as rude by the teacher's standards: Yet, if the student is Haitian (or from many other cultures), avoiding eye contact with an adult is the respectful thing to do. However, care must be taken to ensure that stereotypes are not confused with the teacher's own personal experience with students from non-American cultures. The examples depicted in this book are taken from my own years of personal experience in classrooms in the United States and abroad, as well as those experiences of other teachers. Although overarching cultural tendencies might be representative of a culture at large, your classroom experiences might be entirely different. Please keep this thought in mind as you read the scenarios. The reference book called *CultureGrams* (2001), and now newer editions published by Brigham Young University, is an excellent source for teachers to use to learn the basics about the cultural traits of a wide variety of countries. This book has been a great reference source.

3. The teacher must know the students' educational and literacy background, the first and second language(s) spoken, and what language they use in specific environments and circumstances. For example, what language do the students use when they are playing or interacting with family members? Perhaps they speak their native language with the parents and speak English with their siblings.

4. Cultural beliefs will shape the students' classroom behavior and interactions.

5. The teacher must know the basics about how first and second languages are learned. The student will go through stages of language acquisition, and interference from the first language will transfer to the second. This is normal and should be expected. Many factors such as age and personality of the learner will shape the learner's path. Age will affect the student's accent and might confuse the teacher. The younger students may sound like native speakers yet have limited ability to perform academically. Older students may speak with heavily accented English yet be far beyond their English-speaking peers academically. This book is not intended to be the "be-all and end-all" of second language acquisition; however, it gives teachers enough information to decipher the main areas of their students' language difficulties. Teachers do not have to be researchers to understand the basic differences between social and academic language.

6. The final crucial issue is that of valid assessment. How do we know we are assessing content or language proficiency? For example, if you want to evaluate whether a student can perform a word problem in math, you may have him or her read the word problem. If the answer the student gives is incorrect, how do you know if the learner has a problem with the math concept or with reading? This is not a valid assessment of math. The same principle applies to issues of assessment in language proficiency. How do we grade language learners? Are the students being assessed by how well they perform as compared to native speakers? Is it possible for new language learners to get 100 percent on a test if they have many language errors? It is possible if you grade holistically. Teachers must know that language learners will "kill" the language before they dominate it.

These issues are only a few of the concerns teachers have to address when educating language learners. However, it is a good start toward providing teachers with a solid knowledge base of language learning. They will be aware enough to ask: "Is this issue a problem because of language, culture, cognition, or the individual personality?"

After learning about the previously mentioned factors, the educator can begin to teach. The content must be modified for the English learner, and strategies for presenting content must be implemented. This book demonstrates how to accomplish this task.

Finally, with the myriad of diverse ethnic groups present in the United States, I would like to explain why I chose to highlight the sampler of cultures mentioned in this book. All cultures are distinct, yet within a general group, overarching tendencies do exist. We must be vigilant about not stereotyping members of a particular group, while simultaneously recognizing that their cultural values may be easily perceived but may be perplexing to the mainstream teacher. I chose to talk about Spanish speakers because they are the fastest growing minority group in the country. Undoubtedly, at some point in time, teachers will have Spanish speakers in their classes. I chose to write about Haitians and Muslims because I believe they are misunderstood, and I want to share my understanding of their cultural and religious values. Native Americans, as all students, reflect their cultural beliefs in the classroom: Teachers who are aware of these beliefs will be better prepared to teach in ways that are congruous with Native American customs. Asian Americans comprise a multitude of ethnic groups. I have taught students from many Asian cultures, and each ethnic group demonstrates unique qualities. As a teacher, I have experienced fascinating and delightful encounters with all my Asian students, but I notice the focus of information is usually on Japanese and Chinese students. In the past several years, I have noticed a dramatic increase in the number of Koreans in my classes, which might be due to economic reasons. Therefore, I chose to focus a bit more on Koreans and share experiences I have had with this cultural set. Additionally, because believers of **Confucianism** and Buddhism are guided by similar principles of ethics that influence social conduct, this identity is recognizable in all groups who follow these social and ethical philosophies. Last, the Indian population is rapidly increasing, yet we don't hear about Indian students very often. By knowing more about the Indian culture and belief systems, we will feel more comfortable with those global English/multilingual speakers who walk in our midst on a daily basis, yet who may be relative strangers to the mainstream American culture. As always, I encourage readers to expand their horizons by learning about the other, less represented cultural and ethnic groups and by being careful, nonjudgmental observers of their students' cultural identities.

PART ONE

Classrooms of Today

CHAPTER 1

Voices from the Classroom

This chapter highlights the insights shared by several teachers in today's classrooms. They share their observations about their teaching careers, about the challenges they face today, and about the changes they have seen over the years. They note the myriad of cultures reflected in classroom behavior and learning styles. Their students come from a diverse range of educational, literacy, and socioeconomic backgrounds, and all have their own history of educational continuity. Teachers have to reconcile these differences with their personal approach to instruction.

Ms. Allen's Elementary School Teaching Experiences

Ms. Allen taught elementary school for ten years in a small town in Massachusetts. She took a five-year sabbatical to begin her own family, and she eagerly returned to the classroom when her own children started elementary school. She reports:

> I became a teacher because I love children and enjoy the look of excitement I see in their faces when they learn. Over the years, I have seen many changes that challenge teachers, such as the ubiquitous state-mandated standardized tests, the lack of respect for teachers by students as well as their parents, and the overwhelming amount of paperwork with which we are burdened. In any other field, an individual who had this quantity of paperwork would have a secretary. I chose to be a teacher because I had a burning desire to teach, but that is the last thing I get to do. Class sizes have increased, yet I have no paraprofessional assistant. Sometimes I don't even have enough books, desks, or supplies for my students. I am not a special education teacher, but I am responsible for teaching students with exceptional needs, learning disabilities, and emotional and physical handicaps. Some of my students are well prepared before they enter my class, but others have never even held a book. I am expected to treat my students as intellectual and socioeconomic equals; however, I am blamed if my students fail academically.
>
> I question why politicians dictate policies for teachers, when most have never set foot in the classroom. I don't believe these policy makers who make laws about education have any clue about what it is like to be a teacher today. They should be made to take the standardized tests just to see if they can pass.

Carol Chursenoff contributed material for this chapter.

Since returning to the classroom, I am amazed at the influx of students from diverse linguistic, ethnic, and cultural backgrounds. I want to understand them, but many of them are so different from the mainstream children I usually teach. Often they look and sound differently and sometimes they might even smell differently. But the hardest part for me is when they don't speak English at all, and I can't speak their language; or they can sound like they speak perfect English but cannot compete academically with the native English speakers. I am responsible for their instruction, and I worry about the best way to reach them. But how can I teach them when I don't speak their language and we can't even communicate?

Ms. Chursenoff's Fifth-Grade Class

Ms. Chursenoff is a seasoned fifth-grade mainstream teacher in Las Vegas, Nevada, in the Clark County Public Schools. Along with her native-English-speaking students, her class is comprised of many ELLs. She shares her experiences with Hispanic families as they relate to the U.S. educational system.

With regard to interdependence, I've always been pleasantly amused during conference times. My Hispanic students are always accompanied by a parent, frequently both, and also a grandparent or two, who all appear at the student's conference time, along with all siblings! This is very different for me, as my American parents almost never bring children to a parent-teacher conference. I have learned to respond to this situation by making sure I have crayons, paper, and picture books available to keep the little ones busy. The student who is being conferred about frequently is expected to "take care" of the brothers and sisters, particularly if the student is a girl. The family members who have attended these conferences are unfailingly polite to a fault and appear very proud of their children, even when their children's academic performance is suffering.

I have noticed another important clue to effective instruction, which is recognizing how a cooperative learning style culturally complements the Hispanic child. My Hispanic students do not seem to openly want to show what they know for fear of embarrassing those who do not know. For my students, it appears that a Hispanic family does not encourage children to excel over siblings or peers; rather, it is considered bad manners. The teacher of Hispanic ESOL students should become familiar with a variety of cooperative learning strategies (Pajewski & Enriquez, 1996). My experience has always been that most Hispanic students are not competitive with one another and love to "partner up" in completing tasks. They are generally very gracious toward each other and are congenial and well mannered in class.

In the classroom, my Hispanic students demonstrate a distinct pattern of interaction when I am lecturing and posing questions for discussions and comprehension. They are frequently very quiet and look somewhat intimidated at the thought that they might be called upon individually; consequently, they will often freeze and get confused or embarrassed as they try to answer (Pajewski & Enriquez, 1996). One student last year began crying the first time she was asked to come to the board to solve a simple math problem. She was exceptionally bright and motivated, knew the answer, but "fell apart" when singled out for any interaction. Her shyness was painful to watch. Even the gentlest interaction she and I had in private was difficult for her. With respect for her "silent stage" of language acquisition, I did not push her. By the end of the year, she actually performed in a skit for a social studies unit and could almost be heard by the audience!

Based on my experience as classroom teacher, it appears that Hispanic students feel much more comfortable responding in groups and helping each other. Girls may not feel comfortable responding when boys are in the group; therefore, the teacher might not know that the girl really does know the answer. I always try to find out if this is the case, or if it is lack of comprehension.

Through implementing instructional strategies that are congruent with Hispanic cultural traits, such as cooperative learning situations in the classroom, teachers can help students upgrade their social and language skill. By listening, encouraging them to support each other, giving constructive feedback, and checking understanding, teachers can take steps to ensure success. Providing teaching and learning approaches that embrace Hispanic tradition and culture will encourage recent Hispanic immigrants to participate more comfortably, because they can express themselves as a group and not as individuals, thus promoting interdependence yet forcing them to become individually accountable.

Table 1.1 shows an example of the variety of educational backgrounds students bring with them from their home countries. This is an actual representation of the students in Ms. Chursenoff's fifth-grade class. The challenge for the teacher is to address and to successfully instruct this wide variety of individuals.

The school is in a very low socioeconomic area of North Las Vegas and is designated as Title I, "At Risk," by the Clark County School District (CCSD). The desks are arranged in two "E" shapes facing each other. The room is a small portable at the far end of the campus. The classroom size does not lend itself to the arrangement of desks in small groups. The student numbers fluctuate between 24 and 28, unusually low this year; the number also changes frequently as students move in and out of this transient area of Las Vegas. The class is comprised of 70 percent Hispanic, 30 percent African American, and no Caucasian students this year.

Backgrounds of Profiled Students

Karina is a bright and motivated girl who has recently asked to be tested for the gifted program. She has been in the CCSD system since kindergarten. Although her speaking skills are good, she still has below-grade-level grammar and writing skills despite having been in this system for six years. Her reading level is also below fifth grade. She loves school and her teacher, and she always strives to understand academic concepts and to improve her English.

Anahi also loves school, is hard working, and is exceptionally polite and helpful. She began her education in Mexico and entered the CCSD system at the beginning of third grade. Like Karina, she speaks fairly well, but has great inconsistencies in her reading and writing ability. She and Karina, along with several of the other Hispanic

TABLE 1.1 Educational Backgrounds of Students in Ms. Chursenoff's Fifth-Grade Class

Grade	Karina	Anahi	Maria	Jose	Alejandro	Juan
5	CCSD*	CCSD	CCSD (arrived in spring)	CCSD	CCSD	CCSD
4	CCSD	CCSD	none	CCSD	CCSD	CCSD
3	CCSD	CCSD	Mexico (retained in 2nd)	CCSD	CCSD	CCSD
2	CCSD	CCSD	Mexico	Mexico	CCSD	Mexico
1	CCSD	Mexico	Mexico	Mexico	CCSD	Mexico
K	CCSD	Mexico	none	Mexico	CCSD	Mexico

*CCSD denotes Clark County School District.

girls, are good friends and excellent role models in class. This group of girls helps each other with assignments, which helps reinforce the use of English in the classroom, except when occasionally explaining concepts in Spanish.

Maria was enrolled in the class in late spring, but she did not show up for school until several days after I received notification of her matriculation. She arrived with her mother one morning after class had begun. Maria was crying. I immediately called on several of my sweet, Hispanic girls who settled her in between them at their desks. Maria had not been in school for a year (since fourth grade), and her mother explained that her daughter had medical and emotional issues. Maria had been retained in the second grade. The Mexico school system she attended required that students pass a proficiency test before entering the next grade. Clearly, my school inappropriately placed her in my fifth-grade class. My immediate attempts to rectify this situation fell on deaf administrative ears. I referred the problem to our ESOL facilitator, but instinctively I knew Maria would remain in my classroom for the duration of the year.

Jose has been in the CCSD school system for almost three years. He is a good math student but is working at a second-grade level in reading and language arts. He can calculate and perform algorithms successfully; however, because of his poor reading comprehension skills, he fails all story and word problems in math. He is affable and well mannered. He understands more English than he can speak. His attendance record is very poor, and by the end of the school year, he has missed forty-eight days. He simply didn't care to come to school, and even with repeated calls to his mother, it appeared that no home supervision was forthcoming. On the decision of my principal, he was not retained in fifth grade, despite our district's requirement that students not miss more than twenty unexcused absences. Jose was nonchalant when asked why he didn't come to school. He just shrugged his shoulders and smiled.

Alejandro has been in the CCSD system since kindergarten. He is exceptionally bright; when I requested that he be tested for G.A.T.E. (our gifted program), he was accepted. His skills are very good, and he is extremely motivated. He rarely smiles and is always obsessed about completing his work as quickly as possible. He does not take criticism easily, but with cajoling will finally accept positive feedback. Alejandro is still designated by CCSD as a "limited English" speaker and has not been tested in two years, which is the only way to change the label in his cumulative file. Efforts on my part to intervene on his behalf have not worked because the ELL facilitator is extremely backlogged. I'm hoping this problem won't affect Alejandro's placement in middle school or beyond. Alejandro loves to work hard and complains that the work isn't challenging enough. Unfortunately, I have too many students to attend to all of them in the way they should be served.

Juan has been in the school system for three years. He is quite immature in his peer relationships, and his academic performance is poor. He will sit doing nothing, unmotivated, even when an assignment is clear and simple. He actually appears to like school and says that he does, but his actions belie his words. He is not well liked by the other students. His parents are both non-English speaking, and he appears to make little attempt to try to better his understanding of English. He doesn't seem to have a great curiosity about learning or to demonstrate recognition of the need to work on improving English acquisition. I am not sure if it is because he does not care or because he does not know how to go about learning English better.

In looking at these six children, one sees a range of ability and motivation. Although those who have attended CCSD throughout elementary school appear better adjusted, their academic skills are not necessarily reflective of where they should be with regard to literacy. With possibly the exception of Alejandro, Karina and her group of friends, who have been at this same school for a number of years, don't appear to me to be at an appropriate level of English acquisition. They are all below grade level. This is partly due to the problems and programs at this school, as well as the school's changing every year or two how it is attacking the bilingual literacy issue. The girls seem to like school very much, but the two boys, Juan and Jose, are far less motivated. Although this may be a gender-based response, it may also be due to not doing well in school and therefore not wanting to try.

A corollary seems apparent between liking school and the enjoyment of learning English. This may possibly be attributed to human nature; we usually like what we can do well. The Hispanic child in my class is most often below grade level, has been retained one or two times, and frequently "fails" assignments and other academic work. A fifth grader who is reading on a second-grade proficiency level knows it. Jose was a big boy, fairly mature for his age, and already hanging out with his older brother's gang-related friends. Why would he want to come to school?

In addition to all the other issues mentioned, the Clark County School District has now instigated a new and "profound" system whereby any student not working at grade level cannot receive a grade higher than a D. This system, of course, affects my African American students in this low socioeconomic area, as all of them in my classroom last year were unable to do fifth-grade work. When we turn to my Hispanic second language students, with few exceptions, none of them could begin to master the fifth-grade curriculum, let alone pass the state standardized tests. Try and explain to hard-working Anahi that she was receiving all Ds, even though she buried herself in her attempts to complete assignments, because she tested at only a third-grade level in reading. Prior to this mandate, English learners were designated as such in their cumulative folder (CUM) and on report cards so that teachers could grade according to effort. One can only imagine what parents must think when their child comes home with grades below satisfactory. Would they think that Anahi did not even try?

Although attempts are being made on national and state levels to solve issues such as not passing students who don't meet grade-level requirements, the efforts are entirely missing the point and do not address the problems we face in the classroom. Interesting, too, is the fact that teachers have been disregarded as the individuals who have the clearest understanding of what needs to be done to successfully educate students in today's world. Go figure.

Ms. Diaz—A Puerto Rican Teacher and Her Mexican Students

The mainstream teacher, as well as the new student, might feel culture shock, since both are thrust into new cultural scenarios. Wilma Diaz, a Puerto Rican teacher with a class of Mexican students, says that she realized the only way she could help her students to become successful in learning a second language was by learning what she did not know about their culture.

> I began to understand what I had been reading about. . . . how important it was for the students to feel connected with the teacher. But it was just as important for me, as their teacher, to learn about their customs, habits, religious beliefs, values, and even the foods they eat. I also realized that the history of their country plays an important part in who they are as individuals in my class. To learn about the culture of my students, I decided to immerse myself in the study of their culture. I interviewed students in formal and informal settings, and we engaged in class discussion about their culture.
>
> In their journal entries, they wrote about the different aspects that they thought would be of interest to me. We spoke about their favorite holidays and foods. We had group discussions about their culture and how it is different from the American culture. These activities brought class unity and formed a class community. I also shared with them many things about my Puerto Rican culture that

are different from the Mexican culture, which I hold dear to my heart. I learned about their cultures as they learned about mine, which taught us to respect each other's values. I interviewed some of the Mexican volunteers at my school: Ms. Sanchez, an Ameri-Corp worker, and Ms. Ortiz, a PTSA volunteer parent, who were both very helpful in clarifying cultural concepts for me. I researched many articles and books to verify the information I collected from students, school personnel, and parents. I learned about important issues, such as why the students had such difficulty saluting the flag every day. Initially I assumed they were in conflict about saluting the American flag because of their allegiance to the Mexican flag. What a shock to learn that it was due to a religious reason, not political. I had no idea that by saluting the American flag, my Mexican students thought they were praying to something other than the Virgin Mary. Because they were so far away from their homelands, they were trying to maintain their cultural belief and heritage. The more we learned about each other, the closer and more cohesive we became as a united classroom. The impact on me confirmed my aspiration to refrain from judging others through my own cultural lens.

Caveat to Mainstream Teachers

Learning the language of the country is essential for success in the adopted country; it empowers the newcomer and facilitates achievement of goals in life. However, if the children of non-English-speaking parents do not embrace the idea that English is necessary for achievement, no impetus to try to learn the language exists. Wilma Diaz learned that if students believed that the family could be successful without knowledge of the English language, the students assumed they would be successful without English, too. With no motivation on the students' part, it is very difficult to teach them the language. The following examples illuminate the rationale behind her students' resistance to learning English:

- Students believe that if their parents own small companies they too could be business owners without mastering the English language.
- The English language is not necessary for survival.
- Lack of second-language comprehension is not an obstacle to finding a job, nor does it interfere with completion of their tasks as employees.
- Family residency in the United States is temporary. The family plans on returning to the homeland. Students want to return to Mexico and do not see urgency for learning the English language.
- The family fears cultural amalgamation.
- Parents fear young children will lose the native language.

Therefore, acquisition of the second language may not be regarded as a necessity for survival in the United States for these newcomers. This attitude may or may not prove true, however. Generally, not knowing the language of the host country makes it very difficult to advance oneself. The responsibility then falls upon the shoulders of teachers to ensure that both native language and English are supported. In school, modifications to language-learning strategies must be made for these students, while at home, parents should be encouraged to provide a rich first-language experience both verbally and through literacy.

These teachers are not alone in their assessment of today's classroom. In addition to the myriad of administrative duties, the population is ever changing, numbers of students have swelled, funding has been reduced or eliminated, and high-stakes standardized tests have been implemented in many states. One of the toughest obstacles for the mainstream teacher to face is that of teaching students who do not speak English or have limited knowledge of English. According to the National Clearinghouse for English Language Acquisition (NCELA) (2006, as cited in Crawford & Krashen, 2007), about one in ten American students is an ELL, which represents a 65 percent increase of this segment of the student population in the last decade. According to Crawford and Krashen (2007), "If these trends continued at current rates, by 2043 one in three of the nation's students would be ELLs" (p. 13). Monolingual teachers who have limited exposure to cultures outside their own may have difficulties understanding and meeting the needs of these diverse students. Bilingual education is rapidly losing ground, but federal laws such as *Lau v. Nichols* (1974) still mandate that all students have the right to comprehensive instruction and equal access to the curriculum (Crawford, 1999; Crawford & Krashen, 2007). It becomes increasingly apparent that all teachers need to learn effective instructional strategies to successfully teach English language learners, even though the teacher might not speak the students' native language. Today's teachers need help in the classroom without having to get a master's degree in ESOL (English to speakers of other languages). They need immediate answers and basic guidelines to follow for success in our multicultural, multilingual climate.

This book is a roadmap for general K-12 educators who have "nonmainstream" students. Teachers will learn the very least they need to know to teach students from other cultures and will learn to understand what they can expect from non-native English learners (ELLs). By increasing critical knowledge of their own American cultural values, the reader will better understand the different cultural values of their students, especially as they relate to schooling and the classroom. By correctly interpreting the cultural cues and body language of their students, teachers will understand why students of other cultures might behave differently. Raising our cultural consciousness leads us to understand different behaviors and helps us to adapt classroom instruction according to the language acquisition process English language learners undergo. Only after much exposure to the issues and language acquisition process of ELLs will the teacher be able to correctly distinguish learning disabilities from problems in simple language acquisition. Finally, the reader will learn how to implement appropriate and effective strategies that ensure comprehensible instruction and assessment for the student who is not yet academically fluent in English.

DISCUSSION QUESTIONS AND ACTIVITIES

1. Individually or with a group, decide how you would teach ELLs even if you cannot speak other languages. List ten strategies, methods, or approaches you might use.
2. Discuss how the United States should attempt to solve the problem of students who do not meet grade-level requirements due to lack of language proficiency, but are nonetheless passed on to the next grade.
3. Based on what you know so far, discuss what you believe to be the most challenging issues for mainstream teachers who have ELLs in the classroom today.

2

Cultural Diversity in the Mainstream Classroom

Ethnocentricity

This chapter addresses the concept of *ethnocentricity*, which is common to every cultural group. We usually base our perceptions on our own cultural perspectives; thus, we judge others according to what is familiar. This applies to cultural beliefs as well as "foreign accents." Many people may not have much experience with other cultures or foreign languages; as a result, miscommunication occurs both inside and outside the classroom. This perspective stays with us wherever we go; therefore, when we go outside of our country we tend to interpret what we see through our own comfortable, cultural lenses.

Luis, from Brazil, a high school student who is going to school in the United States, works part-time as a troubleshooter for a large telecommunications company. His job includes working with small businesses and unhappy people who call him when their telephone lines are malfunctioning. He has to defuse the potentially volatile situation, track down errors, and get the lines up and running as soon as possible. One very busy day, Luis answered the phone, "Luis Rocha, Small Business Repair. May I help you?" The man on the other end of the phone barked at him, "Get me someone who speaks English. I don't want to deal with any outsider!" Luiz answered him politely, "But sir, I am speaking English. I just have a Portuguese accent."

Many Americans believe that the United States is the best country in the world. People from other countries may feel the same about their homelands as well. This type of thinking is called **ethnocentrism**, and it colors our outlook on the rest of the world, including our interactions with immigrants to the United States, with people who speak English as their second (or third, or fourth . . .) language, and how we feel about "foreigners" or people with "foreign accents" in general.

The schools in the United States are grounded in beliefs shaped by the mainstream, dominant culture that is white, European, and English speaking. Therefore, the hidden curriculum in schools reflects the underlying values of the mainstream culture, thus unwittingly creating barriers for minority students (George & Aronson, 2003). Newcomers to the country are bound to encounter cross-cultural conflicts in every area of life, especially in the classroom. All components of their culture, such as language, behaviors, beliefs, and values, may be incongruent with the host country.

Non-native speakers of English automatically are marked as newcomers. Instinctively, people who have no conspicuous accent are understood and maybe accepted as "one of us." Someone who has an accent, no matter how good his or her English is, may never be accepted as an "American." One who speaks English well is also expected to know the rules of the American culture. We may "forgive" the person with the accent when making an inappropriate social or cultural blunder, but the person who speaks native-like English is expected to behave like a native English speaker within the American paradigm and cultural rules.

While in Spain, Mark, an American study-abroad student, is invited to visit his Spanish friend's family at a restaurant for a 7:00 P.M. dinner. Excited to feel a part of the Spanish culture, he goes to the train station for information about the train schedule. The clerk shrugs his shoulders and tells him that the train will be there when it arrives. Uncertain about what he should do but not wanting to arrive late for dinner, he decides to leave at 6:00 P.M. He believes an hour should be plenty of time to traverse the city. As it turns out, Mark's train is stopped on the track for quite a while, and Mark doesn't arrive until 8:30. After finding the correct address, he enters the restaurant to find no one there. He can't believe his bad luck; the dinner party is over already, and he is so disappointed to have missed his new friends. He decides to sit down and order a *bocadillo de tortilla* (egg omelet sandwich on long, white bread). Surprisingly, wine is included with his meal, but he has to pay for the glass of water he orders. He lingers over an *infusion* (herbal tea), and at around 10:00 P.M. he gets up to leave. As he is leaving, his friends arrive and exclaim, "Ya comienza la fiesta!" (Now we can start the party!) Mark is dumbfounded!

Looking at Our Own Culture—U.S. Values

We may not truly know our own culture until we leave it or until our cultural values are challenged. Mark's experience above shows how he is trying to navigate Spain using the only cues he knows, those from an American perspective. His belief system does not apply to situations he encounters in another country. Let's analyze what has happened to him. When invited to a dinner in the United States, it is important to arrive on time. Common knowledge dictates that, if you are very late for dinner, it is rude and you might miss the meal. In Spain, if an invitation is for a certain hour, everyone operates under the assumption that the affair won't start until several hours after the specified time. Obviously, Mark did not know this. Time is treated differently in many other cultures. In the train station, when Mark asked what time the train was going to leave, the clerk couldn't even tell him a schedule. In the United States, public transportation operates on a scheduled time, and the schedule is something to which people must adhere. Time is money, as the adage goes, and American life is geared to that mindset.

Returning to Mark's not-so-excellent adventure, he discovers that, not only had he not missed the party, it hadn't even started yet. When he ordered a *tortilla*, he expected a Mexican tortilla, which he had eaten in Mexican restaurants in the United States. (If he had ordered a taco, the waiters would have been stumped because in Spain the word *taco* means foul language.) The wine was free; this surprised him, as alcoholic beverages are usually quite expensive in the United States. At home, water can be ordered in unlimited quantities, but cocktails are costly. Then, just as Mark was heading home, his friends arrived and were ready to start the party.

Kohls's (2001) popular book *Survival Kit for Overseas Living* mentions traits that are ascribed to typical Americans by cultural outsiders (Table 2.1). Each cultural group is known for its own personal traits and characteristics. However, individual idiosyncrasies, capriciousness, or uniqueness of character can account for the distinctive behavior of some people. We have to be careful not to incorrectly assume or stereotype individuals.

If you are a teacher in a U.S. mainstream classroom, you will see many of your cultural beliefs challenged on a daily basis. For example, if you expect your students to be on time for school and your students function on the principle that being late is not a negative thing, clashes are bound to occur. You may have carefully scheduled appointments with parents, only to have them arrive late, cancel without notice, not show up, or arrive with the entire family with whom you must try to carry on a conference. Other examples of cultural miscommunication will be presented throughout this book.

If a teacher has students from many different cultures, it is difficult to have in-depth knowledge of them all; however, at the very least, a general understanding is a must for successful intercultural communication. Cultural sensitivity can level the diversity playing field. If a teacher is from the mainstream population, those students who are not from the majority population may be forced to play by, and be judged by, rules of which they might not be aware. Cultural proclivity will guide the teacher's approach to teaching, just as it will guide the student's approach to learning. What steps can the teacher take to mitigate misunderstanding and promote cultural understanding? Some of the following recommendations emanate from Brown University's Education Alliance for Culturally Responsive Teaching:

■ Get to know the culture of your students by researching their backgrounds, the countries they are from, their languages, values, behaviors, beliefs, holidays, traditions, customs, and foods. In other words, learn about their **surface culture** (e.g., food, dress, and music) as well as the **deep culture** (values, family roles, expected behaviors, male and female roles, etc.). When teachers possess profound cultural information about their students, they are better able to discern behaviors and to provide effective instructional strategies.

■ Try to make home visits to get to know the family and the students' living circumstances. Usually the family appreciates the interest the teacher shows, and the dynamic among the teachers, students, and family becomes more of a partnership. The knowledge gained from the home visit can be translated into effective instructional practice.

TABLE 2.1   U.S. Cultural Values

1. Personal control over the environment/responsibility
2. Change seen as natural and positive
3. Time and its control
4. Equality/fairness
5. Individualism/independence
6. Self-help/initiative
7. Competition
8. Future orientation
9. Action/work orientation
10. Informality
11. Directness/openness/honesty
12. Practicality/efficiency
13. Materialism

Source: Kohls (2001).

- Attend neighborhood and local cultural events. Get to know cultural insiders; ask questions and conduct your own research on the culture in question. Ask your students probing questions about their own cultural practices: Their consciousness will be raised to recognize and reflect on their own habits and beliefs.
- Teachers can focus on inquiry-based and discovery-oriented thematic units on topics that relate to the interest of the students and are socially and culturally relevant to student's lives. Relate teaching scenarios, questions, and problem solving to real-life interests and issues pertaining to the students.
- Offer a challenging a curriculum and enough time to complete tasks, but provide scaffolding for students to succeed by activating prior knowledge as much as possible, or provide schema to make the unknown familiar for all students. Provide an equal and equitable academic playing field for all students regardless of linguistic, cultural, or ethnic background.
- Provide ample feedback and call on all students, regardless of English proficiency. Modify your questioning strategies according to the level of the language proficiency of the student.
- Integrate multicultural viewpoints and histories into the daily curriculum.
- Learn about diverse **learning** and teaching **styles** and culturally appropriate classroom behaviors that are associated with each culture. Teach students to recognize and actively participate in their own learning.
- Try to encourage learning within appropriate sociocultural and linguistics situations. Don't hesitate to incorporate the students' native language within the class learning situations. Become aware of the classroom management styles that your students are familiar with, and help them to adjust to the American classroom styles and routines. Recognize diverse ways of achieving developmental benchmarks.
- Seek to understand parents of English learners and help them to understand school routines that may be unfamiliar to them. Let them know what services the school offers.
- Develop higher order knowledge and skills within a modified curriculum. Utilize a variety of learning strategies, and establish high expectations for all students.
- Use cooperative, collaborative, and community-oriented instruction as well as individual work within a nonthreatening classroom environment.
- Continuously aim to increase academic language proficiency as well as oral proficiency. Expand oral discourse by modeling and helping students to develop verbal expression.
- Be conscious of your own ethnocentric attitudes. Hone your cultural negotiation skills. Know that language and culture play a vital part in identity formation. Be empathetic, open, and flexible, and demonstrate caring for all your students' well-being and individual differences.

Culture Shock

Diana was excited to go to France to learn French. She had taken basic French and was intrigued by the language. After learning about a French language institute, she decided to matriculate. Her excitement grew as she planned her trip. She would be there for two semesters, live with a family, and be able to practice the language every day. On the day she arrived, no one was there to meet her at the airport, and she had to navigate the bus system to the university. She didn't know how to get the bus tokens from the machine since she had no Euros, and she tried to make herself understood. She didn't know how to use the phone and had no coins to make a call anyway. Finally, she found someone who understood English, and she was able to get some change for the bus.

The trip to the university took hours; she'd had no idea how lost she was. To find the university, she had to changes buses twice, and once a strange man insisted on paying her bus fare. Her next problem was trying to tell the secretary at the university that she was there to register, then to find out who her host family was, and then to get to their house. Even the smallest task was becoming a tremendous obstacle. She sat down and cried. She couldn't speak French; she was there to learn, but everyone kept talking to her in French as if she understood. She felt she had made a terrible mistake. She hated her situation, and she wanted to go home.

Cultural patterns are deeply ingrained in an individual. You can take a person out of his or her culture, but you may have problems trying to take the culture out of the person. When individuals move from one culture to another, very often they suffer from what is called "**culture shock**" (Hall, 1959). In your own culture, you are a functional individual who knows how to do all the things necessary to survive. Suddenly, the "bottom falls out" when all your familiar patterns are skewed. What works at home does not work for you now. You can't ask for what you need; you try to shop and realize you don't know how to ask for a half pound of cheese, sliced very thin. You have to read the money before you use it, and negotiate the price of a taxi ride before you even get into the vehicle. The easiest task at home is insurmountable in the new country. You ask for milk, and it doesn't taste the same. You can even go into McDonald's, a mainstay of the United States, and the hamburger tastes different. "For here or to go," takes on new meaning, as you can't ask the counterperson to wrap it to go. Perhaps they give you only one napkin or don't have artificial sweetener.

Newcomers to the United States suffer the same fate. Culture shock (Brown, 1994a; Oberg, 1998) typically starts with the honeymoon stage, when the traveler is excited about the trip. Next comes the *hostile* or *aggressive* stage, as the newness of the situation diminishes. Being frustrated, anxious, and angry about the inability to function are symptoms of this stage, which can last an indefinite amount of time. During this time, the newcomer will want to go home, criticizes the host country, the food, the language, and the people, and blames the country for any problems encountered. If this period becomes intolerable, the individual might return to the home country before adaptation occurs.

Recovery is the next period; the newcomer adjusts to the language and the host culture, as well as the new environment. The last stage is a period of *adjustment* when the individual accepts the new culture as just another way of life; anxiety is minimal, the new language, food, culture, and habits of the country are acceptable, and adjustments have been made.

Newcomers of all ages can suffer from culture shock. Teachers may see symptoms of reactions to culture shock, such as irritability, exhaustion, upset stomach or headaches, poor sleep, impatience, and great concern over minor pains. Learning a language is exhausting, and students might fall asleep in class from sheer fatigue.

Implications for the Classroom

It is important for the classroom teacher to know and recognize the symptoms of culture shock and to expect to see manifestations of each stage. The teacher can help students adjust by maintaining a positive attitude about themselves and celebrating the noticeable cultural differences. Teach students expected classroom and societal behaviors, and show sensitivity by protecting the newcomer from unkind behavior from other students and by highlighting the newcomer's culture. Use the opportunity as a learning experience for the whole class. Express positive values in whatever appears "foreign" to the other students. Present the newcomer's music, food, dress, and other surface values that can be seen, while learning to appreciate the deep cultural values that can present potential conflicts. See all situations as "teachable moments," and exploit the circumstances in the best light possible. Try to get to know the families, and invite them to the classroom so the other students can see them as family instead of strangers. Finally, try to introduce the family to American expectations while appreciating the richness of the culture they bring to us.

Classroom Behavior

Ms. Bingham was scheduled to teach fourth grade in Pompano Beach, an area highly populated with recently arrived Haitian children. She had taught English language learners in her practicum and was prepared to modify her instruction with ESOL strategies. She entered the classroom, and her students stood up as if on command. "Please sit down," she suggested. They did as she asked. Deciding to use one of the boys to model how they should salute the flag, she called out, "Pierre, please come up to my desk." Pierre stood up and walked toward the teacher, his head hung low, averting his eyes from the teacher. When he approached her, he held out his hand expecting the punishing slap of a ruler. She had not expected this and didn't know what to make of this misunderstanding.

Students who come from other countries bring their expectations and understanding of classroom behavior with them. The students mentioned above come from a rigid school system where they must respect the teachers by standing when they enter and where corporal punishment is the norm. Naturally, Ms. Bingham was shocked to learn that the student was expecting a slap for some alleged discretion. Averting the eyes away from an adult is the polite way to behave for a Haitian child. Had he looked into Ms. Bingham's eyes, members of his culture would have considered him rude. In his country, the classroom desks are connected, side by side, so the rows are horizontal instead of vertical. Students learn by rote memorization, and they repeat chorally. They are expected to memorize whatever material they are assigned, and they are punished if they have not done so. Multiple-choice tests are unheard of, and tests in Haiti always consist of essay questions. Much pressure is placed on tests, and the scores of individuals are published and announced on the radio so the entire village knows how everyone has done. American classes are very different, and the students will eventually learn the customs of the American classroom. They will learn that students can question the teacher, that students are expected to work independently (otherwise they might be suspected of cheating), and that taking initiative is usually rewarded. Expectations that are in direct opposition to rules of their home will cause discord. For example, American children are usually taught to tell the teacher of another youngster's trouble making instead of fighting. However, a male child from Mexico is taught that "men" never tell on each other, no matter what, and they will fight to defend a sister's honor. These discordant behaviors can cause miscommunication if not understood by the teacher. Knowing the expectations of the student's culture can demystify the most complex situations.

DISCUSSION QUESTIONS AND ACTIVITIES

1. You can experience culture shock by going to another country, by going to another region, or even by changing jobs or schools. For example, moving from the north to the south or from the east to the west, one can feel disoriented. Have you ever experienced culture shock? Where? Discuss how you felt and what you did to orient yourself to the new culture.

2. In trying to help your students, what signs of culture shock will you look for? Plan five activities to help your students recover from culture shock.

3. Look at news headlines, advertising, textbook content, classroom and school rules, etc. Do you notice any obvious American values? For example, a poster in a store window shows a dog licking his owner's face. This would be contrary to many other cultures in which animals are considered not as family members but rather as animals that should not be in the house. Think of five examples to share with your group.

4. If the teacher in a mainstream classroom discovers that students in the class have divergent cultural beliefs, what methods should be used to alleviate cultural miscommunications?

Cross-Cultural Understanding in Academic Settings

Research shows that teachers are often at odds with students from other cultures because the students' ways of life are discordant with the values and behavioral expectations of the teacher. This incongruence can lead to miscommunication as teachers unwittingly inflict their perception of reality upon students who interpret life through a different paradigm. The miscommunication occurs not only verbally but also through body language, gestures, facial expressions, personal space, and movement. Trying to decipher what another individual is truly conveying without knowing the "rules" to the other's cultural "game" is difficult.

Banks (2001) uses the metaphor or an iceberg to describe culture. Looking at the part of an iceberg that is not submerged, one can see only about one-tenth of it. This fraction depicts surface culture, or the outward vestiges of culture, such as clothing, food, and music. The other nine-tenths of the iceberg reflect the components of deep culture, which includes values, gender roles, and religious beliefs. We are often unaware of how profound and deep-rooted our values are until they are unexpectedly challenged. At that point, major misinterpretations can occur, which often wreak hurt feelings, outrage, anger, and disbelief that someone else could be so "wrong."

> While the tip of the iceberg represents the individual's conscious understanding of his or her culture, the submerged part symbolizes the larger, more subconscious influence of culture in one's life. Coming to an understanding of this subconscious influence requires some inner exploration.

Vignette 1: Mr. Thomas, a Caucasian American teacher from Minnesota, is young and shows a natural zest for life. He feels great respect and fascination for Native American cultures, and he leaps at the opportunity to begin his teaching career in a school located on the Native American reservation in Oklahoma. He prepares his classroom to look friendly, warm, and intellectually interesting. On the first day of class, he feels ready and well prepared. He introduces the concepts he is going to teach with a **KWL chart** (what you know, what you want to know, and later, what you learned). He asks Little Flower a comprehension question, but she does not know the answer. In an effort to engage the class, Mr. Thomas asks someone else, but the student lowers his eyes and remains silent. Again and again, Mr. Thomas gets the same response from the rest of the children. He does not understand the defiant attitude, and he is truly baffled by their behavior.

The explanations for the above scenario are simple. The Native American students in Mr. Thomas's class hail from a cultural lifestyle that is more group oriented and where learning takes place in a method that is more self-directed and exploratory than is found in his own Anglo cultural background. Because one student does not know the answer, the other students will not answer in an attempt to "save face," or not embarrass Little Flower. Even if they really know the answer to the question, they will not answer to try to "outdo" each other. The value of this uncompetitive principle is reflective of the belief that no one should be singled out because the group as a whole is the most important identity. The tribal elders sit in a group, sometimes not speaking, and are comfortable in their silence. If children are raised within this environment, they demonstrate these behavioral patterns. Problems arise in the classroom only when the cultural styles of the students counter those of the teacher.

Teachers who are not from the same culture as their students may find difficulties understanding the beliefs, behaviors, or values demonstrated in their classrooms (Ogbu, 1988; Pajares, 1992). Knowing the learning and cultural styles of your students helps to explain behaviors that can cause misunderstandings. Although on the surface this appears to be a simple explanation, in reality the situation is quite complex. Teachers need to understand diverse learning styles in the classroom. However, as useful as this information might be, mere knowledge of learning styles is not a panacea for the myriad of issues found in the classroom of today (Bennett, 1990). The students' home language, culture, heritage, family beliefs, previous education, and experience are only a few of the components necessary to consider in creating an effective formula for instruction.

Nonverbal Communication

Making assumptions of cultural meanings based on your own perception of cultural reality can result in incorrect interpretations of another's intentions. Using Banks's iceberg metaphor, this chapter further discusses surface culture as well deep culture and nonverbal communication, which can be misinterpreted if we apply significance from our own cultural values to the actions of others.

Vignette 2: Mrs. Sato, an American-born teacher of Japanese descent, has relocated with her husband and children to Framingham, Massachusetts, a city with a high population of Brazilians. Being from Hawaii, Mrs. Sato has had much experience with students from diverse cultures, so she is welcomed into the public school system as a high school teacher. Mrs. Sato is teaching a lesson on economics and is trying to describe the inflated housing pricing in Hawaii. After giving an example, she concludes by saying, "So, you need to have a lot of this (making the 'OK' sign with her thumb and forefinger) to get a house in Hawaii." Her American students look puzzled, her Brazilian students gasp with embarrassment, and Mrs. Sato is wondering what has just occurred.

In fact, the difficulties of communicating with someone from another culture arise not only from language differences but from cultural differences as well, including **body language**. When we talk about nonverbal communication, the problem compounds because each cultural group has its own set of symbols, and the meanings of the same symbols may and often do vary across cultures. Although Mrs. Sato was born in the United States, she was raised with much Japanese influence. From the Japanese reference point, the "OK" symbol refers to money. To Brazilians, this gesture is obscene and vulgar, referring to something sexual; in the mainstream American culture, this widely recognized symbol just means "OK." Unfortunately, not until Mrs. Sato accidentally discovered this difference in meanings did she realize how badly misconstrued nonverbal communication can get.

Renowned anthropologist Edward T. Hall is best known for his seminal works in nonverbal communication. *The Silent Language* (1959) depicts culture as having its own system of communication with different meanings. Teachers can better understand their students from other cultures if they have knowledge of the underlying significance of nonverbal communication.

Nonverbal communication can be classified into categories known as **kinesics** (the study of body language), proxemics (conscious and unconscious use of personal distance); **paralinguistics** (vocal effects that modify speech; elements of speech), **haptics** (communication through touch), and **chronemics** (perceiving and using time). Additionally, cultural beliefs can be further subdivided into categories of surface culture and deep culture (beliefs about how families should function, attitudes about religion, health, life, death). A note on kinesics: Each culture demonstrates body language in a different way. When greeting each other, Asians bow, Americans shake hands, the French kiss each cheek three times, and Hispanics kiss on one cheek or two, depending on the country. In Asia, the custom of bowing has more subtleties that are decipherable to the unsuspecting Western eye. The person with the higher rank in society (the employer or an elder) will be bowed to by someone younger or by someone who holds a subordinate position. A Thai will press hands together, steeple style, and bow the head. If a Thai is bowing to a higher-status individual, the hands will be raised higher. Americans appear informal to more formal cultures. Newcomers to the American society may have difficulty judging whether the situation is formal or not because Americans appear informal when actually an unspecified hierarchy does exist. Teachers who are cognizant of potential cultural clashes in the classroom are better equipped to deal with everyday issues that can cause misunderstandings.

Even in the business world, the simple act of exchanging business cards carries cultural significance. How a card is presented to a new acquaintance (e.g., Asians proffer the card with two hands) or whether the card is looked at immediately or pocketed without a glance can represent respect or rejection.

Now let's look at some examples of how each culture determines its own rules of behavior, both in and outside the classroom.

Vignette 3: In an adult ESOL class, Ms. Walsh, the teacher, invited her students to her wedding. She told her students that dress was not formal. The students were excited to go to their first American wedding. Ms. Walsh's Columbian student, Henry, who usually dressed quite formally, arrived an hour late. He walked into the function in the middle of the ceremony, wearing jeans, a T-shirt, and tennis shoes. He was mortified and insisted on going home to change. When the teacher said the wedding was not formal, she was implying that tuxedos were not required. Henry believed that the word "informal" meant sports clothing. He did not have the background knowledge to distinguish the degrees of formality implied in the American culture.

Vignette 4: Ryoko, a Japanese student, was thrilled to go to Disney World on her first visit to the United States. Stopping in front of a roller coaster, she stared up in surprise as she watched a grown man shouting excitedly. She said, "It is shocking to see a grown man yell on the ride! In Japan, men do not shout out."

Display of emotion is unique to each culture. Many individuals must hold their grief inwardly because it is not for public display. However, in other cultures people may openly keen when in grief. This is obvious in televised American trials: When the accused does not openly demonstrate grief or remorse, it is well noted according to media and it appears almost as an indication of guilt. The individual is judged according to "typical" American response to grief. Smiles can be deceiving, too. In the United States, we often smile at strangers just to be polite. If Asian people smile, it may be their attempt to cover up embarrassment, pain, or grief. Some individuals display grief, shock, or happiness openly, while others are expected to hide their feelings.

Kinesic differences are evident in the classroom in more ways than one. How? When a teacher tries to affectionately pat an Asian student on the head, the student may recoil because many people believe that the head houses the soul and must not be touched. For individuals from many cultures, to show the bottom of the feet is an insult because they are the dirtiest part of the body. If a teacher requests the students to remove their shoes for any reason, this might cause conflict for some students. Sitting on the floor is another area of potential conflict for students.

For certain Arab cultures, offering your left hand for a handshake is an insult because this hand is considered "unclean." The right hand is preferred for eating, while the left hand is used to clean the body after going to the toilet. In many Arab or Islamic countries, the crime rate is low because in accordance with to the Koran, punishment is very severe. For example, if someone picks a pocket in Morocco and gets caught, the right hand might be cut off, ensuring that the person, left with only an "unclean" hand, will be shunned for a lifetime.

Eileen and Mary, teachers from Massachusetts, were in Morocco touring the labyrinth of street markets. From all sides, vendors yelled out invitations to buy their wares. One vendor, upset that the ladies were ignoring him, began to curse them in English. (Remember that non-native speakers of English will use words that hold no deep meaning for them but will be offensive to native speakers). The leader of the tour group chastised the vendor and told him to apologize to the women. The vendor replied, "Of course," and held out his left hand for a handshake with Mary. She quickly refused, saying, "I know what that means."

In the classroom, children from cultures that maintain a closer physical proximity may crowd around the teacher and will not know it when they have crossed the personal boundaries of the teacher. If the teacher backs up, which may be an unconscious response, the students may feel rejected or think that the teacher does not like them. Hall (1966) coined the term **proxemics** to describe the use of personal body space. For example, Americans have a certain personal space surrounding their bodies that others must not penetrate. It is unspoken, but everyone knows that to get too close to an American is an uncomfortable declaration of intimacy and may even be considered a threat. The American will become uncomfortable, or even hostile, and will back off. If Americans touch each other accidentally, they immediately say, "Excuse me" or "I'm sorry."

At the end of the summer session at the English language institute, Ms. Clark held a goodbye party for her students from Korea, Taiwan, Peru, and Brazil. As the teacher, she had enjoyed learning about the cultures the students came from. When the party was in full swing, she scanned the room and looked at the group of students in wonder as she realized how different they were from each other. The Brazilian girls were trying to get everyone to dance. Two Korean young men were sitting on the floor, backs against the wall, with their arms draped around each other, and the Peruvian and Taiwanese students were deep in discussion. The Peruvian girls stood very close to the Taiwanese students, and it appeared that the Taiwanese boys were shying away from the girls. Ms. Clark noted with amazement and delight the students were behaving naturally, according to their individual cultural patterns, which is what they had discussed in their cross-cultural communication classes.

DISCUSSION QUESTIONS AND ACTIVITIES

1. Plan four questioning strategies that you can use to make sure all students have a chance to contribute to the class discussion, despite their different cultural backgrounds. If students do not know what to say, what will you do to make sure they don't feel embarrassed in class? Show examples of:

   A. Kinesics
   B. Proxemics
   C. Chronemics
   D. Paralinguistics
   E. Haptics
   F. Surface Culture
   G. Deep Culture

2. Imagine you are in a classroom with students who come from different countries. What can you do to get to know their beliefs? How can knowing their beliefs make you a more informed teacher?

3. Brainstorm possible cultural misconceptions your students might display in the classroom. Refer to the situation with Henry wearing the wrong clothing at the wedding. Give five examples of situations where students might misinterpret situations in the classroom.

4. One student leans so close to you when you are sitting at your desk that it makes you feel uncomfortable. Another student recoils when you pat her on the head. A third student stands so close to you, he "shares his breath" with you. How would you handle these situations?

5. As you correct a student from Japan, she keeps smiling at you. What would you think this student is feeling? How can you find out?

4

Diverse Learning Styles

This chapter's focus highlights the reflections of **home cultures** on learning styles. Teachers are better prepared to understand their students' instructional strengths when they are conscious of the influences that cultures have on how students interact in an educational setting. With this knowledge, teachers can plan the most effective instructional practices.

Howard Gardner's (1993) seminal work on learning styles has made us aware that every student has strengths in different areas of learning. Learning style inventories (Dunn & Dunn, 1978) are available to determine what kinds of learners we are; as a result of this awareness, we can learn how to modify teaching and learning strategies for all our students.

Students' learning styles often reflect their cultures as well as how they are treated in their homes. Since **personal independence** often is a salient characteristic of the American culture, American children may be encouraged to be more independent than children from some other cultures. The example below illustrates a different cultural outlook on what children should and should not do for themselves at a given age.

As an English/Spanish bilingual teacher in the first grade, Ms. Zelden was amazed at the behaviors of some of the parents of her Hispanic students. She noticed that some parents would carry their children into class, hand-feed them, carry their books, take their boots off, and some children even had pacifiers and baby bottles. She noticed that this heightened dependence was also reflected in the way the children approached their assignments. The teacher would give a set of multiple directions, and the children would check with the teacher at each step. For example, if the directions were (1) go to the crayon box, (2) choose the crayons, (3) choose the drawing paper from the bin, and (4) draw a picture of your favorite play place, the children would question the teacher after doing each task. They would ask questions like "What color crayons should I pick?" "What should I draw?" "Teacher, can you draw a horse for me?" On the other hand, the American children seemed to act more comfortable with choice and took the initiative to proceed independently, which apparently was a direct reflection on how they were treated at home. In fact, Ms. Zelden found that the American children were so accustomed to doing things their own way, they often crossed over the acceptable boundaries between teacher and student. Ms. Zelden often had to tell the children, "This is not how we act with a teacher," or "You need to ask permission first before you get up from your seat," or "This is not how we talk to the teacher," because they truly did not know they were overstepping their limits.

Generally speaking, Americans promote and cherish independence. It is looked at as an inalienable right. The country was founded by people searching for the right to be independent. We teach children to care for themselves at a very early age. They contribute to the household by being responsible for chores; they learn how to dial 911 and report an emergency; they are allowed and even encouraged to make choices; and they order their own food in a restaurant. American mothers are expected to wean babies from nursing and bottles as soon as it is feasible.

We might not be aware how we are conditioned to accept our cultural values as the right way of life, but it is evident from infancy and early childhood. U.S. pediatricians often encourage new mothers to wean babies from bottles or nursing to drinking from a cup after about 1 year of age. Mothers in other cultures might nurse or feed their babies from bottles until they are 4 or older. In the U.S. society, we believe that is too old. We look askance at the child who is sucking on a pacifier if the child looks too mature to indulge in that habit. The value placed an independence applies even in our slumber patterns, as U.S. children are usually encouraged to sleep alone instead of being with the parents or the mother in a "family bed." These expectations will enforce the ideas and values of independence. Later, this inculcated behavior will reflect in classroom behavior and the conduct of children in the everyday business of living.

The U.S. values described here are contrary to the values of a culture where dependence on parents and elders is the norm. Again, the students who are more dependent on teacher interaction and direct instruction are usually a reflection of societies that do more for the child, which delays independence.

Field Independence and Field Dependence

As we have read, teachers from the **mainstream culture** in the United States will reflect the values common in U.S. society. Students from **nonmainstream cultures** possess their own value systems, which often lead to incongruence and misinterpretation of behavior, expectations, and learning styles in the classroom. **Cognitive styles** of individuals differ in processing and analyzing information, acquiring knowledge, and reacting to the teaching styles and assumptions of the instructor (Dunn & Griggs, 1990). How we approach problems, address issues, ask questions, and interact with the teacher and our peers may be very different from culture to culture. This can be due to the ways of thinking or behaving that have been modeled for us (Banks & Banks, 1993; Garcia & Malkin, 1993), or it can be due to cognitive or physical disabilities (Grant & Sleeter, 1989). However, within each culture, general characteristics of cognitive similarity can be found (Grant & Sleeter, 1989; Philips, 1983; Ramirez & Castaneda, 1974; Willis, 1993).

Field-independent and field-dependent learners do not differ in intelligence or cognitive ability; however, they differ in learning strategies and the approaches they take to problem solving and interacting with others. Once students enter school, they approach each situation at hand in the way they have been taught at home. If process at school is incompatible with the way the student has been raised, misinterpretation and conflicts will occur (Baruth & Manning, 1992; Vogt, Jordan, & Tharp, 1987). U.S. schools typically have favored an Anglo-European educational style, which reflects the mainstream learner who may need to articulate perceptions but does not pay much attention to social clues. Learning is impersonal. The field-independent approach to education will not be compatible with the nonmainstream minority student, and it may even appear that the minority student is in need of special education (McIntyre, 1993; Rueda & Forness, 1994).

Mainstream European Americans tend to be **field-independent learners.** The tendency is for them to be motivated by impersonal, analytical activities that do not necessitate a group-type approach. They may like competition, individual recognition, show a rational, intrinsic appeal for the task without consulting others, and do best with learning the history or theory of the activity before attempting the assignment (Anderson, 1988; Banks & Banks, 1993; Diaz, 1989; Ishii-Jordan & Peterson, 1994).

Field-dependent learners usually hail from nonmainstream cultures and like to work with others to achieve a common goal, very often while interacting with the teacher (Ramirez & Castaneda, 1974). These learners are more sensitive to the feelings, opinions, and ideas of others and may like to assist one another in a group effort. They like to practice and learn by experimentation as opposed to engaging in conceptual discussion before attempting the task (Anderson, 1988). Students from cultures that are African American (Banks & Banks, 1993), Arab American (Nydell, 1987), Hispanic (Banks & Banks, 1993), Native American (Utley, 1983), and, often, Asian American (Hvit-feldt, 1986) tend to be field dependent and are greatly influenced by the teacher. This type of learner may prefer a global perception and be more attentive to social clues.

When the cultural mismatch occurs, teachers may assume students are less competent than they really are, which can result in cultural bias or students' being labeled as having behavioral disorders (Gollnick & Chinn, 1990; McIntyre, 1995; Rueda & Forness, 1994).

With differing ideas of appropriate behavior, it is easy for teachers and students to misunderstand each other. For example, the field-dependent student comes from a culture that appreciates helpfulness and cooperation between members. A student may try to help another student by sharing work or answers or letting a friend copy his or her answers. This is perceived as cheating in the individualist-oriented mainstream American culture.

Mainstream teachers usually expect silence, while people from other cultures, such as those that are Arab or African American, may demonstrate a more contributory, vocally responsive or physically oriented style of behavior (McIntyre, 1995; Nydell, 1987; Ogbu, 1988). Other issues, like the importance of being task oriented, time conscious, and prompt can also be misconstrued. The student who is rushed may not finish work on time, or the student who needs to finish work at his or her own pace is definitely not appreciated by the teacher who is obligated to stick to a strict schedule. Additionally, consider the student who is not accustomed to asking questions or is not comfortable participating verbally in class. For example, a teacher may ask an Asian student if he or she understands a concept. To "save face" and avoid public embarrassment for the teacher for not explaining it well enough, or because the student was not capable of understanding the concept, the student will say "yes" (Wei, 1980; Woo, 1985). That student may fail the assessment, which indicates that he or she did not really understand the assignment, and the teacher might think the student was lying. Alternatively, very often, the student might say "yes," then go home and try to figure it out alone.

Modifying Instruction for All Learners

Although students may be prone to one style of learning, they can be taught to be bicognitive. That is, the field-dependent student can learn to be more field independent and the more field-independent student can learn to become more field dependent. Although we must not categorize all individuals according to their ethnic groups, it is essential to keep in mind what type of learner the student is more likely to be. For example, in a list of characteristics that determines what a "gifted" student is, one of the measures mentioned was taking initiative to begin a task without being prompted. That is a typically "American" value, and a gifted minority student might not behave according to that "American" gifted-student criterion. Success for both types of learners greatly depends on the teacher, who should keep in mind that the instructor's own teaching style usually reflects his or her own learning style.

Field-dependent teachers are usually student centered and try to use positive reinforcement as opposed to negative feedback. They often use a hands-on, participatory approach with student discussion as opposed to lecture or discovery methods of teaching.

Field-independent teachers may focus more on the subject, use a negative evaluation approach, and prefer inquiry or problem-solving methods of instruction, and the teaching situation may be more impersonal.

To reach all students, a mix of both styles should be taught so that instructional methods can complement the cultural style. For those students who would thrive in more physically oriented tasks, implement activities that incorporate group work that depends on a hands-on activity, a project-based task that necessitates active participation, perhaps with a kinesthetic objective. Students can role-play a courtroom scene or a session in Congress or put on a play that portrays a historical event that they have researched and written about themselves.

For students who are more comfortable with field-dependent types of learning, introduce them to a more field-independent task by taking a systematic process using the discovery approach, or create a competition using groups instead of an individual contest. Know which approach your students seem to prefer, and incorporate that as much as possible.

Once cognizant of the differences in learning styles, teachers should reflect upon their own teaching and learning styles to see if they need to adjust their instructional practices to include a wider variety of strategies. Teachers can provide various opportunities for their students to experiment with more diverse instructional styles. At the same time, teachers can guide students to discover for themselves what types of learners they are, which can lead to their becoming more autonomous learners.

DISCUSSION QUESTIONS AND ACTIVITIES

1. Describe your preferred learning style. What kind of teaching and learning situation are you most comfortable with? Why?
2. Create five activities you could incorporate in your class to help field-dependent learners become more independent, and vice versa.
3. Gardner's (1993) Multiple Intelligence learning styles are as follows:

   - Visual/spatial intelligence
   - Musical intelligence
   - Verbal intelligence
   - Logical/mathematical intelligence
   - Interpersonal intelligence
   - Intrapersonal intelligence
   - Bodily/kinesthetic intelligence
   - Naturalist intelligence

   Keeping in mind cultural and age differences, create one activity that utilizes each intelligence.

PART TWO

The Experience of Learning Another Language

5

What Teachers Need to Know About Language Acquisition

Scenario one (mother and child in conversation):

CHILD:	"Mommy, take me a bath."
MOTHER:	"You mean **give** you a bath."
CHILD:	"Yes. Take me a bath."

Scenario two:

MOTHER:	"We have to go to Miami."
CHILD:	"Then after we go to your ami, can we go to my ami too?"

Scenario three:

CHILD:	"I want to wear my Batman jamamas to bed.
MOTHER:	"You mean pajamas."
CHILD:	"Yeah, **jamamas**."

Researchers used to believe that children learned their first language by listening and repeating what adults said. These beliefs are based on a **behaviorist theory**, made famous by Skinner (1957), who argued that language learning is culturally determined and is a behavior learned by imitation of adult speech. Linguists questioned this belief, because it means that children would not produce novel utterances they have never heard before. It is impossible to attribute to imitation the creative forms of language children use, such as the language described in the examples above.

Later, the **nativist** theorist Noam Chomsky (1979) offered another explanation that promotes the idea that children are born with a basic innate language learning capacity, called the Language Acquisition Device (LAD). Chomsky's hypothesis espoused that children are born with innate structures that allow them to figure out linguistic rules of any language they are born into. As shown in the scenarios above, the children do not respond to error correction but correct themselves in their own developmental time frame, as if it were an internal syllabus. The nativist and behaviorist theories are compared and contrasted in Figure 5.1.

If we look at how children start to speak, we can see that crying, cooing, and babbling are the first signs of speech because they are intended for communicating messages. Later, the children begin to produce one-and two-word utterances like "Mommy go," "Doggy bye bye." Negative sentences are produced by adding "no" to an utterance as in, "Mommy no go." Questions are formed by using a rising intonation like, "Baby sleep?" Children actively construct more advanced speech forms that are developed over much time and after prolonged exposure to adult language.

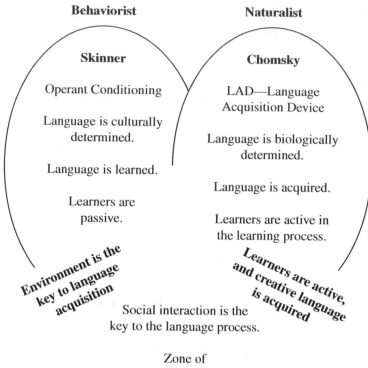

FIGURE 5.1 Theory Comparision Chart

Source: Ariza (2002).

The language acquisition process develops in predictable stages at the children's own speed, but their understanding is usually grounded within the immediate context of their environment.

Another theory of language acquisition is **social interactionist theory**, which assumes that the child's linguistic environment is instrumental in language acquisition. A social environment of speech between a parent and child (**motherese** or **parentese**) is believed to promote active negotiation of meaning as they interact. This same interaction of conversational strategies can be seen between a native and non-native speaker (foreigner talk) as they use language and paralinguistic devices intentionally to promote meaning. The Soviet psychologist Lev Vygotsky (1962, 1978) describes this type of development as the zone of proximal development, which infers that what learners can accomplish today with help, they can do alone tomorrow. By using strategies and materials that target students' individual zones of proximal development, teachers can move them from their actual developmental level to their potential developmental level. An example of this expansion is when a child makes a simple statement, such as "*Doggie.*" The mother expands the statement by saying, "Yes, see the doggie. What a big doggie! What does the doggie say? Does the doggie say 'Woof, woof'?" Although some cognitive theorists (Bialystock, 1978; McLaughlin, 1980) maintain that Vygotsky's ideas are too simplistic, Krashen (1981) incorporated a similar hypothesis into his theory of second language acquisition, which is discussed further.

Theories of Second Language Acquisition

Brain-based theories emphasize that learning a language is complex and includes more issues than just cognitive functions. There are numerous factors influencing language acquisition, including age, motivation, comprehensible input, affective conditions, and the methods used in teaching and learning. Krashen's (1978) theory of second language acquisition encompasses ideas that focus on the differences between acquisition and learning of the language. It proposes five hypotheses: **Acquisition Versus Learning Hypothesis,** **Natural Order Hypothesis,** the **Monitor Hypothesis,** the **Affective Filter Hypothesis,** and the **Input Hypothesis.** The latter is also known as (i+1) theory, i being the input and (+1) being the message a bit beyond the learner's level of language proficiency (Krashen, 1981). Krashen argues that creating comprehensible input that is slightly challenging will push the learner further on the language development continuum. With this comprehensive theory in mind, Krashen and Terrell created the Natural Approach for learning a second language. As a result of their work, the direction of classroom teaching has been altered to include methods that aim to provide comprehensible input for second language learners.

Implications of Krashen's Work for Classroom Learning

According to Krashen's theory, classroom teaching contributes to acquisition only if it provides comprehensible input that entices students' interest. Optimal input in the classroom is especially important for students who live in literacy-deprived environments. Listed below are some implications arising from each of Krashen's hypotheses:

- Drill and practice are not as significant as natural communication. The *Acquisition Versus Learning* hypothesis implies that, just as very young children take time before they produce any verbal output, second language learners go through a silent stage. Teachers should be patient with students who are still in their silent period because "real language acquisition develops slowly, and speaking skills emerge significantly later than listening skills, even when conditions are perfect" (Krashen, 1982, p. 7).
- Grammar need not be the center of instruction. Acquisition of correct language will evolve gradually and naturally within the school curriculum. The *Natural Order Hypothesis* suggests that certain rules are learned before others and are acquired gradually, so they do not have to be formally taught.
- The *Input Hypothesis* implies that when learners understand the language (comprehensible input) and are exposed to information just a little bit beyond their current level of comprehension (i+1), language acquisition takes place. Comprehensible input is afforded by the teacher's use of scaffolding through visuals, realia, graphic organizers, less complex language structures, modifying curriculum, paraphrasing, clear and slower pronunciation, buddy tutoring, and so forth.
- The *Monitor Hypothesis* refers to an error-correcting mechanism in the brain that edits the utterances of the language learner. This helps the learner to focus on correct form, but this can only occur when the learner knows the correct rules of the language. Corrections by teachers and native speakers may not be internalized until the learner is developmentally ready. Because errors are a part of the natural order of acquisition, second language teachers should not overemphasize them during instruction. To try to correct every error is the fastest way to impede a learner's natural inclination to communicate. Remember, the individual is competent in his or her native language. To be suddenly reduced to feeling stupid because of one's inability to communicate is demoralizing.
- The *Affective Filter Hypothesis* means that the learner must feel secure and "unthreatened" in the learning environment. Teachers should identify topics and

practices to which students will relate most positively. Collaborative and noncompetitive environment is ideal for students to receive input and to produce language output (Krashen & Terrell, 1983). It is important for language teachers to identify and utilize the practices that motivate students, lessen their anxiety, and sustain their interest in learning. As I mentioned previously, the learner will "mangle" the new language until he or she "dominates" it.

Understanding Social Language and Academic Language

As clearly put by Spolsky (1989), "the important issue surrounding second language acquisition can be summarized in one question: 'Who learns how much of what language under what conditions?'" (p. 95). There are many theoretical approaches to second language acquisition, but according to Cadiero-Kaplan (2004), the theory that is most popular among practitioners promotes the distinction between social language and academic language (Cummins, 1981b, 1982, 1994). Educators can use Cummins's considerations about language proficiency as a guide to understanding their students' needs, and to successful instructional planning. Figure 5.2 depicts the distinction between the social and academic language in a visual mode.

Quadrant A of Figure 5.2 list tasks that are simple, and the English learner can determine meaning by looking at the speaker's face and gestures. If an ELL cannot understand the words, the speaker can modify or repeat the utterance. In quadrant B, the tasks are cognitively simple, but the ELL has no way to negotiate meaning from the context. Thus, comprehension is more difficult. Context clues are **embedded** in quadrant A but not evident in quadrant B. Social conversation can take place, but no indication of the students' true academic ability can be determined because they sound as if they possess proficient language skills. Compound this ability with a native-like accent (which will be likely if the student has had exposure to English before puberty), and the teacher has no idea of the student's true academic skill level.

In quadrant C, notice that the tasks involve more advanced cognitive abilities, but context clues are embedded with the task, making comprehension clear. Students are able to perform the academic tasks because of visual and graphic scaffolding. In quadrant D, no context clues are embedded within the activities; students will begin to fail because they lack the academic language necessary to complete the academic task. The longer they are in school, the more they fall behind; these are long-term English language learners who are at a high risk of failing and dropping out of school. This phenomenon is very common with English learners who go through the U.S. school systems (Thomas & Collier, 2002).

I learned my second language relatively late in life, so I have experienced how painful the process of language learning can be for an adult. As a bilingual teacher of ELLs and a teacher educator, I still learn from my students, from the teachers I train, and from reading new books in the field. When I first learned the difference between **Basic Interpersonal Communication Skills (BICS,** or social language) and **Cognitive Academic Language Proficiency (CALP,** or academic language) (Cummins, 1981b), it was an epiphany for me. Even as a bilingual/ESOL teacher, I was one of those teachers who asked, "This child speaks perfect English; why is he in ESOL?" Understanding the reasons why students should not be advanced from the transitional bilingual class to the mainstream class answered many of my questions.

Many teachers make the logical mistake of trying to push their English learners into more advanced classes. Because the English learners have a good foundation in social language (and the younger they are, the more native-like they may sound), teachers are under the impression that the students know more English than they actually do. Although learners might be accomplished speakers and sound native-like, academically they might be years behind the native speakers. This lag may be explained by weak or interrupted schooling in the students' home countries, by months of not comprehending academic instruction delivered in English, or by the combination of both factors (Freeman, Freeman, & Mercuri, 2002).

Before I became a bilingual/ESOL teacher, I did my internship with a wonderful third-grade teacher of a mainstream class. We had a lovely English-speaking student whose problems appeared in his spelling tests. When writing words, he was spelling phonetically, and they looked like this:

apul (apple)
skul (school)
bar (bare)

Inventive spelling is common among beginning writers, but this situation was odd because the student was a bright third grader. My cooperating teacher was baffled and believed the boy had some sort of disability. I suddenly had an idea and

FIGURE 5.2   Social and Academic Language

Cognitively Undemanding (BICS) Social Language

Context Embedded	**Context Reduced**
• Survival language (playground, simple ordering of food; inability to communicate needs by speaking, but can indicate needs by pointing, gesturing, etc.).	• Telephone conversations (because they are not communicating face to face).
• Can follow directions if a model is provided.	• Filling out a job application with no model to follow.
• Can negotiate understanding by the **speaker's actions, facial expressions,** gestures, etc.	• Reading directions without illustrations.
• TPR (Total Physical Response).	• Simple written text.
• Choosing the correct answer when asked questions, such as: Do you want the red one or the green one (and the speaker is pointing to the items)?	• **Simple homework assignment with** nothing to connect it to the work done in class.
A	**B**
C	**D**
• Book reports using a template format.	• Standardized tests.
• Instruction through graphic organizers, visuals, realia, role play.	• Text without visuals.
• Presenting an academic paper.	• Lectures.
• Dramatic scenes where students memorize lines (a play).	• Listening to the news.
• Doing hands-on experiments through scientific inquiry.	• Math word problems.
• Math with manipulatives.	• Mainstream content text.

Cognitively Demanding (CALP) Academic Language

Source: Adapted from Chamot & O'Malley (1987); Cummins (1981b).

asked him in Spanish if he spoke Spanish at home. He answered, "Si. Señora. Mis papás son de Puerto Rico." Because Gabriel's parents spoke perfect English and self-identified as native English speakers, there was no indication on the child's cumulative folder that he came from a second language background. It is possible that teachers will have second-language learners in their classes without realizing it because, when they learn languages early in life, children are able to speak with accents that are native sounding. The assumption that children have a "critical period" (Lennenberg, 1974) of language learning that enables them to gain native-like fluency before puberty is often a cause for mistaking it for academic ability in the second language.

To reiterate, learning about Cummins's work on the distinction between social language and academic language was pivotal for me as an educator. Cummins looked at standardized scores of ELLs and compared them to native English speakers. He found that, although the ELLs could acquire social English rapidly (within two years), it took five to seven years for them to acquire academic language. Compound these findings with a child who speaks with no foreign accent, and what teacher would not suspect any problem other than one with language? Cummins (1984) later clarified the terms BICS and CALP through a theoretical framework, that encompasses the concept of Cognitive Academic Language Proficiency (CALP) within a larger theory of **Common Underlying Proficiency (CUP),** as opposed to Separate Underlying Proficiency (SUP). CUP as opposed to SUP assumes that knowledge and literacy skills learned in the native language will transfer to the target language. This is the foundation for the main argument for bilingual education: When a learner receives academic knowledge in the first language, it can be transferred to the second language. If a student has a strong academic foundation in a native language, it is assumed that the transfer of knowledge to the second language is more a question of language learning than of knowledge learning. Keeping this idea in mind, it is understandable that a child who learns to read in his or her native language first, regardless of the native language, understands the concept of reading. Therefore, in the ESL reading class, the concept of deciphering print is already understood; only the new language needs to be learned. Cummins's idea of Common Underlying Proficiency also explains why an international high school student with a strong academic background from the native country might fare better academically in an American school than a second language learner who was brought up in the United States. Although the U.S. student will sound more American, the foreign student could conceivably achieve a higher level of academic success.

Stages of Second Language Acquisition

Other **brain-based research** has revealed that adults and children use different parts of their brain when learning a second language. In the idea of **parallel distributed processing (PDP),** the human brain is thought to be capable of processing multiple pieces of information simultaneously. These and other ideas are offered in an attempt to explain how languages are learned, but the fact is, researchers have found that very often second language learning parallels the developmental stages of first language acquisition (Hill & Flynn, 2006). Hill and Flynn speak of five stages of second language development: preproduction stage, early production stage, speech emergence stage, intermediate fluency, and advanced fluency. According to Hill and Flynn (2006), it is critical for teachers to know and understand their students' stages of language acquisition in order to differentiate instruction successfully.

Classroom Implications of Language Development Stages

Preproduction is the silent period. According to Hill and Flynn (2006), although students do not speak, they may possess up to 500 words in their receptive vocabulary. Students in a silent stage may repeat words after the teacher and copy words from the board, but not every action will reveal comprehension of material. These children may get tired after a short amount of time because their brains get exhausted from trying to make meaning from the unfamiliar language. Teachers should assist those students by speaking clearly, stating key words more than once, and helping them build more vocabulary. It is unreasonable to demand that these children begin speaking English immediately, as the silent stage may last up to six months.

The *early production stage* usually occurs between six months to a year of learning English. During this stage, students bring their receptive vocabulary to active use while learning up to 500 new words. They also attempt to combine these words into phrases or repeat memorized utterances, although the grammatical usage may not always be correct. They can use short language chunks that have been memorized, but these chunks may not always be used correctly. Some of the activities suggested for this stage are using realia and visuals to support instruction, asking yes/no questions, accepting short responses, adapting content material, and encouraging writing using sentence frames.

At the stage of *speech emergence*, which occurs between the first and third years of learning a second language, students communicate using simple sentences and phrases. By then, their vocabulary has grown to about 3,000 words. Although the usage of words and grammatical constructions is not always correct, the students are able to ask simple questions, participate in some classroom activities, and carry our short conversations with classmates. They will understand easy stories read in class with the support of pictures. On this stage, it is important for teachers to engage students in modified content area activities, buddy reading, journal writing, and vocabulary-building activities.

During the stage of *intermediate fluency*, which normally takes place between the third and fifth years of learning English, a student will have an active vocabulary of 6,000 words. During this stage, students attempt to use more complex sentence structures, ask comprehension questions, and share answers in class. Because students' production increases, it is easy to notice the elements of transfer from the native language to the second language. It is especially evident in students' writing, which may contain chunks directly translated from the native language. Teachers should use students' mistakes as a tool for learning, suggesting improvement and modeling appropriate usage. As children's comprehension in content areas increases, teachers should model helpful learning strategies that students can use independently in class and at home.

It takes students between five and ten years to achieve *advanced fluency* in a second language, which also manifests itself in grade-level performance in academics. By that time, most students have been exited from ESOL or support programs. Student at this stage will have mastered complex structures of the language, applying them in speaking and writing. However, at the beginning of this stage, these students still need teacher support, such as checking comprehension often, modifying learning strategies, suggesting study guides and materials to reinforce comprehension, and so on.

While other researchers may offer a different breakdown of elements related to second language proficiency, the universal agreement is that the second language acquisition process is complex. In fact, any time second language acquisition is discussed, it is impossible to ignore students' "individual differences (e.g., ability and attitude), the skills and competencies being learnt (e.g., grammatical accuracy, conversational fluency and literacy), contextual and situational factors, linguistic inputs and learner processes (e.g., code switching)" (Baker, 1996, p. 114).

Implications of the First Language on the Second

For a classroom teacher, it is important to know how a student learns a language so we can align our teaching according to the developmental states of language acquisition. Although you may not know the student's language, if you understand how language is learned, you can adjust and correlate your instruction to the student's level of proficiency. Often you will hear, "All you have to do is immerse yourself in the language, and you will just pick it up." If that is true, I can say the following words to you all day, and you should eventually understand them.

Круговорот воды в природе является одним из грандиозных процессов на поверхности земного шара. Вода находится в постоянном движении. Испаряясь с поверхности водоемов, почвы, растений, вода накапливается в атмосфере. Рано или поздно, она выпадает в виде осадков, пополняя запасы в океанах реках, озерах и т.п. Таким образом, количество воды на земле не1 меняется—она только меняет свои формы—это и есть кругов орот воды в природе.

According to the submersion theory, you should be able to understand it now, especially after hearing it several times. I could also put this concept in another written form, which you might be able to understand better if you are literate. Try reading this:

Известно, что 90% всех испарений воды поставляют океаны. Испарение также происходит в преснов одных озерах и реках. Водянои пар, поднимаясь в атмосферу, конденсируется в облаках и возвращается на землю в виде осадков. Осадки—это дождь, снег и град. Когда выпадают осадки, вода пополняет водоемы, проникая через почву, питает подземные воды земли. В итоге, вода вновь возвращается в океан речным и подземным стоком. Растения, питаясь дождевой и грунтовой водой, затем листьями выделяют воду в атмосферу в виде пара. Так продолжается круговорот воды в природе.

Is there anything in the above text that gives you a clue to what is being said? Unless you read Russian, you probably will not understand any of the above text no matter how many times I read it to you. According to Krashen (1981), unless it is accompanied by comprehensible input, it does not matter how many times you hear a message in another language. If you hear someone talking at you, it is just "blah, blah, blah." Once there is something to connect meaning to the words, we can begin to learn the language. Babies are immersed in the sounds of their native languages for at least a year before they are expected to speak. Yet the newcomer to a language is expected to repeat words without being given the chance to internalize the sounds.

Language researchers such as Fillmore and Snow (2000) believe that teachers who know educational linguistics, that is, how language impacts teaching and learning, will make a greater impact on the learning achievement of English language learners. This idea makes sense because the teacher will understand why the English learner is having difficulty, and she or he will be better prepared to engage in proactive teaching, thus facilitating literacy development.

Morphology

Morphology is the study of word formation. Certain languages do not have the same word tenses or words that denote gender. For example, in Haitian Creole "he" might be used to refer to a female or an inanimate object because "she" does not exist. The English verb to be in "to be hungry" is conjugated "I am hungry," "You are hungry," and so forth. In Haitian Creole the morpheme (smallest unit of meaning) "be" is not utilized, and the Creole speaker would say, "I hungry," instead of "I am hungry."

In my experience teaching English as a new language, one of the most difficult concepts for students to learn is how we use "do" in all its forms. Picture the conversation between two native speakers:

> **Do** you **do** your homework?
> Yes, I **do do** my homework.
> **Do** you really?
> Yes, I **do**.
> No, you **don't**.
> I **do** so.
> You **didn't do** it last night.
> I **did do** it last night. I just didn't do it the night before.

Imagine trying to explain how to use "do" correctly. Did you ever wonder how English-speaking children pick this up naturally? Test your English learners to see how much they know about the usage of "do" by asking them, "Ask me what I did on my birthday last year." Chances are, they will give you an answer like this, "What you did on your birthday last year?" The native speaker will instinctively ask, "What did you do on your birthday last year?"

Another problem across English morphology is the use of prepositions. In Spanish, for example, the word en means "in," "on," "at," and "inside." Trying to decipher which preposition is the correct one to use in English takes a long time, especially with such nuances as "**in** the morning" but "**on** Monday morning." Additionally, in French, Spanish, and some other languages, the same verb is used for "to make" and/or "to do." The result of this confusion winds up with the student saying, "I made my homework."

Syntax

Syntax refers to the word order in a language. In English, the writer or speaker must be clear to express what he or she really wants to say. In every language, a word pattern exists. In English it is subject, verb, object (SVO): For example, *John has a black car*. In a language such as Spanish, this sentence is not stated in the same order. The order would be translated to *John has a car black*, or *Juan tiene un carro negro*. Additionally, English speakers must avoid ambiguity within sentences, as shown in the following examples:

> Dr. Weaver inspects documents in the Department of Education.
> There is nothing odd about the number of students who fail.
> John and Bob took the exam, but he failed.
> To be served shirts must be worn.
> The boys fed the snakes rabbits and mice.

And my personal favorite:

> Woman, without her, man is nothing. (By changing the punctuation, the meaning changes:)
> Woman, without her man, is nothing.

Semantics

Semantics is the study of meaning, words, and phrases. The idea of semantics is complex to a native speaker, but can be absolutely confounding to a non-native English speaker. The new language learner needs "the appropriate cultural knowledge to process language that contains special connotative meanings, idiomatic expressions, and ambiguous sentences, as well as the relevant real-world knowledge to comprehend messages in a second language" (Ariza, Morales-Jones, Yahya, & Zainuddin, 2002, p. 89). Words, idioms, or metaphors hold special meaning for each culture. If the teacher says, "It looks like we're not in Kansas any more, Toto," only the person who is familiar with the Wizard of Oz is going to relate to the true meaning of this phrase. How many other expressions do we use that are culturally pertinent that an outsider may not understand? "Let me say this about that . . . I am not a crook" (former President Richard Nixon). "Read my lips . . . no new taxes" (former president George Bush). We get "paid under the table," driven "up a wall," and give someone a "piece of my mind." How many non-native speakers can finish this: "Jack fell down and broke his _____"? What do we mean by saying, "It's not over til the fat lady sings"? Would a non-native speaker know these phrases? Would a younger person know these phrases? Watch a movie such as *Good Morning, Vietnam* with a group of students. Older students who lived through that era will laugh hysterically in places the younger ones will not, because the older ones have background knowledge and schema. Or if you have the opportunity to see a movie in English with subtitles in another language, you will find yourself reacting differently than the non-native English speaking audience because your background knowledge gives meaning where simple words will not. Our common knowledge of background meaning is pervasive and colors our understanding whether we realize it or not.

A young man lost his passport overseas. When he went to the U.S. consulate to apply for another, the consul wanted to test his cultural knowledge to see if he was really an American. Instead of asking him to recite the Pledge of Allegiance or to sing the U.S. anthem, the consul asked him one question. He told the young man to finish this sentence: "M&Ms melt in your mouth . . ." The young man answered correctly, "Not in your hand," thus proving that he indeed was from the United States.

Teachers must be vigilant in their speech and oral instructions to be sure no special, culturally specific, or nonliteral meanings are necessary for understanding. This attention to nonliteral significance must also include instructional materials.

Always ask yourself if the meanings of the topics are perfectly clear. Will your student understand that "lid" is another word for "top or cover"? Some of our native English speakers won't even know that. What about "teacup and saucer"? Maybe they use a mug. Depending upon our area of the United States, we use different meanings for the same item. Look at the definition of the following words: *a fire escape on a city building in New York* (the stairs on the side of the building that can be accessed by the windows), *tonic* (soda or soft drinks in Boston), *sleet* (hard, frozen snow falling in very small pellets), *lanai* (a porch in Hawaii), *porch* (the landing outside the front or back door of a house such as those found in New England), *hearth* (the flat surface in front of a fireplace), *basement* (the underground room in a house), *attic* (the room or space in the highest part of a house), *dungarees* (jeans), *cobbler* (one who fixes shoes or a dessert made with fruit), *bubbler* (water fountain), *Florida room* (a sitting room in a house that is sunny and usually faces the outside), *mudroom* (the first small room you walk into in a house located in a state with snowy or inclement weather, where you will take off your boots or shoes before entering the house), and *dumbwaiter* (a small elevator within a wall that you utilize with a pulley to deliver dishes, trays, etc., between floors of a house). These words are all culturally pertinent, and without prior knowledge, you or your students (both native and non-native English speaking) will not know what they mean. Imagine an assignment such as this: *Write about what the cobbler did after he went to the bubbler in front of the mudroom.* Without knowing the meanings behind these words, the student is set up to fail.

Phonology

Phonology is the study of the sound system of a language. The English pronunciation of learners will be imperfect because the sound system of the first language gets in the way of the second language. Unless the person has learned English at an early age and has no accent, the new English speaker will approximate the sounds that are the closest to the native language. The speaker cannot "hear" or form the same exact sound because it does not exist in the native language. For example, in Spanish *B* and *V* are pronounced the same. The speaker can be understood but still can get into linguistic trouble. Imagine the Spanish speaker saying, "I have trouble with my bowels," when he really means "vowels." Stress and pitch are also included in this troublesome area. One of my students tried to tell me he was "unique" but he stressed the first part of the word, so he really said "eunuch."

Pragmatics

Pragmatics is the study of how people use language within a certain context and why people use language in a particular way. Would you approach your minister, the Reverend John Simmons, with "Yo Rev"? If we apply for a job, we dress as nicely as we can and put our best foot forward. When we are asked what our weaknesses are, we probably will not tell them that we are lazy, even if we are. We know what the employer is looking for, and it is probably not a lazy employee. We know we need to impress the interviewer, and we usually learn how to do this within our U.S. cultural experience. If people from other cultures (such as Asian societies that encourage humility) were asked questions such as the above, they would be modest and self-effacing. Americans are trained and encouraged to promote themselves, whereas the humble person might be perceived as insecure or inexperienced. These are culturally learned behaviors that work in one culture but are incorrect behaviors in another. Picture these verbal scenarios, and decide where they occur:

- How many in your party?
- For here or "tago"?
- Will that be thin, thick, or traditional?
- Regular or black?
- One lump or two?
- Paper or plastic?
- Say, "aaahhh."

Answers:

- Seating in a restaurant.
- "Will you be eating your food at the restaurant or do you want to take it out?"

- "Do you want your pizza with thin, thick (stuffed with cheese), or traditional crust?"
- "Do you want cream in your coffee or would you like it black?"
- "Do you want one or two lumps or sugar in your coffee?"
- "Do you want your groceries in a paper or plastic bag?"
- The doctor is looking at your throat.

How do you know what these phrases mean? You know because they are all common phrases used in U.S. culture. We learned the right thing to say at the right time because we have grown up within the context and have the background knowledge to know what is correct. If you came from another country, you would have to learn the background to understand this "cultural code." The following is a true example of understanding the background context to interpret meaning:

Lina, from Colombia, was working at a store on Martha's Vineyard when a customer asked her, "Is this a dry town?" Lina answered, "No, the beach is just down the street."

Lina did not realize that a "dry town" is one that does not serve alcohol.

If a small child hears an obscenity and repeats it, adults may react with shock or embarrassment. The child does not know the meaning of what he has said; he only responds to the listener's reaction. He will probably repeat the obscenity at the most appropriate time, so it looks as if the child knows what he is doing and understands what he is saying. If an English learner says a vulgar word in English, chances are it means only that he or she has heard it within a certain context and has repeated it. It holds no meaning for the non-native speaker; the meaning is held within the native English speaker. In the classroom, a teacher must deal with this situation but take into consideration that the student is only repeating what he or she has heard. This is a pragmatic interference; the newcomer has not learned the pragmatic rules of the target culture.

From culture to culture, pragmatic rules differ. In English, very often we use indirect speech. When the teacher says to the student, "Do you want to sit down now?" it is really not a question but a command couched within a question. But the student might answer, "No," without realizing that it was not a question. The U.S. teacher says to the student who is doing nothing, "Have you finished your work?" Although the question appears to ask if the student has finished, the true implication is that the student should be doing something else to stay on task or to keep busy. Doing nothing is not a valued thing in the U.S. culture. In another culture, it might be a true question. But until students learn what the teacher really means, cultural miscommunication can occur. In the home culture, perhaps the teacher would be praising the student for finishing the assignment.

Bilingual Basics

The newcomer to the class with no English ability at all is at an obvious disadvantage, as is the teacher who must provide the same curriculum for the nonspeaker as well as the fluent speaker. Yet the home language needs to be supported as well, because bilingualism is an asset that should be cherished and is not in any way a liability. Being bilingual has cognitive, social, cultural, and economic advantages (Hakuta & Pease-Alvarez, 1992). Very often young children lose the ability to speak their native language when they begin schooling in English. Wong-Fillmore (1991) points out that children who do not maintain their bilingualism are in jeopardy of losing the ability to communicate well with their parents and grandparents. Although promoting bilingualism will enhance the richness of their students' lives, teachers should be aware that bilingual individuals may not be balanced bilinguals, and language can be lost quickly if it is not used (Wong-Filmore, 1991). One language is typically used in each domain; for example, English is used in school and the native language is used at home.

At times it may look as if a child is limited in both languages. If the child does not use the home language enough, it may stunt the richness of native language knowledge that could be transferred to the second language. If the child does not know the age-appropriate amount of second language, it may appear that that child is proficient in neither language. Eventually, the language will become more balanced. However, it is in the best interest of the child if the teacher does everything possible to help the child maintain the home language. This means exposure and usage in sufficient amounts. Encourage the parents to speak the native language at home, even if the child seems to resist.

Additionally, it is helpful if teachers know that "**code-switching**" is a normal occurrence even though it may appear that students are getting their languages confused. Sometimes students will be speaking English and will interject a word from the native language or vice versa. For example, Spanish speakers might say:

- *I am going to averiguar to see if I can go.* (*Averiguar* means "to find out.")
- *Yo tengo un part time.* (I have a part-time job.)
- *He wants to aprovechar the time and get his homework done now.* (*Aprovechar* means *to* "take advantage of.")

Code-switching is actually a sophisticated communicative device that follows rules and demonstrates meaning (Pease-Alvarez, 1993).

Language Interferences

Although the native-English-speaking teacher will notice the errors English learners make in speaking and writing, learning *why* they make these mistakes lends great insight to understanding the process of second language acquisition and to realizing that the students can still make academic gains.

Language learners will make mistakes when they try to transfer knowledge from their first language to their second language. When this process works, the teacher will not recognize that this **positive transfer** has taken place. When the student transfers the native language into the new language and it does not apply, then **negative transfer** has taken place. The errors we see the new language learner making are understandable. With some knowledge of how language is learned, teachers will understand why the first language often interferes with the second language.

DISCUSSION QUESTIONS AND ACTIVITIES

1. Create your own 2 x 2 grid based on Cummins's (1981b) Social and Academic Language theories. Brainstorm individually or with your group and come up with at least four activities that reflect the language abilities depicted in each quadrant.
2. Positive transfer happens when the language learner tries to use a concept from the native language (L1) and successfully applies it to the second language (L2). Negative transfer occurs when the learner tries to relay a word or idea from the first language to the second, but it does not apply. See the examples in Table 5.1:

TABLE 5.1

Example	Spanish	English
Positive Transfer	horrible	horrible
	terrible	terrible
Negative Transfer	actual	now, currently
	carros rojos	cars reds

With your group, research and come up with ten examples of interferences that can happen as a result of language learners' applying the principles from their L1 to their L2. Show morphological, phonological, syntactic, and pragmatic examples of positive and negative transfer.

3. Think of examples of idiomatic expressions that might be difficult to translate, such as the examples below:

   I'm going to give you a piece of my mind.
   He drives me up a wall.
   He took off like a "bat out of hell."
   How might these expressions confuse the English learner?

4. Think of a subject area and a topic of a lesson. Create examples of comprehension questions you can ask the new language learner at each proficiency level:

   ■ Preproduction
   ■ Early production
   ■ Speech emergence
   ■ Intermediate fluency
   ■ Advanced fluency

CHAPTER 6

The School Experience for the English Learner

When non-native speakers of English enter your classroom, you need to know as much background as possible about them. In the publication *Reading and Adult English Learners: A Review of the Research* (Burt, Peyton, & Adams, 2003), the authors offer a chart of the types of native language **(L1)** literacy and their effects on second language **(L2)** literacy. Although it specifically mentions adults, it is as revealing as the types of English learners that are described in the publication by Freeman, Freeman, and Mercuri (2002), *Closing the Achievement Gap: How to Reach Limited Formal Schooling and Long-Term English Learners*. Both depict the very special characteristics and levels of language proficiency in L1 and L2 that English learners bring with them when they begin their studies through English in the United States. Educators who are aware of the specific characteristics of these groups of learners will be better prepared to construct effective instruction to meet these learners' needs (see Table 6.1).

TABLE 6.1   Literacy Characteristics

L1 Literacy	Explanation	Special Considerations
Preliterate	L1 has no written form. Indigenous, African, Australian, and Pacific languages.	Learners need exposure to the purposes and uses of literacy.
Nonliterate	Learners have no access to literacy instruction.	Learners may feel stigmatized.
Semiliterate	Learners have limited access to instruction.	Learners may have had past negative experiences with literacy learning.
Nonalphabet literate	Learners are fully literate in a language written in a nonalphabetic script.	Learners need instruction in reading and alphabetic script and in the sound–syllable correspondence in English.
Non-Roman alphabet literate	Learners are literate in a language written in a non-Roman alphabet (e.g., Arabic, Greek, Korean, Russian, or Thai).	Learners need instruction in the Roman alphabet to transfer their L1 literacy skills to English. Some, such as readers of Arabic, will need to learn to read from left to right.
Roman alphabet literate	Learners are fully literate in a language written in a Roman alphabet script (e.g., French, German, or Spanish).	Learners need instructions in the specific letter-to-sound syllable correspondence. They read from left to right, read English, and recognize letter shapes and fonts.

Source: Burt, Peyton, & Adams (2003).

TABLE 6.2   Types of English Learners

Newly arrived learners with adequate formal schooling.	▪ Recent arrivals (less than five years in the United States). ▪ Adequate schooling in the native country. ▪ At grade level in reading and writing. ▪ Able to catch up soon academically. ▪ May still score low on standardized tests given in English.
Newly arrived learners with limited formal schooling.	▪ Recent arrivals (less than five years in the United States). ▪ Interrupted or limited schooling in native country. ▪ Limited native-language literacy. ▪ Below grade level in math. ▪ Poor academic achievement.
Long-term English language learners.	▪ Seven or more years in the United States. ▪ Below grade level in reading and writing. ▪ Mismatch between student perceptions of achievement and actual grades. ▪ Some get adequate grades but score low on tests. ▪ Have had ESL or bilingual instruction, but no consistent program.

Source: Freeman, Freeman, & Mercuri (2002).

Compare Table 6.1 with Freeman, Freeman, and Mercuri's (2002) chart in Table 6.2 (which they based on Olsen & Jaramillo, 1999) that describes types of English learners (children as well as older English learners), and you can begin to appreciate the range of students and literacy issues you will encounter in your classes.

Understanding Your English Learner

Typically, students who come to the United States with a strong academic background have had the economic or political means to have received a thorough education that readily transfers to English (Cummins, 1982, 1994; Krashen, 1981, 2002b). However, with the variety and diversity of political, financial, and educational backgrounds of students entering the United States, there is no guarantee that any students will bring an uninterrupted, complete education. The idea that basic knowledge in the native language can transfer to the target language makes educating ELLs less difficult, but that is the best-case scenario and is just not the reality in many cases.

The time required for students to acquire social language (up to two years) and academic language (five to ten years) greatly effects academic achievement (Cummins, 1981a, 1982). Students who arrive in the United States with strong educational foundations easily transfer that knowledge to English; therefore, they are apt to perform better academically. Students who come to the United States with limited or interrupted educations will have a more difficult time catching up to their English-speaking peers academically.

To classify students further, another group of students called **Generation 1.5** (Harklau, Losey, & Siegal, 1999; Rumbaut & Ima, 1988) are described as non-native English speaking students who sound native-like and may have been in the United States educational system for many or most of their scholastic years but are still unsuccessful academically because they lack the academic language needed to be successful. These students usually have better English proficiency than their first-generation immigrant parents, and they may sound like native speakers because they learned English at an earlier age. They are not truly native English speakers, yet they are more than international students. They are bicultural with the traits of both the first- and second-generation immigrants. They don't fit the profile of the typical ELLs: therefore, they may not have had the benefit of ESOL classes and, consequently, are still not prepared to do academic work in English. They may not have a strong connection with the homeland, yet are not quite "American" enough to fit in with the native speaker. Since the ESOL class, or a remedial or developmental class, has a negative connotation for them, they will resist taking those classes. The further they go along in school, the more at risk they are of failing and of dropping out of school. Although orally fluent, bilingual or multilingual, they lack adequate competence in reading and writing. This is the "hidden" population of students that may go unnoticed as their teachers might think they are intentionally lazy or avoiding their work. These are the students who cause a teacher to say, "If Tony would just apply himself, he could do much better in school."

School Registration

In an effort to determine placement of a new student, many schools provide a Home Language Survey for parents to complete when registering their children. Another scenario depicts a non-English speaking parent who tries to register her children at the neighborhood school. As she approaches the counter, she begins to tell the secretary what she is there for, but the secretary does not speak German. Imagine what the parent must be feeling.

PARENT:	*Frau des gutenmorgens. Ich bin hier, meine Kinder für Schule zu registrieren.*
SCHOOL SECRETARY:	Hello folks. Welcome to our school.
PARENT:	*Verzeihen Sie mir bitte. Ich verstehe nicht Englisch, aber ich muss meine Kinder für Schule immediatelz registrieren.*
SCHOOL SECRETARY:	Yes, well here are the forms you have to fill out. You need their birth certificates, social security numbers, proof of residency, and the grades from their last school. Please answer the questions that ask about the children's home language. That will tell us if they need to be tested for the ESOL program or not.
PARENT:	*Verzeihen Sie mir bitte, aber ich sehe, teh Formen aber kann nicht sie lesen, weil sie auf englisch sind. Ich kann nicht sie übersetzen. Haben Sie jemand hier, wer mir auf Deutsch helfen kann?*
SCHOOL SECRETARY:	I am sorry, I can't understand a word you are saying and no one here speaks German. You will have to get someone to help you because I can't. I am truly sorry. I wish I could speak your language.
PARENT:	*Lieber Gott im Himmel. Was ich annahmen, um jetzt meine Kinder zu tun sind, die Neigung zur Schule gehen und sie müssen i Nocken zu diesem Land für ein besseres Leben erlernen, aber meine Kinder können nicht eine Ausbildung sogar erhalte.*

The parent walks away dejectedly. No one has asked the children if they can speak English. If they did, they would have learned that the children understood what the secretary was saying. However, in many cultures, the familial hierarchy would be disrupted and the parents would lose face if the child were to interpret for the parent.

Picture yourself entering a school in any non-English-speaking country to register your children, but you don't understand the language. You would not be able to fill out forms or ask about the teacher, proper placement of your children, or school procedures. What would you do?

Background the Teacher Needs to Know

When students are registered for school, a Home Language Survey, such as the one in the Florida schools, asks simple questions such as the following:

1. Is a language other than English used in the home?
2. Does the student have a first language other than English?
3. Does the student most frequently speak a language other than English?

These questions reveal the most rudimentary information, yet this does not help the teacher very much. The teacher needs to know more comprehensive and detailed information, such as that asked by the Home Language Survey distributed by the state of Maine. It asks the parents more pertinent questions:

1. What language do you most often use when speaking to your child?
2. What language did your child first learn to speak?
3. What language does your child most often use when speaking to brothers, sisters, and other children at home?
4. What language does your child most often use when speaking to you and other adults in the home? (referring to grandparents, aunts, uncles, guests)
5. What language does your child most often use when speaking with friends or neighbors outside the home?

As a result of learning this information, teachers are provided with more background information to help determine language dominance and proficiency. However, we are still unable to ascertain crucial information about literacy levels. Can the students read and write in their native language(s) and, if so, up to what level? As a good example, the Pennsylvania Department of Education has devised a Home Language Survey (see Figure 6.1) that appears to cover all bases and offers explanations of what the answers determine (survey available at www.pde.state.pa.us).

Schools or individual teachers can create their own Home Language Survey, keeping in mind that the more information the teacher has, the more appropriate the instruction can be for the student. For example, students from Haiti possess a rich oral literacy tradition but may be illiterate in writing. Notice how students of any age hold a book or a pencil, or where they begin to write on the paper. By being observant, teachers can determine much of the student's literacy background. Some students will not know how to hold a book, use a pencil, or turn a page. That would tell us that the person lacks familiarity with books and with writing. A transient student from a family of migrant workers might never have owned a book, or may have experienced interrupted schooling because the parents move around the country to find work. Each student arrives in school with a history. A student may come from abroad, and the parent may have papers that indicate a birthdate that is very different than is indicated by the appearance of the child. The following is a true story shared by a fifth-grade teacher.

FIGURE 6.1   Home Language Survey

Background and Basis

The Civil Rights Act of 1964 Title VI, Language Minority Compliance Procedures, requires school districts/charter schools to identify limited English proficient students (language minority students). The Pennsylvania Department of Education has selected the Home Language Survey (HLS) as the tool to identify limited English proficient students. The purpose of this survey is to determine a primary or home language other than English (PHLOTE). Schools have a responsibility under federal law to serve students who are limited English proficient and need ESOL or bilingual/bicultural instruction in order to be successful in academic subjects. Given this responsibility, school districts/charter schools have the right to ask for the information they need to identify these students. If not given to previously enrolled students, the HLS must be given to all students enrolled in the school district/charter school and then can be given at the time of each new student's enrollment. The HLS is placed in the student's permanent record file and remains there through the student's graduation.

Suggestions

The school needs to maintain a reasonable balance between the family's privacy interests and the school's need to know information about the child in order to carry out its responsibilities. After a student is identified as a PHLOTE (primary or home language other than English), the school may request additional information about only the student for whom it is needed.

Home Language Survey Questions

The questions listed below are in logical order. The first three questions are necessary to determine minimum information.

What was the student's first language?

Does the student speak a language other than English?

If yes, specify language _____.

(Do not include languages learned in school.)

What language(s) is/are spoken in your home?

If identified as a PHLOTE, a student with a primary home language other than English, additional questions may be asked to get information about the student's academic experiences.

Additional Questions (Optional)

What language(s) does your child read?

What language(s) does your child write?

What language(s) has your child studied in school?

What language(s) do you use when speaking to your child?

Does your child understand, but not speak, a language(s) other than English?

What language(s) do you (parents/guardians) read? *This is important for determining the language of documents you send home and the need for a translator.*

Do you (parents/guardians) read English? *Some parents/guardians may have a good command of written English, but are not able to speak it fluently. They may want documents sent home in English.*

What language(s) do you (parents/guardians) write?

What language(s) do you (parents/guardians) speak? *This will determine if the school needs to use an interpreter for parent conferences, telephone calls, etc.*

Parent/Guardian Signature: _____

I teach fifth grade, and I have a little Haitian boy in my class who is much smaller than his classmates. I wonder if he is developmentally delayed because I can't even seem to teach him how to write his name. He hangs on my leg; I know there is something wrong with this situation, but his father will not talk to me. The boy does not speak much English at all, but I sense that there is something else going on with him.

As is turned out, the youngster should have been in first grade but had arrived in the United States using an older child's papers and birth certificate. The father was afraid to be truthful for fear of being deported. After much deliberation and talk with a Haitian Creole interpreter, they convinced the father to let the boy go into third grade and they would retain him at at the end of the year. By that time, school personnel hoped the boy would be caught up enough with his classmates so that he could function at the correct grade level.

What the Teacher Needs to Know to Teach the ELL

One of the most baffling ideas is to imagine how a teacher can teach a student when neither one knows the other's language. Yet with the elimination of bilingual education and the advent of the No Child Left Behind Act of 2001, legislators, who are almost never educators, demand that mainstream teachers instruct students who don't speak English and then hold the teachers accountable for the students' academic success. This act stresses a number of federal requirements that many states have already addressed.

Given the plethora of research (Collier, 1989, 1992; Cummins, 1981a, 1982) that indicates a period of five to ten years is required for non-native English speakers to approach or equal the academic abilities of native English speakers, ESOL educators have serious concerns about the prospects of success for this plan.

The teachers who are responsible for the task of educating ELLs must know teaching strategies that integrate language within content. Unlike older methods of foreign language teaching, researchers today emphasize that a natural approach to language learning can be accomplished by learning English through the content area. Most of us remember wearing headphones in the high school foreign language lab, trying to learn by repeating words that the speaker was saying, usually at too rapid a pace, and feeling the frustration of not being able to complete the phrase. Personally, I always hoped the teacher would not be listening in on my booth because I could never complete the entire sentence and would just mumble along. We were supposed to repeat the speaker's words and, by some miracle, learn the language. Currently, when I ask my university students how many years of a foreign language they have taken, many will indicate two to four years. Then when I ask them how many can speak the language today, not one will answer affirmatively. What happened to those two, three, or four years of language learning? The fact is, that is not the way we acquire a language. Not one of us learned English by memorizing: *I am, you are, she is, he is, you are, we are, they are.* Yet that is how our schools tried to teach us foreign languages.

Learning rules of reading, writing, listening, speaking, grammar, and pronunciation, one structure at a time, is not necessarily the best way to become communicatively competent in the target language. **Communicative competence** (Hymes, 1972) means the speaker knows how to use the language and address individuals appropriately throughout all settings and situations and within the correct context. There is a difference between linguistic competence, which means knowing about language forms, and communicative competence, which recognizes that social and cultural contexts of language are just as important to successful communication (Bachman, 1990; Canale & Swain, 1980). Background meaning, or schema, is critical. Anyone who has studied a foreign language has experienced this situation: After studying the foreign language, you think you know how to speak it, only to visit the country or talk to native speakers of the language and not understand a word the native speakers are saying. As an example of how one can formally study a language but not become proficient, I share my experience below.

I first decided to go to Mexico because I liked Spanish. After studying Spanish for two years in college, I was ready to go study Spanish formally at the Universidad Nacional Autonoma de Mexico in Mexico City. Upon my arrival, I immediately called my friend, Victor, who could speak English. I was proud of myself for having mastered the telephone procedure with foreign coins and all. When someone answered, I said, "Por favor, puedo hablar con Victor? (Can I please speak to Victor?). The woman replied, "Victor no se encuentra." I was clueless as to what that meant because, if he wasn't home, I thought she would have said, "No está", or "No está en casa." I tried again, "Victor, por favor?" Again she said, in a rush of words, "Lo siento. No se encuentra." I was in serious trouble now. I didn't know what she was saying, and all I understood was the word, "No." I decided to negotiate an alternate communicative route with the memorized phrases I knew. Taking a guess that I might get more information I could understand, I asked another question I was sure of: "A que hora esta en casa?" (What time will he be home?). Finally, I hit pay dirt! She said, "A las tres." (At 3:00). Wow, and I thought I could speak Spanish! I finally understood how people who come to the United States feel when they study English in their home countries yet can't communicate when they encounter native English speakers.

The focus should be on learning a language through authentic texts and situations, in other words, through the use of materials that have not been specifically produced for the purposes of language teaching (Nunan, 1989). A more "communicative approach" offers a natural emphasis where learners are actively engaged in "comprehending, manipulating, producing, or interacting in the target language" (Nunan, 1989, p. 10). By using authentic materials, more genuine communication can take place.

Many of the older methodologies of language teaching, such as the Audio Lingual Method, are based on structure and form, error correction, native-like pronunciation, and eliminating any use of the native language, rather than on meaning. The Communicative Language Teaching approach concentrates more on meaning within the authentic context, with fluency, acceptable language, and communication being the immediate goal, rather than speaking the language perfectly.

Having established the point that language should be acquired in the most natural and authentic manner, how do we approach this task? First, the teacher has the crucial responsibility of making the learner feel comfortable in taking language risks. New language learners will make mistakes; this is inevitable and expected. Teachers have the responsibility of facilitating language learning in the classroom by planning for interaction to take place and for assisting the learner to move from "total dependence to relatively total independence" (Brown, 1994a, p. 162). Eventually, students will learn language appropriate to the classroom settings as well as outside the classroom.

DISCUSSION QUESTIONS AND ACTIVITIES

1. Individually or with a group, create your own Home Language Survey. What important questions do you need to ask to obtain information about your new student? What do you need to know to be able to teach this student?
2. Your new students have different backgrounds. One studied extensively in her homeland, and another was uprooted from his school when war broke out in his country. What differences do you think you will encounter? How will you address the needs and issues of these two students?
3. Have you studied a foreign language? How well did you learn it? Describe your experience. What would have been a better way for you to have learned the language?

PART THREE

Learning English Through Academic Content

CHAPTER 7

Why Integrate Language and Content

Language and content must be integrated—you cannot wait until the student knows enough English to start studying academic content. The law says teachers must provide the same curriculum for the new ELL as for the native English speaker, in a manner comprehensible to the student and at his or her level of proficiency, without diluting the curriculum. The Council of Chief State School Officers (CCSSO, 1992) determined that success for English language learners "hinges upon gaining access to effective second language learning opportunities and to a full educational program" (p. 4). In an effort to ensure that ELLs have the same opportunities as English-speaking students, CCSSO recommended that, although supportive language-assistance programs may help develop language proficiency, schools must provide a way for English learners to "continue to learn and expand their knowledge of new content and, therefore, not fall behind peers whose native language is English" (p. 6). Consequently, this attitude corresponds to federal laws that insist all students, regardless of native language, receive comprehensive curriculum in a manner that they can understand.

In many states, bilingual education is not an option; language teachers and subject area teachers have begun to collaborate to prepare curricula that will include ELLs in the mainstream classroom and keep students on grade level while developing English proficiency. Several approaches have offered teachers resources for integrating language with content, such as books, training workshops, courses for ESOL endorsement, teacher development inservice programs, professional conferences, presentations, seminars, and training in ESOL techniques. Content-based instruction does not focus on discrete-point language training such as grammar rules and memorizing vocabulary lists. Rather, teachers use regular content topics as the framework for instruction that complements language learning. Another approach, Sheltered English or Sheltered Instruction, is geared for intermediate-level (of language proficiency) students who are all ELLs; the teacher adjusts the instructional level to that of the students' capabilities. ESOL techniques are utilized to make the content understandable or **"scaffolded"** to make learning understandable to the English learner.

In the integrated language and content class, the focus is on communication through reading, writing, listening, and speaking. More concrete instructional techniques such as visuals, demonstrations, graphic organizers, prewriting, and prereading skills are utilized. Students are taught **cognitive processes**, such as how to think and how to develop study skills, which actually helps all learners (Brinton, Snow, & Wesch, 1989; Crandall, 1993; Short, 1991). A buddy system for peer support is offered for companionship and translation if possible, and authentic and meaningful situations are provided for communication to take place through social interaction and contextualized communication. In other words, meaning can be constructed because communication takes place as it is embedded within the situation.

More detailed information about language and content lessons will be discussed later in this book. Appendix I is a sample of a lesson plan format that integrates language and academic content. This approach is called **Sheltered Instruction Observation Protocol (SIOP)** from the book *Making Content Comprehensible for English Learners: The SIOP Model* (Echevarria, Vogt, & Short, 2004).

Strategies for Teaching ELL Beginners

Teaching the English beginner calls for certain strategies. The students who are in the **silent stage** or the emerging language stage may appear to understand or pretend to understand when they do not. More proficient students might act the same way, so it is imperative that the teacher constantly check for understanding. If you say, "Do you understand?" the student very often will say yes. The best comprehension check is to have the student show you that he or she understands by acting out what he or she is supposed to be doing. Fillmore and Snow (2000) recommend a list of strategies for the teacher to use with the beginning English learner. These strategies will be referred to and expounded upon throughout this text.

- Use demonstrations, modeling, and role playing to teach the appropriate language to make polite requests, apologize, express thanks, and so forth for particular circumstances. For example, a real telephone can be used to show how to use appropriate telephone language, a table can be set with real cutlery to practice authentic language, and so on.

- New information should be presented within the context of a situation (**context clues**) the student already knows. Themes and materials for reading and other instructional activities should be appropriate to the students' cultural background and are best presented embedded within the context of the here and now (Cummins, 1982). For native and non-native speakers, vocabulary should never be presented in isolation. Present words in context so the students can better determine their meanings.

- Paraphrase and extend language utterances as you would with a native English speaker learning a first language. Whatever the student says, repeat the utterance but elaborate and extend upon it. Model correct language when errors are made. For example, the student might say, "She name Susie." Then you could say, "Her name is Susie? Susie is a lovely doll. She is very pretty. What a beautiful face she has."

- Use simple language structures and avoid complex sentences. When paraphrasing, we often use more complex grammatical construction. I remember listening to a teacher give an orientation to a new group of English language students. In trying to explain the rules, she said, "This is a fire extinguisher. If you want to play with it, it will cost you 50 bucks." I interjected, "Mrs. Johnson wants you to know that it is illegal to play with fire extinguishers in this country because the firemen will come, and you will have to pay a fine or penalty of 50 dollars." If I say, "The boy, who is from Morocco, is going to buy a book," I really am saying two sentences because one is embedded within another. I am saying: *The boy is from Morocco. He is buying a book*. It is easier to understand simple sentences than ones with clauses. Stories and language can be just a little bit above the students' language ability, but not so much as to be frustrating.

- Use repetition of sentence patterns and routines. Songs and rhymes are wonderful for promoting language development because students will learn what to expect within the repetitions. Classroom routines with predictable language are good for students to attach meaning to the words. Common classroom imperatives are repeated again and again, and students can look around them to see what classmates are doing if they don't understand the words. Some examples:

Take out your book.
Close your book.
Take out your pencil.

- Ask questions according to the language level and participation of the student. If he or she is in the silent or preproduction stage, tailor your questions to correspond with his or her ability. In the order of simplicity, the easiest language forms are yes/no or one-word answers, which are great for beginners. According to the levels of difficulty, the order of questions will range from *what* to *where, when, how,* and *why,* with *why* questions being the most difficult to answer. Teacher response will train the learners in the appropriate protocol for questions and answers.
- Finally, be tolerant of students' mistakes. They may be developmental and will self-correct with time. Understanding the message initially is more important than perfect speech.

Methods for Teaching ELL Beginners

One of the most useful approaches to teaching the beginner is using the **Total Physical Response** method (Asher, 1972). Asher, a psychologist, conjectured that people learn better when they are incorporating physical and mental processes. TPR is quite fun for students, as it satisfies their kinesthetic needs; they are not expected to speak, only to obey and to respond to physical commands. Think of the game "Simon Says." Imagine the teacher giving a command in English and the students responding. The teacher can model the behavior first, then students follow. After a few times, the teacher may stop modeling and just state the commands. Students who do not understand will look around at other students and follow their actions. With much repetition, all students will eventually understand what is being said, yet they are not expected to say a word. The following commands are an example. Commands can be built upon little by little:

Stand up.
Sit down.
Turn around.
Raise your hand.
Touch your head.
Pick up the book.
Put down the book.
Walk to the door.
Walk to the door, touch the door, turn around, and then sit down.

After much practice, not only will students respond to the command, but they might want to play being the teacher. As they begin to utter their own commands, their language proficiency develops. It is easy for me to discern how much exposure to the language the students have experienced prior to being in my class; those students with little or no exposure seemed to merely "approximate" the pronunciation of the word, and it sounded similar to how a deaf person sounds. In my experience, it appears to me that young children who are not native English speakers but have been raised listening to *Sesame Street* and *Barney* in English have internalized the sound system and will sound more native-like in their pronunciation.

Visuals, pictures, objects, realia, pointing out, choosing, organizing, classifying, grouping and regrouping, and rearranging pictures are only some of the other components that can be used within TPR. Teaching prepositions (put the book ON the table, put the pencil UNDER the table) is easier when the students see the concrete meaning for the word. Although TPR is focused on listening comprehension for those students in the silent or preproduction stage of language proficiency, the teacher can introduce reading and writing the commands as well. From positive statements, you can go to negative statements and even to questioning formats.

After the students are very certain of the commands the teacher has chosen, they can be written on the board so that the students can see what the spoken words look like in written form: for example,

> *Give me the book.*
> *Paul, give Helen the book.*
> *Paul, give her the book.*

Seeing the written form of the pronounced word will help reinforce reading, pronunciation, and writing. With writing, the next stage of grammatical development can be teaching negatives by seeing the action; this can then develop into a question format by watching the expression and action of the teacher.

> *Paul, give Helen the book. (Give the book to Helen.)*
> *Do not give Helen the book. Give the book to Juan.*
> *Give Tran the book. Do not give the book to Tran. Give the book to Manolo.*

Pictures work well within TPR. Comprehension is shown after giving a command and the correct actions are done.

Vocabulary can be expanded by giving the students an array of pictures and saying:

> *Raise (or hold up) the picture of the apple.*
> *Put the picture of the orange on your desk.*
> *Stand up if you have the picture of the watermelon. Walk to the bulletin board and hang the picture.*

With a little imagination, you can create any type of activities for your ELLs and include their classmates as buddy tutors. Collect and laminate pictures of every type of vocabulary a new student is likely to need to know. *Bathroom, faucet, desk, locker* (most students from other countries do not have lockers or cubbies in their schools), *pencil, pen, hall, closet, chalk, eraser, computer, computer keys,* and so forth are all common vocabulary words that your students will need to know for survival. I used to take my students on unconventional "field" trips into the bathroom, the kitchen, the cafeteria, the playground, the students' lounge, and name whatever I was doing. On a trip to the bathroom, I would talk my way through what I was doing: for example,

- *I am opening the door.*
- *I am entering the bathroom.*
- *I am sitting on the toilet.* (I act as if I am going to sit down. This might seem obvious to you, but a little Chinese girl I know used to sit in the reverse position on the toilet because no one had ever told her the right way to sit.)
- *I am taking the toilet paper off the roll.* (Show the student how much to take. Use your own discretion, and consider the age of the student. At times I pantomime what to do.)

- ▪ *I am flushing the toilet paper down the toilet.* (Many students do not know that it is permissible to flush paper down the toilet. Numerous countries do not have a septic system that can support flushing toilet paper. On the other hand, you must also indicate what is not permissible to flush down the toilet.)
- ▪ *I am turning on the faucet.* (Show and let them feel the hot and cold water. Depending on the country, they might not expect the hot water. Actually, in many bathrooms around the world, you cannot even find paper or soap. Everyone knows to bring their own toilet paper, or there may be an attendant who sells toilet paper by the piece.)
- ▪ *I am wetting my hands.*
- ▪ *I am washing my hands with soap.* (Have you ever noticed that every soap dispenser is different?)
- ▪ *I am rinsing my hands.* (Every faucet is different as well. How would someone know that all you have to do is stand in front of the sink and the water would go on?)
- ▪ *I am drying my hands.* (Again, this may be with individual paper towels, a warm air blower, or a towel on a roll.)

Two exchange students from Italy came to the United States to study English. They lived together in a homestay situation. When the director of the language school asked them if their living arrangements were satisfactory, they said that they loved the family, but they were glad they were living together so one could guard the other when they went to the bathroom, because there was no door. The director was horrified and called the host family. The mystery was solved when the host mother told the director that their house had pocket doors that slide into the wall. How could the students be expected to figure out something about which they had no prior knowledge?

Being prepared before the first day of school ensures that you will not be caught off guard when your ELL comes into the classroom. It is a lonely feeling to sit in a class and have nothing to do because the teacher cannot speak to you or is too busy with the other thirty kids in the class. That is why visuals, TPR, and buddy systems are wonderful methods to use for the ELL. Language master machines (machines that show a picture as a voice pronounces the name of the picture) and computer programs are also excellent tools for beginning language speakers. Do not assume, however, that the new student will know how to operate a computer. Have an assigned buddy help guide the student if you cannot get to the student individually. Teachers can utilize partner work, group work, or entire class work to maximize opportunities for language practice.

DISCUSSION QUESTIONS AND ACTIVITIES

1. Write a script using TPR (Total Physical Response) for a beginning-level student: for example,

   Stand up.
   Sit down.
   Pick up your pencil.
   Go to the door.

2. Show by role playing how you could teach prepositions, nouns, and verbs using TPR.

3. Take the dialogue you have used for question 2 and manipulate the language to write sentences, questions, and negatives. Show how you would turn a TPR activity into a writing lesson. Using the sample lesson plan in Appendix I, create modified lessons for ELLs in

   - The silent stage.
   - The emergence stage.
   - The intermediate stage.
   - The advanced stage.

CHAPTER 8

Differentiated Instruction for English Learners

Research and recent legislative mandates dictate that students need to learn English through the content area, and teachers must have the ability to modify mainstream content textbooks. Overall, bilingual education may no longer be an option. Therefore, teachers must be skilled in modifying lessons that will scaffold learning subject matter through another language. Language integrated approaches to teaching must provide opportunities for cognitive growth as well as language practice. This chapter provides examples of lesson modifications, shows how to critically analyze mainstream textbooks for appropriateness, and gives guidelines for adapting materials.

A native English-speaker and ESOL teacher, Ms. Silva fell in love with the Spanish language while she was visiting Mexico. After completing her elementary education program, she decided she wanted to be a bilingual teacher. She taught in Puerto Rico, Spain, Colombia, and Mexico before feeling comfortable enough with the language to teach native speakers of Spanish in the United States. With the influx of Spanish speakers into the U.S. school systems, she was quickly hired as a bilingual first-grade teacher. The principal thought he had struck gold by finding a teacher with ESOL, elementary, Spanish, and bilingual certification.

Ms. Silva learned much during her first year of teaching in the United States. She learned how to handle the situation if no supplies were available for her young charges; she learned how much she loved the Hispanic children in her class; and she learned about politics. She quickly discovered that being able to speak two languages did not make her feel "bilingual." Even though she had studied Spanish for years and could live in a Spanish-speaking culture, the 6- and 7-year-old children often knew more Spanish than she did. She also did not feel comfortable teaching writing in Spanish. They laughed at jokes she didn't understand, even though she knew every word. Simply, she realized how much she did not know. She could converse well, but when it came to underlying meanings and understanding jokes that required previous schema, she knew she was at a loss. Speaking Spanish and knowing pedagogy of bilingual teaching and the second language learner were two very different issues. Fortunately, she had a native Spanish-speaking assistant who could help her with the nuances of the language.

Ms. Silva did her best throughout the year. She believed that if she said everything in Spanish and then again in English, the children would understand and learn the language at the same time. By the end of the year, she switched to only English, as the children understood everything she said; they sounded like native English speakers, even parroting Ms. Silva's Boston accent. At the termination of the school year, she recommended that thirty-four of her thirty-seven children be mainstreamed into monolingual. The principal was shocked and told her that would be impossible.

Ms. Silva's scenario is embedded with issues. First, she doesn't realize that, although the children may speak flawless English, they are not ready to be mainstreamed. They need academic support and modifications with ESOL strategies to continue to be successful. Even though you may hear, "Why is this child in ESOL? He speaks perfect English," research shows a great cognitive difference between social language and academic language (Cummins, 1981b). In fact, Ms. Silva found the same thing happening to her: She could speak Spanish very well, but had difficulties when abstract concepts where involved. Her social language was excellent, but understanding language is more than just possessing an extensive vocabulary.

Ironically, when the principal said it would be impossible to mainstream thirty-four children the next year, he was not referring to language issues at all. His main concern was political; he did not want to lose the position held by the second-grade bilingual teacher. If the children went to the mainstream class, they would not need a bilingual teacher, and she would be out of a job. No other mainstream teacher was available. Probably more important to the principal was the fact that he received funds for each student who was in his bilingual program. If the children were exited, so was his funding. It was a hard but valuable lesson for a new teacher to learn.

With bilingual education losing favor, more mainstream teachers bear the responsibility of teaching English learners in the classroom. Although some schools have English for non-native speakers as a pullout program or even bilingual programs, the short time these specialized teachers spend with English learners is not sufficient enough to grasp the social language, never mind the academic language of the subjects taught in schools.

Students from other countries come with a kaleidoscope of varying abilities in academics and language proficiency. I see a recurring pattern of students who seem to fall into the following categories:

- Strong academic background in their native language, ready to transfer this knowledge to English
- No previous school experience or interrupted schooling, with poor language and academic proficiency in their heritage language
- American citizenship or residency, but speaking a language other than English
- Fluent English, born in the United States, but with poor academic skills

Regardless of the academic language or diversity of your students, they will be in the same classroom with all the other students of varying abilities, languages, and individual issues.

The mainstream teacher is mandated by law to teach all students in a comprehensible manner. This means that the teacher will have to integrate language learning through the content area. The most important phenomenon about language learners I have ever learned was that it takes five to ten years to become as proficient as native speakers in a given academic area (Cummins, 1981b; Thomas & Collier, 2002). If this is the case, a teacher may see students enter the class in first grade and go through until eighth-grade graduation without ever seeing them gain sufficient English proficiency to become academically successful. This fact also begs the question: Why are we forcing students to take standardized exams without English language proficiency? It is ludicrous, yet every year we hear more and more about the government's stand on "raising the bar" for teaching and learning through the ubiquitous, if not misguided, standardized test, the "cure all" for "poor teaching." Teachers are faced with incredible odds, including poor pay, long hours, students who are not motivated, parents who are ready to sue if the child is chastised for improper behavior, and lack of administrative support, which robs the teacher's power to maintain discipline in the class.

From the thousands of preservice teachers who have passed through my classes, one constant remains: Teachers are drawn to the profession because they have a burning desire to teach. Quite often, teaching is the last thing educators get to do in the classroom. Class sizes have swelled, students with behavioral problems must be monitored, students with exceptionalities and limited English proficiency are mainstreamed, and it seems like every new teaching and learning fad that comes along is adopted before proven successful. Yet, teachers still desire to teach because of their passion for helping students.

Federal laws mandate that all students must receive an education that is comprehensible to them, regardless of native language. Deciding that separation of races in schools was not really "separate but equal," *Brown v. the Board of Education of Topeka, Kansas* (1954) guaranteed equal protection under the law for all races, students with handicaps, and the linguistic and culturally diverse populations. In the case of *Meyer v. Nebraska* (1923), the Supreme Court determined that instruction in the native language was not immoral or injurious and should be allowed. Consequently, the landmark case *Lau v. Nichols* (1974), where 1,800 Chinese children filed a class-action suit in California, established a precedent stating that having the same textbooks and curriculum did not imply equality of education, because the students could not understand instruction in English. At that time, special language programs were developed across the nation. Therefore, this chapter is dedicated to teaching educators how to modify the curriculum for English language learners so they can learn language through the content area.

A language-integrated approach to teaching content will allow teachers to use the same curriculum that is used for the mainstream class; however, scaffolding with ESOL strategies is necessary. Many publishing companies are now providing strategies for language learners and students with disabilities in the teacher's edition, but it is not probable that every bit of material will come with these provisions. Additionally, in an effort to provide authentic resources, teachers will have to modify their own materials. In my university's ESOL-infused teacher education program, we emphasize a list of common teaching strategies that is by no means comprehensive but is recommended by Broward County Schools (see Appendix A). I have also included the classification and descriptions of language proficiency levels to determine how much modification is necessary (see Appendix B).

As in teaching any students, the teacher must nurture the development of cognitive skills and provide avenues for student participation for language practice. Researchers have studied language immersion programs and determined that students can attain high levels of language proficiency while learning content matter (Lambert & Tucker, 1972; NCBE, 1990). Students understand the material because the teacher uses visuals, realia, demonstrations, hands-on learning, manipulatives, and cooperative strategies where students have to participate in their own learning. Instead of traditional foreign language learning that focuses on isolated classes of grammar, reading, writing, listening, and speaking, learning language through content allows background knowledge, or **schema**, to be built on. The students then can process the information more holistically, top down (Carrell, 1983) instead of bottom up, or piecemeal.

Hoover and Collier (1989) have created a list of suggestions for selecting and adapting materials for ELLs. However, these strategies work well for all students with special needs.

- Be aware of each student's language abilities.
- Make sure appropriate cultural experiences are reflected in the material.
- Ensure that the material progresses at a rate that is commensurate with the needs and abilities of the student.
- Document the success of selected materials.

- Experiment with the materials until you find the most appropriate for your particular student.
- Make a smooth transition into the new material.
- Follow a consistent format or guide when evaluating material.
- Be sure to become knowledgeable about the cultures and heritages of your students to ensure appropriateness and compatibility of the material.
- Evaluate the success of adapted or developed materials as the individual language and cultural needs of the students are addressed. (p. 253)

Many teachers want guidelines for adapting materials. Although this chapter shows actual examples of how to adapt text, other tips include the following (Harris & Schultz, 1986; Lewis & Doorlag, 1987; Mandell & Gold, 1984):

- Develop your own supplemental materials.
- Tape record directions for the material so students can replay for clarity.
- Provide alternatives to responding verbally to questions (e.g., use prearranged signals, give them a card to hold up, a flag, or any indicator they can use instead of speaking).
- Rewrite sections of the text to condense the reading for those with lower proficiency levels.
- Outline the material for the students before they read.
- Teach students the meaning of using bold headings, italicized words, subheadings, and transition words (*first, last, however, although,* etc.).
- Use graphic organizers for preinstruction.
- Reduce the number of pages or items to be completed by the student.
- Break tasks into smaller subtasks.
- Provide additional practice to ensure automaticity and mastery of the material.
- Substitute a similar, less complex task.
- Develop simple study guides, rubrics, and templates for uniform assignments.
- Develop study guides for all students.

After presenting the content to be learned, the teacher can focus on individual concepts such as grammar or obvious language interferences. Students demonstrate competence on a daily basis within authentic situations as they interact with class members. Using this method challenges students and teaches them how to use learning strategies.

Preparing to Teach the Standard Curriculum

Ms. Aldrich was frustrated and annoyed. Henri, from Haiti, had been sitting in her classroom all year, and she could not seem to motivate him to produce work. He barely uttered a word, and she wondered if there was something wrong with his hearing or if he had other problems of which she was unaware. She knew he would not be able to take the test on the Civil War with the other students. She passed out the test to the rest of the class. When she got to Henri, she tossed a piece of paper on his desk, and said, "Here, draw a picture." He took out his colored pencils and began to doodle. When the bell rang, he shyly put his paper on her desk. When she picked it up, she was speechless. Henri had drawn a gorgeous pictorial of the entire Civil War, from start to finish. He had grasped the lessons, but did not participate in the class work because he was unable to write in English.

All classroom teachers are going to face the same types of problems; therefore, it behooves teachers to collaborate with each other. A thematic approach will unify content throughout the grade levels, and all teachers will be focusing on the same topics. Initially, look at the content you are expected to teach. What are the objectives? Note the language used. Look at the pictures, if any. What realia can you use to enhance the concepts being taught? Will your students be able to understand what is written? Note the language proficiency levels in Appendix B. If a student cannot speak because he or she is in the silent stage of language acquisition, it will be up to the instructor to modify the content to make it comprehensible. What key terms are the students expected to know? You will have to simplify and adapt the text to fit the appropriate language level of the student, from beginner to intermediate to advanced. Using the strategies found in Appendix A, teachers can present information clearly and systematically, so the learners can count on daily structure and format that does not change. Routines will make the ELLs comfortable, and soon they will be able to follow the predictable class schedule.

Begin your lessons by writing objectives on the board so students can see what they are expected to know, to do, and to learn. Then, as in good teaching everywhere, list the steps they need to follow to complete the assignments. Use visuals wherever possible, with lists, charts, diagrams, templates, concept maps, and concrete examples. Review frequently; finally, have the students show you what they know through verbal discussion, in a drawing, or in any other acceptable way.

We are often advised to incorporate multicultural factors in our daily academics. Familiarity with your students' culture will allow you to include and refer to situations, matters, and issues that are important to them. All students feel more valued when their teacher knows what is important to them and their families. In the United States, we are taught that it is our job as teachers to reach out to the students, to determine their preferred learning styles, to appreciate the diversity of our learners, and to modify what we can to ensure academic success. The educational culture in the United States stipulates that we adopt a student-centered approach that allows the students to be more responsible for their learning, while the teacher is more of a facilitator. A constructivist method of teaching allows the students to form their own opinions in a type of inquiry approach to learning. Students from other cultures may see this as not really teaching, and will comment to their parents that they are "waiting for the teacher to teach." Thus, learner training is encouraged so the students are cognizant of the class objectives and will understand that the teacher does know how to teach, even though the students might have been asked their opinions about what or how they wanted to learn.

In many countries, going to school means that the teacher lectures while the students sit and copy notes to be used for a test later. In American classrooms, the ideal approach is to allow students to speak to facilitate interactive language practice. With ELLs, language has to be very clear and direct. They need time to think, to process what is being said in one language, and then to find an answer. The typical English speaker may speak too fast to be understood by the ELL. When we ask one question, we need to make sure it is one question. We have a tendency to ask a question in this way: "So what would have happened if we had not won World War II? What would life be like today? How would we be living, and who would be controlling our country? How would you feel if some other country were controlling the United States?" The student does not know which question to answer.

We need to reduce the amount of teacher talk, ask one question at a time, give plenty of wait time for the question to be processed, rephrase the question if necessary, and create authentic opportunities for students to speak interactively. Know that language learners will make many mistakes; I always tell my students that language learners are going to mangle the language before they dominate it, so do not expect perfection. Expect and encourage trial and error, and take this into consideration when grading. Think globally. Can you understand what the student is trying to say? If the

ELLs are making themselves understood, that is something to celebrate. Beginners should not be corrected unless the mistake interferes with understanding. For example, "That is a nice chair," when it is really a table, needs to be corrected. "He like she; she pretty" is very clear. You can correct this by saying, "He likes her? Yes, she is pretty," which is a good modeling strategy.

Asking pertinent questions is an art form. It is tempting to ask cognitively lower level questions, such as, "How many people were in the play?" A more profound learning experience can be elicited by asking, "What can we learn from this play?" Think out loud so the students can see your cognitive process. According to Bloom's (1984) taxonomy, critical thinking skills such as hypothesizing, analyzing, predicting, inferencing, reasoning, summarizing, and justifying will help with comprehension of reading and academic content. Always keep in mind that cognitive skills have nothing to do with language skills.

Preparing students for instruction is an important element of effective instruction. Help them become successful by giving them tools to sharpen study skills. Ensure your students will grasp the concept of the lesson by motivating them before instruction begins. Start at the students' level of listening and speaking ability before transitioning into reading and writing. Teach them what steps to follow to solve problems and how to infer meaning from a textbook through the bold print, subtitles, illustrations, graphs, table of contents, and index. Teaching study skills will help all your students, regardless of native language. Develop questioning techniques that will assist students to develop a higher level of cognitive skills instead of expecting them to answer lower level questions. Watch your students closely, and analyze their learning styles. Remember that students from different cultures will reflect a variety of learning preferences. Experiment with a variety of alternative activities, and note the methods students prefer. Check comprehension by using methods such a cloze tests (where they fill in the missing word), completing a template (an outline that the student completes with missing information), filling out a timeline, drawing a picture, or any other method that shows comprehension of the subject matter.

Review vocabulary and key concepts with a graphic organizer, a **KWL chart**, a semantic web, or a concept map. Concept maps will help direct and categorize thoughts, while providing schema or background knowledge for your students. KWL charts will give you the opportunity to see what students already know about a topic. To complete the KWL chart in Table 8.1, ask the class what they think they know about rainforests, and fill in the first (K) column. Ask what they want to know, and fill in the details in the middle (W) column. At the end of the lesson, to review and summarize,

TABLE 8.1   Example of KWL Chart

Rainforests		
K What I know:	**W** What I want to know:	**L** What I learned:

ask students what they have learned. This summation will go in the last column (L). You will be astounded to learn what preconceived notions students have about a topic.

All students will be able to engage in the topic if they possess some background knowledge that will connect concrete concepts to abstract ideas. Teachers can make a subject come alive by offering an enticing initiating activity to open a lesson. Imagine the interest students may show when they enter the classroom and encounter a large, artificial tropical tree, hanging "vines," tropical "animals" hung around the room, and music of the rainforest and wild animals playing. The teacher is decked out in a safari hat with rations of food to carry around the room. The book *The Great Kapok Tree* is displayed and read from, and everything in sight is labeled. Students are surrounded by vocabulary of the rainforest as pictures, collages, maps, and evidence of realia is everywhere.

An opening approach like the one described above is apt to whet the interest of even the most intransigent student. Vocabulary is easily demonstrated by looking at the labels, pictures, and models. When the teacher initiates the KWL chart, students will be eager to offer what they know; their memories are prodded as they understand what the rainforest includes and transcend into the "rainforest" mood. The teacher can start with a group task, engage students in discussions, invite them to share previous knowledge, and examine tactile artifacts found in a rainforest. The Internet can be utilized to find pictorials of "live" rainforests, and students can be invited to engage in various activities to begin the thematic unit.

Although language learning techniques are used in the language learning class, the same or similar methods can be incorporated in the content class. Typically, the younger the student, the more realia is used. However, as the students get older, less embedded information that gives clues to understanding is present in the text. Unless students have extensive vocabularies, they will soon become lost. Therefore, even the older students will appreciate the scaffolding built in to enhance understanding.

Short (1991) offers ideas taken from traditional ESOL techniques for content teachers to incorporate in their classes. She recommends the following:

- Realia.
- Demonstrations with action (e.g., science experiments, model language functions in context).
- Filmstrips, video and audio recordings with books and headphones, computer programs.
- Hands-on activities (e.g., role play, TPR, laboratory experiments, art, story sequences, comic strips, creating math word problems, creating templates to be filled in).
- Incorporating Big Books (social studies, science, stories) into lessons.
- Using jazz chants, music, dance, rap songs, poetry; have students write their own rap and poetry about subjects or people being studied.
- Sustained silent reading (SSR), where students are allowed to read material of their choice.

Teachers must provide comprehensible content matter for students. The regular classroom curriculum can be used if modified for the ELL. Short (1991) provides excellent strategies for simplifying and adapting materials and encourages teachers to begin with presenting the main point of the text in clear, simple, understandable language:

- Decide what should be learned by comparing text information with the curricular objectives.
- Eliminate unnecessary details (start by presenting concrete references to abstract ideas).
- Try to relate information to students' backgrounds.
- Use visual representations.

Rewrite the text using these guidelines (Short, 1991):

- Topic sentence, then supporting detail.
- Reduce words in the sentence, and sentences in a paragraph.
- Use subject-verb-object word order.
- Simplify vocabulary, while retaining key concepts and technical language.
- In the text, avoid using many synonyms, which can confuse the reader.
- Use clear vocabulary definitions repetitively, while giving clues by connecting new vocabulary with known vocabulary.
- Use simple verb tenses (present—*I eat*; past—*I ate*; simple future—*I am going to eat*).
- Use the imperative form. (Sit down, please. Take out your books, please. Stop talking, please.)
- Use active, not passive voice. (*Active:* John hit the ball. *Passive:* The ball was hit by John.)
- Use pronouns only when you can tell to whom they are referring. (John went to the store. Tom went to the game. He got lost on the way.)
- Avoid *there, it, or that* at the beginning of the sentence. They are ambiguous words. (*Don't use:* There are many cars in the garage. *Do use:* Many cars are in the garage.)
- Avoid relative clauses with *who, which,* or *whom* in sentences. Make the clause into a sentence, since it creates an embedded sentence. (*Example:* John, a man who is from Texas, is a doctor. *Better:* John is a man from Texas. He is a doctor.)
- Use negative judiciously, especially when testing. (*Avoid:* Which of the following does not belong . . . try to use the form of negation that includes the verb, as in *don't cry*)
- When the students' language level warrants readiness, teach sequence markers (*first, second*), transition words (*although, however*), and terms that prioritize (*most important, best of all, the least likely*).

Content Area Analysis and Evaluation

In most classrooms, the required texts do not arrive with modifications for diverse learners. This will be up to the teacher. Examine the text to ascertain the adaptability of the text for your class. Figure 8.1 shows an example of how a high school text can be examined to determine how it should be modified. An elementary text would be scrutinized in the same way. Examine the sample of the text analysis in Figure 8.1, developed by Jennifer Peffer. As a result, the teacher can determine whether the book is appropriate and how the book needs to be modified for the ELLs.

Short's (1991) training manual is an excellent resource that offers steps to develop lesson plans, adapt material, and incorporate ESOL strategies and techniques for integration of language through the content area (her model is used in Appendix D).

FIGURE 8.1   Analysis of a Textbook to Be Modified*

Name of Textbook:	United States Government—Democracy in Action
Publisher:	Glencoe/McGraw Hill—Congressional Quarterly
Content Area:	American Government/Civics/History
Grade Level:	High School Grades 9–12

*Contributed by Jennifer Peffer.

1. Content Objectives of the Book—Scope and Sequence:

United States Government—Democracy in Action introduces the key concepts required to understand the history and composition of the American governmental system. These concepts include Federalism, Separation of Powers/Checks and Balances, Civil Rights and Liberties, Constitutional Law, Political Processes, Comparative Government, and Economics. The book also highlights a variety of critical thinking, writing, and technology skills used to study American government. Examples include understanding cause and effect, decision making, interpretation of poll results, taking notes, outlining, writing reports, and using computers for research.

The teacher's edition begins each chapter with a "Bell Ringer." This activity is used to motivate students and to get them involved in the chapter. It introduces the key concepts to be discussed. The book is organized into nine units and twenty-six chapters. The student is guided through the book beginning with the origins of American Government. The next three units focus on the three branches of government: Legislative, Executive, and Judicial. Unit Five spotlights the Constitution and civil rights. This appropriately leads into government participation and policy. The book finishes with an overview of state and local government and a comparative look at different political and economic systems that exist throughout the world.

Every section begins with a series of questions designed to focus the reader's attention to the important ideas present in the reading. The sections end with vocabulary and key people reviews as well questions about the reading. Critical thinking questions are also placed at the end of each section. Each chapter has a review of facts, key terms, and concepts. There are also critical thinking exercises, technology activities, and government participation assignments.

A. Chapter: The Constitution
   Four sections:
   1. Structure and Principles
   2. Three Branches of Government
   3. Amending the Constitution
   4. The Amendments
B. A large number of concepts are covered in this chapter because the Constitution is the basis of the entire American Government, which is a conglomeration of many interrelated concepts. Each chapter reviews many of the concepts that were previously introduced, solidifying the reader's comprehension.

Thirty new ideas and vocabulary terms are to be mastered in Chapter 3. Some of these are jurisdiction, popular sovereignty, judicial review, checks and balances, federalism, impeachment, ratify, probable cause, due process of law, and warrant. After completing the study of Chapter 3, students will be able to

- Summarize the historical origins of the Constitution.
- List the major parts of the Constitution.
- Define the major principles involved in the formation of the Constitution.
- List the three branches of government and the expressed powers of each.
- Define implied powers and give examples of each by analysis of the Constitution.
- Explain the concepts of checks and balances and why the system is important to a stable government.
- Outline the amendment process and explain why it was designed to be a difficult one.
- Identify the ten amendments that make up the Bill of Rights.
- Differentiate between a right and a privilege.

(continued)

FIGURE 8.1   Continued

▪ Classify the amendments into ones that affect governments, personal rights, and societies.
▪ Explain the concept of judicial review and give examples of its affect on citizens today.

2. Unfamiliar Cultural Assumptions:

The study of American Government presents concepts that might be unfamiliar or even uncomfortable to some people from other nations. Notions such as freedom of speech, women's rights, popular sovereignty, and capitalism are all concepts that are foreign to many nations. These concepts are addressed from a very basic level. Most of the exercises require at least a basic understanding of the concepts after they are covered to fully answer the questions. The author's examples are well explained and are accompanied by a good amount of background information, which allows the student who might be unfamiliar with the material to answer the questions and participate fully.

One area that would prove difficult for some ELLs would be the political cartoons. Much of the humor is characteristically American and might not be grasped by students from another nation who do not have schema pertaining to American popular history.

A group of women in a museum are standing around a portrait of men. The caption on the cartoon reads, "Founding Fathers! How come no Founding Mothers?"

Students might be from countries where women are not expected to play a role in government and therefore might not understand the significance of this cartoon.

For the most part, this book is free from cultural assumptions in the testing and review questions. The role of the text is to portray the culture of American government and the history that led to its development. After teaching the core concepts, students should understand the evaluation exercises, despite their initially unfamiliar ideas.

3. Higher Order Thinking Skills:

Many exercises in this textbook require higher order thinking skills (see table):

Example	Skill
1. What is the relationship between the principles, concepts of federalism, and the separation of powers as detailed in the Constitution?	*Analyzing* the two concepts of federalism and the separation of powers as detailed in Constitution. *Relating* two concepts to another.
2. Have students keep a journal of their daily activities for two weeks. At the end of the period, ask students to name activities that would have been restricted or impossible under a repressive government or a government that does not have a constitution based on the major principles discussed in section one.	*Analyzing* the Constitution to draw a conclusion of what rights are protected as they relate to students today.
3. Which principles or provisions of the Constitution allow students to carry out their daily activities without fear or punishment?	*Making* predictions. *Drawing* conclusions. *Relating* applicable concepts.
4. How would the federal system of government be affected if the Supreme Court did not have the power of judicial review?	*Making* predictions. *Drawing* conclusions. *Relating* applicable concepts.

a. Modification of Question: These exercises are appropriate for ELLs. The wording may be a little advanced, but simple rewriting of the question would assist the students by clarifying what is being asked.

An example would be another version of question 1: *How are federalism and separation of powers the same? How are they different?* This would make the question easier to understand and would allow the student to focus on the concept and not the language.

The second question also would be appropriate for ELLs, with language modification to ensure comprehension. This task allows the students to practice writing in a nonacademic arena and also to take time to analyze and formulate their answers, free from the language issues.

4. Text Evaluation:

This text is visually oriented, which makes it comprehensible. Over eighty maps and charts complement the text, as well as pictures on nearly every page, a boon for teaching students of other languages and the visual learner. The book is also in tune with issues that are pertinent to today's society. Many news stories and illustrative examples highlight relevance of the subject matter to the students' lives, including censorship, civil rights, and equal protection under law. The text also establishes important vocabulary and terms at the beginning and end of each section. Important words are highlighted in bold when they are introduced within the text. What would help would be making review answers available to the students to allow self-checks for understanding as they continue to study.

The teacher's addition has many supplemental activities that are appropriate for different academic levels. The author also focuses on Gardner's (1993) multiple learning styles and has activities that focus on the different intelligences. Many resources are available to accompany the book such as a DVD that contains video and audio material to complement each chapter, transparencies, and computer software with review activities. The text also offers supplemental materials that would be particularly helpful to ELLs, including lecture notes that outline the chapter content and guided reading activities with graphic organizers to help convert the reading into comprehensible input.

The text was well organized and appropriate for ELLs as well as the general student population. The variety of activities that are available to solidify the concepts being taught is impressive and will allow the teacher to reach students of all levels. The activities are labeled by difficulty (levels 1–3, with 1 being basic for all students and 3 being advanced) in the teacher edition. The text is sensitive to students who need more vocabulary assistance and focuses on concept building and relating those concepts to concrete, real-life situations. This book will be a valuable tool in teaching the ESOL population as well as English proficient learners.

Note: See Appendix F for template.

Note: In Appendix D, Honey Smith shows how she adapted text from a book on government. She created a PowerPoint presentation with pictorials and modifications for the English learner in the mainstream class. Because of copyright issues, I am unable to include the visuals she used. However, I have included the text slides along with the websites with wonderful clipart that can accompany the text.

DISCUSSION QUESTIONS AND ACTIVITIES

1. Describe the steps you would take to discover what background knowledge your students possess. What activities would you offer to connect their prior learning with the lesson you are going to present?
2. Choose three books. Using the Content Area Textbook Analysis form provided in Appendix F, analyze the main objectives of the books. What unfamiliar cultural assumptions do you find? (Remember that your students will not come from an American mind frame. Everything might be different.) Name three higher order thinking skills that are present in the text. What is your overall evaluation of the books for English learners?
3. Choose a paragraph from a text. Using the methods prescribed in the chapter, simplify the language for beginning, intermediate, and advanced language-proficient English learners.
4. Create an alternative assessment for each level of language proficiency (beginning, intermediate, and advanced). Why do you think these assessments are valid?

CHAPTER 9

Literacy and the English Language Learner

SUSANNE I. LAPP

Liza, a 7-year-old Russian girl from a well-educated family, arrived in the United States at the beginning of the school year. Her father was a physician and her mother was a graduate student in the United States. Liza's parents set high expectations for their daughter's academic achievement in the United States, and they expected her to quickly adjust to her new learning environment. Before coming to the United States, Liza had completed four years of preschool in her native country. The Russian preschool program focused on socialization skills and encouraged children to think creatively. Among other activities, the students spent the day singing songs, participating in dramatic play activities, and completing art projects. Liza was also beginning to learn the Cyrillic alphabet. Liza knew most of her letters and was experimenting with inventive spelling at the time her family left for the United States.

Upon Liza's arrival in the U.S. first-grade classroom, Liza's teacher, Ms. Drake, made an attempt to gradually introduce her to classroom rules and procedures. Instead of seeing her Russian classmates' artwork, writing attempts, and dramatic play centers, she encountered a classroom that was completely foreign to her. Liza found desks arranged in a traditional style with four rows and four columns. She discovered that her teacher created the seating arrangements according to how each child behaved and that, if she displayed good behavior, she might have the opportunity to move to a different seat. Ms. Drake told the students that they were expected to remain in their seats throughout the day, and they had to ask for permission to leave their seats. Liza was shocked by all the rules and requirements. In Russia she was able to access a number of centers in the classroom when she desired to explore. In her U.S. classroom, her freedom to move around the room was curtailed and controlled by the teacher.

Ms. Drake believed that learning could not take place in a noisy classroom, and she made a strong effort to control behavior. She expected that eventually Liza would become adjusted to the course curriculum, which consisted of teacher-directed activities, with Ms. Drake controlling classroom instructional techniques and assignments. Students played passive roles and were not given the opportunity to interact and collaborate with each other or in groups, as they became too noisy. The teacher's style of instruction was most noticeable in her approach to teaching reading and writing. She taught reading and writing by concentrating on the graphophonic cueing system approach, focusing most of her instruction on teaching letter–sound relationships and rules for decoding words. Ms. Drake began the daily writing assignment by discussing a particular letter, describing its shape, and writing an example of the upper and lower case of the letter on the chalkboard. Then she would pronounce the letter, and the children would be encouraged to repeat the sounds. After pronunciation practice, the teacher would randomly select four or five words from the students' basal reader and ask students to copy these words in their notebooks. Most of the first graders eagerly tried to please the teacher and completed the assignment meticulously. Liza, however, was reluctant to complete the teacher-directed assignments. Instead, she spent a great deal of time trying to spell her name, draw pictures, and copy answers from classmates. Habits such as these caused her to be late with assignments or resulted in papers that were turned in to the teacher uncompleted. As the semester continued, Liza's negative behavior increased. She displayed frequent outbursts in class, refused to complete assignments, or tried to steal her classmates' assignments. Ms. Drake expressed complete frustration over Liza's negative attitude. She repeatedly contacted Liza's parents and met with her mother on one occasion. Unfortunately, the meeting was unsuccessful and fraught with miscommunication and misunderstanding; the parents accused Ms. Drake of being incompetent and responsible for harming their daughter's educational development.

To avoid a potentially cataclysmic outcome with the parents, the teacher sought the advice of several colleagues and her principal, who encouraged her to consider creating a more student-centered learning environment. They suggested that Ms. Drake needed to embrace the following fundamental rules about student-centered learning environments:

- As teachers, we need to know that all students bring a degree of literacy knowledge to school. This knowledge is unique and related to the student's different experiences using literacy concepts and skills.
- Classrooms need to be designed so that they provide a safe and supportive learning environment where teachers actively model functional and purposeful reading and writing activities.
- Teachers need to be patient and learn to accept and celebrate student progress in their gradual approximations to conventional literacy.
- Teachers need to encourage students to read and write at home and to talk to their parents and families about their reading and writing attempts.

Engaging parents and families in the students' literacy efforts encourages family members to feel that they are significant stakeholders in the student's academic future (Peregoy & Boyle, 2001).

Liza's teacher considered these suggestions as she embarked on a new instructional approach to her literacy classroom. Her initial attempt at implementing new instructional strategies began with the daily classroom routines. Liza's teacher wanted her students to realize that literacy was meaningful and that it fulfilled their everyday needs and purposes. Through this process, the teacher discovered that she was able to explicitly teach actual processes of reading and writing as the students participated in daily classroom activities that enhanced awareness of the forms and functions of print. These types of literacy forms are discussed below.

Morning Message

During the morning message, the teacher has the opportunity to preview the day's activities for students. Activities that are central to the morning message include the teacher's writing the activities of the day on the board, as he or she says the words. This activity models the organizational function of writing (left to right, letter-by-letter sequence corresponding to the spoken word).

Classroom Rules and Procedures

Involving students in establishing classroom rules and procedures at the beginning of the year is another way to demonstrate functional literacy. As the teacher and students negotiate and make decisions, the teacher records the rules on a large sheet of paper. Students have the opportunity to see spoken words written on a sheet of paper. By stressing the important uses of print in day-to-day routines, students learn that literacy is a natural and nonthreatening way to express ideas.

Alphabet/Word Wall Dictionary

Creating word walls is another effective instructional tool to use with early literacy and language learners. Ideally, students need to be seated so that they see the alphabet/word wall chart at eye level. The most effective way for teachers to introduce young children or beginning literacy students to alphabet/word walls is to include students' names in the alphabetical listing. Students are able to recognize their names and those of their classmates. Gradually, they begin to recognize the "power behind the print." Letters and words begin to take meaning, and printed names indicate individual personalities. After a period of time, students will become interested in placing words from songs, poems, and stories on the alphabet/word wall. Students are constantly invited to add new words to the wall from their own literacy experiences, and they are asked to chorally read the words on the word walls (Peregoy & Boyle, 2001). The teacher should check to make sure all students are participating.

As Liza's teacher began to incorporate these instructional changes in her classroom, she noticed the students' level of enthusiasm and interest increase. Prior to revising her instructional approach, the teacher believed that students learned most effectively by participating in carefully scripted assignments, where they were asked to read specific controlled vocabulary and to copy words from the book.

Students' increased interest and positive reactions led the teacher to further reassess her approach to literacy instruction. Ms. Drake began to provide more opportunities for students to listen to authentic literature, and she began to create more student-centered writing assignments.

Reading Aloud

Students of any age are interested in listening to stories read aloud. When teachers read stories aloud, students are introduced to the aesthetic pleasures and functions of print. They are exposed to the literary notions about story plots and characters, and they have the opportunity to observe teachers model the reading process. Although read-aloud activities appear to be aesthetically pleasurable, they do in fact create a heavy cognitive–linguistic demand on listeners, particularly in terms of attention, comprehension, and memory. Teachers need to compensate for these challenges by frequently pausing to discuss illustrations as they relate to a story, to make predictions, and to reconfirm predictions that support comprehension. Repeated readings of the text will also enhance comprehension. Once the story has been read aloud to students, it is likely that they will want to have access to the story to practice some the techniques that they have seen modeled by the teacher. It is advisable for the teacher to have multiple copies of the text so students can access the book for individual reading. In addition, a great way of increasing understanding is to provide each student with a text so he or she can follow along silently with the teacher's words. This will model pronunciation while the student visualizes how the word looks.

Books selected to be read aloud in the classroom need to be age and topic appropriate as well as comprehensible. If vocabulary is too difficult for students, teachers need to clarify, define, and add the new vocabulary to the alphabet/word walls. Pre-instructions of vocabulary will scaffold reading comprehension.

Since students in a classroom have a variety of literacy experiences, teachers need a well-stocked classroom library complete with an assortment of books that will suit a variety of reading levels. Among the types of book to be included are the following:

- Alphabet Books—Alphabet books describe the alphabet in an interesting way and can help students become aware of the alphabetic principle while learning the names of letters and concepts. The most effective books are ones that have enjoyable illustrations that convey meaning and help English language learners make connections between specific letters and the sounds they make in words that they already know.
- Big Books—Teachers will also want to have Big Books in their classroom. Big books consist of large, predictable text. The large format of the Big Book allows students to follow along with the words as the teacher reads the story to the class. Teachers may wish to use frames that allow children to focus on only one word at a time in the book. By framing the word, the teacher provides practice in recognizing the words on sight, as well as the graphophonic cueing system. It is important that the teacher use predictable books with word patterns and phrases to teach or to reinforce sound–symbol correspondences including consonants, vowels, and letter sequences found in rhyming words.

A very popular technique used to enhance oral and written literacy skills includes individually made books. One of the most effective techniques is the **Language Experience Approach (LEA)**. The LEA can be appropriately used at any age, for early learners to adult literacy students. The basic philosophy behind LEAs is that

1. Students who can think, talk, and listen can learn to read and write.
2. What students talk about can be expressed in writing.
3. What students write or have written can be read. (van Kraayenoord & Paris, 1996)

One effective way to initiate LEAs in the classroom is to invite the entire class to dictate a story. The teacher first models this process for the class. As students dictate a story, the teacher writes it down on chart paper. Students are asked to read what has been written. This activity models a host of important reading techniques, including functional writing and reading, illustration of the relationship of sound to speech, sound–symbol correspondence, and development of sight vocabulary. Since students generate the content of the text, it ensures that the assignment is age appropriate and relates to the students' experiences and interests.

Sight Word Activities and Development

LEA can also be used effectively to teach reading and writing skills, such as sight word vocabulary and development and decoding activities. Students develop sight word vocabulary as a result of immersion in meaningful, functional encounters with print found in dialogue journals, morning messages printed and explained, alphabet/word walls, repeated readings of poems and predictable books, and shared writing through LEA activities. Words can be selected from LEA activities and other books to familiarize students with specific sight words. Students may also benefit from working in pairs or in small groups to advance the task of sight word recognition. Sight word tasks might include playing matching games or using flash cards to encourage instant recognition of words. Later, students should be encouraged to use their sight word knowledge to complete authentic writing activities. Readers must eventually learn to recognize sight words instantly. Otherwise, students will spend an unreasonable amount of time trying to decode words, which will negatively affect their understanding of the text (Peregoy & Boyle, 2001).

Decoding/Phonics

The purpose of phonics instruction is to provide the reader with the necessary tools to unlock the construction of a word, thus increasing the students' chances for comprehension. Phonics should be taught within a meaningful context and not for the purpose of forcing students to recite rules or generalizations. The following decoding/phonic suggestions may be effective for English language learners:

- Provide ample time for students to read and write for meaningful purposes, and allow students to develop their own understanding of sound–symbol correspondence.
- Informally assess phonics and word recognition skills your students already possess by observing their reading and writing efforts.
- Always teach phonics and other word recognition skills within a meaningful context. Encourage students to enjoy the story or poem for its meaning first, then attempt to teach the phonic skill or generalization.
- With a focus on meaning, encourage students to concentrate on spelling patterns rather than phonic rules or generalizations.
- Remember that phonics and other word recognition strategies are simply a means to the end goal of comprehension.

Student-Centered Learning Activities

Reading Aloud Strategies in the Classroom

Returning to the vignette at the beginning of the chapter, it was noted that upon arrival in the United States Liza had become a disengaged, apathetic reader. She was disenchanted with classroom activities and failed to complete assignments. As her teacher began to implement newer, more student-centered learning strategies, Liza's interest in literacy began to blossom. Some of the strategies Ms. Drake used are explained here.

One of the first student-centered activities that the teacher used in Liza's classroom was reading aloud to the children. The teacher decided that the best time to read aloud to the children was after they had returned from the afternoon lunch break. The teacher read one of the books from the classroom reading center. Liza attentively listened and enjoyed looking at the pictures. One picture in the book depicted a busy street with many trucks and busses. Liza looked at the picture and claimed that it looked like her home in Russia, "I lived in the town of *Mockba* (pronounced *Muskva*) but you Americans say it [sic], you make it sound like this /moskkooww/!"

Many of Liza's comments about reading and writing appeared to come from previous experiences with the Russian language. During the school day, Liza, along with her native English-speaking peers, attended a 70-minute Russian class where they received exposure to Russian songs, language, literature, and games. At home, Liza's mother spoke Russian and read Russian stories to Liza. Liza was surrounded by the

Russian language and culture; this exposure appeared to be reflected in her second—language literacy experiences as she consistently integrated Russian language in her English writing.

Language Experience Approach Activities

With the positive feedback from the reading-aloud activities, Liza's teacher began to implement writing activities in the classroom. She decided to model the LEA procedure for her students. All of the students actively contributed to the writing activity. Liza thought that the class LEA assignment should include a story of a handsome prince or princess. The teacher wrote down all of the students' suggestions. From the collection of words, the teacher encouraged the children to think of writing a story. Gradually, the students began to place the collection of words into sentences, and the teacher began to write the students' words on the board. As the teacher went along, she pointed out sight words that the students should recognize, and she highlighted some phonic generalizations that the students should know. The children added the new words to their vocabulary notebooks. Once the story was completed, the teacher encouraged the students to write the short story in their books and to then illustrate the story.

The students had favorable reactions to the assignment. After several group LEA activities, the teacher decided to let her students compose their own LEA writings. Liza's teacher also thought this would be a great opportunity to enroll her students in a districtwide Young Authors Program. The students were encouraged to write and draw about any topic. The teacher was willing to provide the students with assistance, but students were responsible for creating and completing the story.

Many of the children in the classroom, including Liza, eagerly attempted to record their literary-attempts on paper. Since many of the children were just beginning to write in conventional English, they included a great deal of inventive spelling and required assistance from the teacher. Although Liza asked for assistance from the teacher, she began to dictate her story to a classmate. Liza drew a picture of a beautiful princess who was planning to marry a handsome prince. In her second drawing, she included a picture of the bride standing near her mother and father. Next to the picture, she carefully wrote the words, MaMa (mama), папа (papa), and Liza.

With the introduction of the LEA in the literacy program, Liza increasingly became more engaged in literacy learning. Liza's continued progress in literacy-related activities began when she was able to see meaning attached to her literacy efforts (Purcell-Gates, 2001). Prior to the change in instructional approach, Liza did not realize that reading could be a personally enriching and satisfying experience. Instead, she believed that reading was getting the correct answer from English experts (her classmates). However, after participating in the LEA activities, Liza gradually realized that she was able to create meaningful text, thereby facilitating comprehension.

Comprehension Activities

Through the interactive and collaborative nature involved in reading-aloud and LEA activities, students were able to develop skills in comprehension. The cognitive demands of listening and responding to stories being read out loud or reading and editing parts of their own stories enhanced the students' interest in striving for meaning and comprehension.

It is important to note that these literacy activities are not exclusively for young English language learners. Many of these activities can easily be applied to adult learners (Kreeft, 1984). Older English language learners might find dialogue journals more intriguing and purposeful. In dialogue journals, students write regularly on a topic of their choice, and teachers respond to the content of the entry instead of the form.

Teachers show interest in students' ideas, ask questions that encourage elaboration, model form and function in writing, and deepen their personal relationships with students.

DISCUSSION QUESTIONS AND ACTIVITIES

1. As a teacher who encounters an English language learner in the classroom, how would you initially introduce the child to the classroom rules and procedures? Create a plan and share it with your group.
2. Find ten other literacy strategies that would be effective to use with upper-grade English language learners.
3. How might you incorporate your English-language-learning students' first language or culture in your English literacy activities? Describe the activities you could incorporate.
4. What English language or literacy activities would you suggest to parents of English language learners to assist in their child's English language development?

10

Teaching Math to English Learners—Myths and Methods

SALLY ROBISON

Many teachers tell me that mathematics should be easy for English learners because the concepts translate across languages. This idea appears to make sense because many ELLs do well in math, even when they are functioning at a rudimentary level of language proficiency. However, language misunderstandings eventually emerge, as mathematics is a subject that has its own vocabulary, double meanings, and idiosyncrasies seen nowhere else. I invited Dr. Sally Robison, a teacher educator in mathematics, to write a chapter highlighting the issues and problems we can expect to find when we teach ELLs math in the mainstream classroom. She guides us to the best ways of teaching mathematics to students who are newcomers to English.

Gloria, a third grader and a native Portuguese speaker, has been in a Florida school for two years. She is bright and apt in math and knows her basic addition and multiplication facts. However, the math vocabulary is different in English, and when she has to show her work, it is always marked wrong, ever though she gets the right answer.

One of the greatest misconceptions about mathematics is the idea that, since it is a universal concept, English learners will have no problems transferring mathematical knowledge to English. Although this might be true with simple, concrete number algorithms (2 + 2 = 4), many other aspects of mathematics might prove difficult because of the language differences. Additionally, the assessment of conceptual understanding of important mathematical concepts may prove inaccurate if the primary method of assessment is the standardized test or the analysis of answers to word problems. Any teacher knows the difficulty that even native English speakers have with wording such as this: "Five times a number is two more than ten times the number." "A number" and "the number" are referring to the same number, yet many students will not decode the sentence this way. Look at this phrase: "The sum of two numbers is 77. If the first number is 10 times the other, find the number." How do students know if the second sentence refers to two numbers or the same number (Dale & Cuevas, 1992)? Therefore, teachers must demonstrate the meaning of these problems with pictures and models as concretely as possible, and explain the semantic differences between "a" and "the."

Modifications for language learners must be provided in mathematics instruction as well as every other content area. However, ELLs need many opportunities to learn all aspects and complexities of mathematics while obtaining academic and communicative competence in English. Lessons must contain both content objectives and language objectives that help students learn language through specific subject matter rather than through isolated activities (Cantoni-Harvey, 1987; Short, 1991). In other words, students do not have to learn English before they commence learning mathematics.

Critical framing encourages learners to evaluate what they have learned, to constructively critique that learning, and to creatively extend and apply it to new contexts (NLG, 1996). Critical framing directly applies to the concept of problem solving in mathematics. Teachers cannot provide every possible scenario in mathematical problem solving, but teachers should provide connections to key problem-solving strategies that assist the students during their mathematical challenges. Teaching students to make connections within the subject and in the real world, to reason mathematically and verify their findings, to solve real-world problems, to communicate their thinking about mathematics, and to represent their findings in a meaningful way formulate the five process standards that encourage "mathematical confidence" as defined in the National Council of Teachers of Mathematics (NCTM) (2000) *Principles and Standards* document.

Diaz-Rico and Weed (1995) explain that the major difficulties English learners have with the language of mathematics are in the area of "vocabulary skills, syntax, semantics, and discourse features" (p. 137). To mitigate these problem areas, Zemelman, Daniels, and Hyde (1998) outline the best practices for teaching mathematics in their book entitled *Best Practice: New Standards for Teaching and Learning in America's Schools*. These practices include

- Using math manipulatives to make math concepts concrete.
- Teaching students to do cooperative group work.
- Discussion of math.
- Questions and making speculations.
- Justifying the thinking processes.
- Writing how they think and feel about math and problem solving.
- Using problem-solving approaches as the most effective type of math instruction.
- Integrating content with math.
- Using calculators, computers, and other types of technology.
- The teacher is a facilitator of learning.
- Using assessment as a learning tool during instruction.

It is evident that many strategies exist for teachers to use that facilitate the learning and application of mathematical concepts by all students, including those who are language enriched. The many strategies mentioned in this chapter have been categorized into the following areas: literacy development, cultural harmony, and effective instruction/assessment. Although the strategies are often intertwined in the teaching process, for ease in explanation of each strategy, the breakdown is beneficial. These strategies will prove helpful in teaching ELL students.

Literacy Development Strategies in Math

The spoken word and the written word require students to be literate in the vocabulary and fluent in their reading so they are capable of comprehending what is read. This is easily said but difficult to accomplish. By incorporating the following strategies, students will improve their comprehension and mathematical skills.

Review Concepts

The teacher will need to review important key concepts whenever necessary, such as mathematical terms that may be abstract or confusing to students. For instance, a lesson on multiplication of two-digit numbers may require an explanation and review or teaching of pertinent vocabulary, such as *product, sum, carry, exchange,* and *equals,* in a contextual setting. Don't automatically assume students know these terms or any others or their synonyms.

Generate a concept table, asking students to identify words that have similar meanings. For example, start off with the word *add* and ask students to create three to five more words that mean basically the same thing. Let them brainstorm on their own, and then bring small groups together to compare their answers.

Add
Combine
Sum
Plus

Vocabulary Building

Introduce pertinent vocabulary in each lesson using realia and demonstrations whenever possible. Before covering a section in the textbook, examine the material to identify terms that will be new to the students or words that will need further explanation. Present any symbols or words that may create problems for the students. The new vocabulary should be repeated often in a meaningful setting and/or paraphrased so that students will retain and use the concepts that are related. Use any synonyms that will assist in their understanding. Capps and Pickreign (1993) recommend a minimum of six exposures to a new word during the lesson and at least thirty additional exposures throughout the following month. Mathematics has often been referred to as a foreign language, possessing its own vocabulary and meanings that have another connotation outside the subject. For example, *simplify* means making something less complex; yet in mathematics, the process of *simplifying a radical expression* may generate a cumbersome process that results in a final answer that appears much less simple.

Teachers need to clarify expressions, words, and symbols that have multiple meanings. For example, the word *reciprocal* is similar to the word *reciprocate* but does not imply the same meaning. The word *rationalize* has a meaning in normal context, yet a totally different meaning in the realm of mathematics. Remember that the repertoire of methods and activities used to teach vocabulary in other areas, such as writing words and definitions, spelling tests, and providing pictures of words, are just as appropriate when teaching a mathematics lesson. Mathematics often includes technical words such as *denominator, quotient,* and *coefficient* or other words with multiple meanings, such as *column* and *table.* Encourage students to talk about their conception of mathematics and to verify and justify their thinking. Verbalizing what they are thinking will give the teacher great insight into the misinterpretations and confusion students may have.

Modeling Mathematical Terms

Model the correct use of appropriate math vocabulary when interacting with students, and encourage students to discuss and use the new concept and role of the word. For instance, *subtraction* is often called *take away, minus,* or *difference.* Help students recognize that the same process can be explained with various phrases. Once again, the use of a concept table will help them identify the relevant connections between the terms.

Accepting the inaccurate phrases students produce will require both patience and flexibility. Teachers should recognize that the written word develops slower than the spoken word. It will be more likely that students learn to speak correctly, although perhaps approximating the words, about mathematics long before they are able to write correctly about mathematics. Although the process is slow, teachers should work toward requiring the mathematically correct use and form of the terminology. In addition, teachers should ask students to explain how they found the "difference" when discussing an example on subtraction. Repetition of the phrases while modeling the action will encourage automaticity of the mathematical process.

Simplify the Words

The typical textbook may be written at the appropriate grade level, yet the ELL student may be reading at a lower grade level in the English language. Assist students by reading the textbook with them to ensure they understand the wording. Asking students to rephrase what was just read will encourage writing and communication skills and will prove to be a valuable assessment tool.

Help students to rewrite word problems in simpler terms and in their own words. Ask probing questions that help them simplify each section they read as well as each portion of the word problem. Read each sentence in the word problem carefully, one at a time, to decipher the meaning and the key elements from the sentence.

Restate complex instructions using simple English that cannot be misinterpreted. The English vocabulary is laden with clichés and slang words that should be avoided. For example, the expression, "You hit the nail on the head," implies the use of a hammer and nail, when the term actually means the person correctly analyzed the situation.

Symbolism and Abbreviations

Abbreviations and symbols can create much confusion. Capps and Gage (1987) call attention to the fact that abbreviations and other mathematical symbols create difficulties in a student's ability to understand. For example, teachers should avoid using traditional symbols without providing an interpretation, such as ~ for similar shapes or the use of the apostrophe for indicating feet. Avoid using abbreviations such as *pt.* for pint, *ft.* for feet, or *lb.* for pound until the students have been introduced to this new symbolism. Repeated use of the symbols and abbreviations will assist them in their proper mathematical usage of these standard items of protocol found in every mathematics textbook and assessment instrument.

The need for teaching the abbreviations and explaining the specific symbolism is a vital part of the instructional process for all students. Make vocabulary charts that include the abbreviations and symbols, and place them strategically around the room where they are clearly visible to the students. Once again, flexibility is in order. If students use *pd.* for pound, which is actually more logical than the traditional *lb.*, identify the error but accept their answers.

Realia

Learning becomes easier when the material being taught is relevant and viewed as personally necessary. The level of concentration and focus are heightened when our interest is aroused. Therefore, selecting vocabulary and performance tasks that relate to the student's own real-world exposure will enhance learning. Common foods, names, items, and traditional holidays can be used making up word problems and examples. For instance, when teaching about fractions, refer to common items such as egg cartons, pies, or pizzas to concretely illustrate the values of halves, fourths or quarters, thirds, and sixths. Follow these activities with the usual mathematical manipulatives used in the traditional classrooms. However, be aware of cultural biases.

Select real situations that include local settings for your instructional lesson. Have students handle money in the school store, identify the time, locate the date on the calendar, and measure their own heights and weights. In addition, use the correctly pronounced names of the students in examples used during instruction. Select everyday activities such as cooking and carpentry that the students will see as pertinent to their existence.

Writing About Math Concepts

Once again, it is important to recognize that the spoken word develops before the written form. To encourage the process, teachers should give students the opportunity to write about their new math concepts. Writing can be used to explain solutions, rephrase instructions, generate word problems, decode existing word problems, and express feelings.

Examining students' written work can be a useful assessment technique. Journals are an excellent way to determine the degree of understanding and to provide the opportunity for students to express their concerns and issues without peer pressure inhibiting their interactions with the teacher. For instance, have them rewrite a textbook sentence in their own words to help them clarify their own thinking. Encourage them to write their own definitions to words, and have them draw pictures to create their own math dictionary. Students should create word problems to share with classmates. This will be a useful way for the students to develop their own interests and understanding.

Encourage students to write often, approximately three times a week, by providing prompts and an audience for whom they should write. If possible, find another class that can become pair partners in reciprocating correspondence with your English learners. Additionally, the teacher should model writing during instruction and class discussions. Above all, allow students to make both grammatical and pronunciation mistakes; however, teachers should be sure to model the correct response back to the students.

Talking About Math

When addressing ELL students, use clear, basic English for all questions and explanations, and enunciate clearly. Give short, concise directions one step at a time, and repeat them as often as needed. Adapt the lesson to simplify each step if complex explanations have been typically used to explain the concepts. For example, expressions such as "one dog, two cats" may be confusing to the ELL student. They may not associate the word you use with number of items, but rather with the type of item referred to.

As previously noted, students may not be reading at the same level as the instructional materials being utilized. Speak slowly and clearly so students can follow along with the instructor. This method will assist in vocabulary building, sentence structure, and comprehension of the material.

Read Slowly Students should to be taught to read their math books slowly and carefully. They often skip past the words and look specifically at the diagrams and examples without utilizing the valuable dialogue that explains key steps and concepts. Teachers should encourage students to use the textbook guides, such as boldfacing, underlining, and the glossary in the back of the book. However, when these tools fail, they should be encouraged to ask for an explanation of a word or sentence they are having difficulty understanding. Persuade them to search for meanings of new mathematical terms by providing a mathematics dictionary, as well as the typical English dictionaries, but avoid routine assignments of looking up words and writing down definitions. Such activities, along with the excessive use of drill exercises, do little to excite or encourage mathematical development.

Pacing It is very important that teachers recognize that ELL students acquire verbal skills faster than writing skills. This is a normal process in learning a second language. Flexibility and acceptance of mistakes are key factors in helping students move forward in their writing. Allow students to write and rewrite their mathematical understanding. First, second, and third drafts should be encouraged to help the students learn the proper way to express their mathematical thinking.

Mathematical Literature Books

Many excellent mathematical resources exist that promote and develop mathematical concepts. In fact, some books are specifically designed to teach mathematical concepts through the use of dialogue and pictures. A good example of teaching math concepts through literature would be *Grandfather Tang's Story* (Tompert, 1990), which uses a theme unit depicting the culture of China. The book incorporates favorite animal characters, concept mapping of the storyline, and stimulates the imagination as the students learn about geometric transformations and tangrams. Connecting literature with mathematics provides an obvious interrelation among subjects that helps students recognize that math is much more than a set of isolated facts.

Math Centers for All Learners

Traditionally for younger learners, math centers are an excellent way to teach math to those who are learning English as well as those who need more concrete examples to comprehend the subject matter. Centers can include a vocabulary component, a review of basic skills for those who need review, individual and group tasks to reinforce the math content, and mathematical enrichment. Centers will encourage students to utilize hands-on activities that are self-paced and student focused. The teacher becomes more of a facilitator of learning while being a guide on the sidelines. A wide variety of activities are available that help to extract theoretical mathematical concepts from textbooks and to translate them into practical use by students.

Centers can be theme driven or relevant to a specific topic or standard they are an excellent way to encourage the use of manipulatives, especially when the teacher does not have enough items for every student. Centers should include an assessment and recording worksheet for easy maintenance, self-checking options, and a choice of the activities. Centers are also called "shoebox math" in some areas.

Culturally Harmonious Strategies in Math

Teachers should identify the background and prior experiences of the students so they are able to apply this information during instruction. For example, in certain cultures, dominoes and card games are a regular activity in the home. Cards and dominoes are excellent mathematical manipulatives and can be uniquely mathematically related, especially those that show one side as a mathematical expression and the answer on the reverse. Conversely, some cultural groups, such as Haitians, may not be familiar with dice. Instead, they will use bones (such as bones from a goat's knee) to count and make certain significant patterns.

Most of the historical figures in mathematics are famous individuals from other countries. Students can explore their own cultural history for significant key personalities who contributed to mathematics or science; they will feel a sense of pride in their culture when they share this information with their classmates.

Cultural differences can interfere with learning as well. For example, pizza is not eaten in every culture, so vary models to be sensitive to cultural differences. Try using pita bread or moon pies that are equally round to represent fractions. Search for foods that are specific to the cultures of your students and utilize them in your instructional examples.

Acceptance

Make sure the curriculum provides for cultural awareness. Some countries focus heavily on computational skills, and others utilize more individual work. The methods used in the United States may seem foreign to some students. Differences in semantics apply as well. For instance, be aware that 7 and 0 may be crossed through at times, 4 may be opened or closed at the top, 2,500 may be written as 2.500, and division may be performed in a reverse order. Subtraction may be done with the indicators of borrowing written on the bottom instead of the top. Adapt, individualize, and modify your classroom while considering the student's level of content, language ability, mathematical expertise, and study skills.

Academic Ability Levels

Teachers will find diversified levels of mathematical knowledge in ELLs. Students may arrive with limited or interrupted mathematical education, or they may possess superior mathematical skills. Prescreening will provide valuable information about the academic abilities of your ELLs. Teachers must consider this diversity in ability levels in their instruction and assessments, and assignments must be varied to meet these diverse levels. Formulate lessons that include a variety of levels so students can obtain some form of success, or individualize homework assignments for your students. For instance, include problems such as *121–34* as well as *12–8*. It is important for the student to feel challenged yet successful and productive.

Process Oriented Versus Product Oriented

In some cultures, the *process* of finding the answer is not as valued as the final answer, so students coming from those cultures will have a difficult time appreciating the teacher's need to see the work process. Teachers should discuss the importance of process as well as product. It might be a contrary concept to some students when their U.S. teachers require them to show their work, as their grades would have been penalized in their home countries if they did not calculate mentally. Additionally, in many standardized high-stakes tests, showing the process of mathematical calculations is mandatory.

Finally, in some countries students can only use graph paper instead of lined paper. This method of writing a number in each box keeps their work quite organized, both vertically and horizontally. Sloppiness leads to many mathematical errors that are avoided by the use of graph paper. Although it is a very good practice, teachers in the United States might accept regular lined paper as well.

Technological Differences

Technology is often readily available and inexpensive in the United States; however, the use, variety, and quality of technology used are disparate in classrooms both in and outside the United States. Globally, philosophical dissention regarding the use of technology has generated huge chasms within curriculum. Just as in a typical mainstream classroom, some ELL students may lack any experience or exposure to using technology, and others may excel in their use of technology. No matter what the circumstances, the teacher should never regard the use of technology as prior knowledge in an ELL class.

Unlike U.S. students, students from other countries usually need to memorize mathematical formulas. Aids such as calculators and computers are gaining in acceptance in the United States, but not all students are able to afford these devices. Teachers will need to recognize the diverse financial situations of their students. Some students will possess all the modern conveniences at their homes, and others may not. Adequate time and access to technology, both inside and outside of the classroom, must be provided.

Effective Instructional Strategies

Effective instructional strategies in the classroom should include encouraging all students to put forth their best efforts. Varying instructional delivery, activities, and assessments while maintaining a regular routine will maintain and heighten student interest. Recognizing that not everyone learns in the same way, and that teaching styles can inhibit or enhance student learning, teachers can provide a classroom environment that is conducive to learning. *Prior planning prevents poor performance* applies to instructional delivery of the mathematical lesson. The following specific strategies are discussed to encourage success for the ELLs.

Visualization

Teachers should always accentuate the visual side of mathematics, because the majority of students may not be auditory learners. Incorporating prompts, cues, facial expressions, body language, and visual aids during instruction will help students to visualize the concept and to form a mental image. Concrete manipulatives, such as base-ten blocks, geoboards, algebra tiles, and snap cubes, and an assortment of models, such as Gummy Bears and M&M candies for children and Popsicle sticks or other countable items for older learners, can be used to develop mathematical concepts. Students will begin to like math when they see it as more concrete and less abstract.

Multiembodiment is important when teaching concepts. Multiembodiment is using different devices or instruments to teach the same concept. For example, teaching addition of fractions with fraction tiles, fraction circles, and fraction bars will all help students to recognize the need for finding a common denominator before adding the unlike fractions.

Concept Charts

The teacher should generate a preinstructional concept map to relate the new topics and words to things students may already know and understand to encourage scaffolding and interconnections within mathematics. For example, the base-ten metric system is easier to learn than the customary units taught in the United States, especially when it comes to converting from one unit to another. By developing a concept map, students make the connections between what they know and what they need to learn for mathematics taught in the United States.

Alternative Algorithmic Methods

A lesson on an **algorithmic process**, such as division or subtraction, may require the teacher to cover the methods used in the United States that may or may not be similar to the students' former knowledge of division. Acceptance of the various algorithmic processes should also be encouraged. However, this will require the educator to become familiar with a variety of alternative algorithms not taught as "standard methods." For example, in Brazil and Haiti, a division problem may be reversed and look like this: $50\lfloor 2$, as opposed to the American stylistic arrangement: $2\overline{)50}$. It is extremely difficult to "think backwards," and yet we are expecting students to do a cognitive reversal.

Recognize that it is extremely difficult to replace what appears to be a logical approach with what seems completely illogical at the time. This does not mean you should avoid teaching the standard algorithmic approach used in the United States. Rather, until the students can learn the "American" style of mathematics, allow them to feel comfortable performing math the way they were originally taught. Teachers might eventually discover that some of the methods from other countries prove to be more logical.

Modeling the Process

Be sure to model problem-solving strategies through real-life situations so students can "observe" your thinking process through a concrete problem that has an authentic purpose for the math learning in which they are involved. The typical problem-solving approach includes reading the problem, understanding the problem, planning a strategy, solving the problem, and verifying the answer.

During instruction, teach and model the many problem-solving strategies while working through mathematical problems. Strategies include acting out the problem, working backwards, guessing and checking, making a table, looking for a pattern, solving a simpler problem, changing your point of view, making a drawing, and systematically accounting for all possibilities so students become critical thinkers in mathematics and develop confidence in their problem-solving abilities. Be careful not to make the problem-solving process appear too easy for you. They need to realize that it is natural to attempt, think through, adjust ideas, and try other approaches when one approach proves unsuccessful. Confusion is bad only when it is terminal.

Heterogeneous Grouping

The benefits of using groups to teach and learn concepts are innumerable. Pairing students into groups of two, three, or five helps them both socially and academically. However, just as it would be inappropriate to group low students together, it is just as inappropriate to group students according to language preference or ability. Heterogeneously arranged cooperative groups can facilitate discussion and peer teaching if incorporated and monitored properly. However, if necessary, be sure to ask a more fluent English speaker to assist in interpreting instructions and questions if learning will be impaired otherwise.

Hands-On Learning

Everyone learns through different modalities; however, many students are tactile learners. These students will learn best with the use of **hands-on activities** involving concrete or mechanical aids that reinforce learning. Manipulatives, computers, calculators, and tape recorders are good devices when selected and used appropriately to reach your academic objective.

Many evaluative instruments can test students to determine their learning styles. Teacher observation can identify learning preferences as well. Understanding diverse learning styles and incorporating students' learning preferences will benefit both the teacher and the students. Regardless of preferences, varying instructional approaches will keep the curriculum interesting and exciting to your students. This is good practice for any teacher.

Assessment

Alternative assessments such as thinking aloud, presentations, interviews, observations, checklists, reflective writing, self-assessment, drawings, and portfolios will help teachers adequately assess and evaluate the students' work. Considering the delay in writing as opposed to speaking proficiency, this is especially helpful in assessment. Encourage students to formulate drawings that translate and visualize the problems.

Students should be encouraged to think aloud and to pair–share their ideas with others as they work through a problem. Open expression is encouraged as students give an oral explanation of their thinking process while solving a problem in a non-threatening environment. Remember, a traditional test that requires competent English proficiency may not truly test the student's mathematical abilities.

Often an English learner may be improperly placed in the math class due to an apparent lack of English proficiency. This placement will result in either a high level of boredom or frustration. Proper assessment must be a vital part of the ESOL program to avoid inaccurate placements. Just because a student is reading and writing two grades below level does not signify that the mathematical aptitude is also below grade level. Often students from other countries are learning algebraic concepts that far surpass those being taught to their American counterparts.

Minimize Anxiety

The most important goal for any teacher should be to create a comfortable, nonthreatening environment for all students. Anxiety and frustration directly affect academic leaning. A lack of success in any subject will generate a dislike and avoidance of that subject. In the United States, it has become culturally acceptable to profess one's dislike for the subject of mathematics. Yet, this openness indicates a lack of successful teaching of the subject matter and should not reflect mathematical ignorance. Too often, the subject has been taught primarily as a set of procedures to follow with little conceptual understanding. Eventually, this approach leaves students in a quandary about the use and purpose of mathematics and with the feeling that it is insignificant in their personal lives.

Sensitivity demonstrated by the teacher and the students will go a long way in helping all students feel accepted and comfortable in the classroom, regardless of mathematical or linguistic capabilities. This attitude will minimize the anxieties within the classroom and will create a more conducive environment for learning mathematics.

Myths about certain cultures and genders being more mathematically capable proliferate in the educational arena. It is true that certain cultures emphasize the importance of mathematics and education in general, but that does not mean that individuals from that culture are more mathematically inclined. This type of stereotyping should be addressed within the classroom. Teachers need to be aware of the cultural and gender factors that have permeated the mathematics classroom. Ensuring gender and cultural equity include providing the same wait time after asking questions, asking the same number and level of questions from all students equally, and encouraging all students to achieve. All students can learn mathematics.

Questioning ELLs

By far, one of the most essential rules to consider is providing ample wait time when questioning ELLs; in mathematics, this applies to all students. Cognitive processing demands extra time for the following to occur in the learner's brain:

Step 1 A question is asked in the target language.

Step 2 The brain translates the question into the native language.

Step 3 The brain calculates the answer in the native language (assuming the student comprehends and is capable of doing the math).

Step 4 The brain then has to translate the information back into English.

Step 5 The learner must speak (pronounce) the answer (Ariza et al., 2002).

In U.S. culture, students are uncomfortable with prolonged silence. Ariza et al. (2002) maintain that, by the time the student is ready to speak, the teacher, thinking the student does not have the answer, has moved on to another student, saying, "Can anyone help Tran with that answer?" Or classmates are wildly raising their hands in the air to give the correct answer.

Some teachers tend to ask multiple questions: for example, "How do you think John would have felt if he couldn't find his lost money? Do you think he would have told his father that he had lost it? Would his father have punished him?" The ELL does not really know what question to answer. To avoid putting a student in an awkward position, the teacher should ask the student a specific question and say, "Think about this question and I will get back to you for the answer." After questioning other students, which gives the ELL time to translate and calculate, the teacher can return to the student for the answer. Of course, you must be certain the student understands the question. This questioning technique can be used on a buddy system so they can work out the problem together.

Summary

By being aware of the above factors, the teacher can make a difference in ELLs' leaning of math by simply focusing on the literary strategies, cultural awareness strategies, and effective teaching strategies. Learning about the best approaches to effectively teach students definitely applies to the ELL students. As you educate yourself about your students' cultural and academic backgrounds, you will be rewarded with a sensitivity and respect for the diversity that exists within your classroom.

DISCUSSION QUESTIONS AND ACTIVITIES

1. Using a teacher's math text, choose a lesson and modify it for beginning, intermediate, and advanced language learners.
2. Find ten examples of word problems and examine them for clarity. Would an English learner have difficulty interpreting the language and solving the problem? Show how you can rewrite the language to make it very clear. Show how you could use manipulatives to make the concepts clearer.
3. Invite people from other countries to demonstrate how they solve addition, multiplication, subtraction, and division problems. How difficult would it be for you to change your way of calculating mathematically to a method that might be the reverse of how you calculate mentally? Discuss how you could teach a student the "American" method of mathematical calculations, which may be very different from how the student was taught in his or he native language. Discuss the issues that may arise.

PART FOUR

Assessment and the English Language Learner

11

Traditional Assessment: Why It Is Inappropriate

The following assignment was presented to fourth-grade students on the writing portion of a standardized state exam:

> Write a three-paragraph essay responding to the following prompt: If you were going out west in a Conestoga wagon, what would your life be like?

This question is obviously biased because it does not elicit what a true writing assignment is supposed to measure. Instead of evaluating students' ability in written expression, it relies on their knowledge of American history, specifically their familiarity with the pioneers' ways of life. Unless the students know that "out west" implies the unsettled American western terrain that pioneers explored, they will not be able to respond to the prompt with the expected level of detail. Clearly, this assignment gives an advantage to children who have had the exposure to the American perspective of exploration of the West, found in popular literature and movies. In other words, this standardized test assesses students' familiarity with the mainstream culture and American history more than it measures writing skills. Although this prompt seems like an isolated example of a culturally biased assessment, the problem is more prominent than one may think. The purpose of this chapter is to demonstrate how some common tests create obstacles to revealing English language learners' understandings and skills, and to offer suggestions on creating meaningful authentic assessments that work in multilevel classrooms.

High-Stakes Testing and ELLs

In an effort to reform the U.S. educational system and to increase the country's overall academic achievement, states have introduced standardized tests (**high-stakes testing**) to ensure accountability. This idea is congruent with the ubiquitous benchmarks and standards developed to make educators and administrators accountable for the achievement of all learners. According to Herrera, Murry, and Morales Cabral (2007), one of the most significant changes in today's assessment practices is that they have become "increasingly standardized, norm-referenced, and institutionalized" (p. 13). Amid this standardization, English language learners have been placed at a distinct disadvantage because their achievement is now measured against the test scores of native language speakers. The evidence is overwhelming that English learners need more than two years to gain skills in academic language (Cummins, 1982); yet in many states, such as Florida, the test results of most ELLs are factored in the schools' achievement data and counted toward the overall school grade. In turn, teachers, who are pressured to make linguistically diverse students produce a certain score, spend much of their classroom time on preparing for high-stakes standardized tests in place of teaching more profound content matter. Unfortunately, these test prep activities also take away time from more meaningful performance assessments in which students are evaluated on the knowledge they demonstrate in the process of creating their product.

If you are reading this book, you are obviously an educated individual. Even though you read and write in English well, have you ever tried making sense or some of the questions found on voting ballots? During the 2002 election, I was expected to vote on a very important question regarding my university's leadership. I read the question several times, but due to the way it was worded, I truly did not know whether I should vote "yes" or "no" to win the proposition. I am a literate, educated native English speaker, and yet I could not extract meaning from the words written in my own language. If I were being assessed on my reading ability, I would have failed miserably.

Language can be so convoluted that even native speakers can misinterpret meanings causing miscommunication among one another. To give you an idea of how misleading assessments can be, let's look at some common ballot questions that create much confusion. The following proposal was introduced in the 2002 gubernatorial election for the State of Maryland. What exactly is it trying to say?

> To amend the Anne Arundel County Charter to remove the limitation that cooperative purchases with other public jurisdictions may be undertaken only by public jurisdictions within the State or with the State of Maryland. (http://elections.state.md.us/elections/2002/questions/anne_arundel.html)

Now, imagine being tested on the meaning of the following convoluted amendment to the Florida Property Taxes. This 498-word revision proposes changes to the state constitution related to property taxation by increasing the homestead exemption. If a native English speaker has difficulty dissecting the meaning from a *small* section of the amendment below, how could a non-native speaker be expected to make sense of it?

> Further, this revision a. Repeals obsolete language on the homestead exemption when it was less than $25,000 and did not apply uniformly to property taxes levied by all local governments. b. Provides for homestead exemptions to be repealed if a future constitutional amendment provides for assessment of homesteads "at less than just value" rather than as currently provided "at a specified percentage" of just value. c. Schedules the changes to take effect upon approval by the electors and operate retroactively to January 1, 2008, if approved in a special election held on January 29, 2008, or to take effect January 1, 2009, if approved in the general election held in November of 2008. The limitation on annual assessment increases for specified real property shall first apply to the 2009 tax roll if this revision is approved in a special election held on January 29, 2008, or shall first apply to the 2010 tax roll if this revision is approved in the general election held in November of 2008.(http://www.votesmartflorida.org/mx/hm.asp?id=VoterGuide_Jan08_Amendment1)

One of the most notorious misinterpretations of language was Proposition 227, given to California voters in an effort to prove that the general public wanted to abolish bilingual education. The wording of the proposition was so misleading that individuals gave answers that did not an reflect how they really felt about bilingual education. By marking "yes" on the Proposition 227, many people voted "for English" because they supported the goal of English proficiency for all learners, not an "English only" ideology. Several studies and polls later confirmed that if many voters had known what Proposition 227 was trying to accomplish, they would have voted differently (Crawford, 1999; *LA Times*, 1998; Krashen, 1999).

Standardized Tests Versus Authentic Assessment

As I have pointed out, assessments can measure content knowledge as well as language proficiency. When used properly, assessments can guide instruction, evaluate the effectiveness of teaching strategies, place students appropriately, determine whether students should enter or exit programs, and diagnose and monitor student progress. Herrera, Murry, and Cabral (2007) define assessment in educational settings as "a range of procedures used to gather information about what students or other individuals know and are able to demonstrate" (p. 3). Assessments can be informal or formal, and they may be used to measure content knowledge or language skills. But what they must be is **valid** (i.e., measure what they purport to measure) and **reliable** (i.e., consistent among different raters as well as over time). Assessment can be *formative* or *summative*. **Formative assessments** are ongoing, and they are designed to guide the teacher in collecting and analyzing student work to determine if instruction is on the right track. They are a barometer of how students are doing so far and include and practice tests, unscored reviews of students' knowledge, etc., to see if reteaching needs to be done. A **summative evaluation** is an assessment of the end result of teaching, as in an end-of-the chapter test. No teacher wants to test a student on unlearned material; the idea is to see how much the students knows, not how much the student does not know.

For language minority students, usually a placement test is given to determine what level of English proficiency the student possesses. This is always a rough estimate because it is very difficult to pinpoint exactly what a student knows. Usually the levels of reading, writing, listening, speaking, pronunciation, and receptive knowledge are unbalanced. English students who have been exposed to English over a long period of time or who may have been born in the United States might have an excellent command or pronunciation and sound native-like but have limited knowledge of reading and writing. I also have had ESL students who have excellent knowledge of reading, writing, and grammar, yet have difficulty communicating orally and understanding American speech. In my opinion, the easier type of students to teach is the latter because they have studied the structure of English and soon will pick up oral skills. Students with English fluency and superb understanding may have ingrained or **fossilized errors** that are almost impossible to correct.

Evaluation Considerations for Testing ELLs

In all fairness, to level the playing field, students new to the U.S. school system must be overtly taught about the school's expectations. In addition to learning the culture of the society, a student who is new to the United States will have to become familiar with the culture of the school system as well. This culture will vary from school to school, as private schools differ from public schools, elementary grades differ from secondary, and the postsecondary institutions are different altogether. Students who enter the school system with the same academic behaviors as in their home country schools will be surprised and confused. Students from other countries often tell me they find U.S. schools to be "easier" than the educational systems in their home countries. Great differences will be apparent in study skills, mechanics of testing, the definition of plagiarism, the morality of doing group work when individual work is expected, and what to expect in order to compete and succeed.

Testing styles will be different in other countries, just as the styles of teaching and learning are different. Often the curriculum in other countries will focus on the students' learning many subjects, and great quantities of detailed information must be learned by rote memorization. U.S. schools have often been blamed for relying on multiple-choice tests instead of more critical-thinking tests. Therefore, schools now try to have students aim toward learning the higher levels of Bloom's taxonomy; tests may include analysis and synthesis, and students will often be perplexed by the possibility of having more than one answer. Students must be oriented and explicitly taught that thinking for the sake of thinking is an educational value. However, if a student is accustomed to essay tests, the idea of taking a test that has an answer sheet with little bubbles that need to be colored in with a pencil will be foreign, and students must be explicitly taught how to proceed. In China, lately, the multiple-choice test format is favored. With a variety of testing procedures pertinent to each individual's country, we will see more academic success if we are sure that all of our students know what they are expected to complete at testing time and why.

When students new to the U.S. schools learn that individual work is anticipated and they come from a country where group work is the norm, they might not grasp the idea that "sharing" someone's work is "immoral" and illegal in the United States. In countless countries (Saudi Arabia, Egypt, Poland, Haiti, Japan) being at the top of the class is a survival tactic. Cheating is not just to get a good grade; someone's future position or career might depend on it. The prevailing norms must be explained so that students are fairly evaluated.

When Oana, a Romanian 9-year-old recently adopted by an American family, was brought to her new third-grade classroom in March, she got scared by the stern looks on the teachers' faces. It seemed that Oana's presence puzzled them, but after talking to each other briefly, they pointed to an empty desk, where Oana sat. Both ladies began to walk around the classroom, looking closely at the students and occasionally telling them something in a strict voice. Then one lady began to pass out white booklets, while another one read something unemotionally out of a thick book. All students picked up their pencils and began to write something on the covers of the booklets. Not knowing what to do, Oana started crying. One lady came over to her and whispered in her ear, "Don't cry. It's OK." Of course, Oana did not know that she entered school not on a typical school day—it was the first day of the statewide high–stakes standardized assessment.

When talking about assessment considerations for ELLs, it is impossible to ignore standardized testing, which is a reality in today's schools. Standardized tests measure discrete items and the fragmented components of language; questions asked on objective tests neglect the complexities of overall learning and cannot accurately measure the ability of English learners. As succinctly put by Crawford and Krashen (2007), "When tested in a language they don't fully understand, students may do poorly because of their limited English or because they haven't learned the academic material. There is simply no way to tell" (p. 57). In 2002, the No Child Left Behind Act was enacted, and each state became frenzied in an effort to use standardized tests to measure academic gains. We have learned that it takes several years for English learners to make academic gains equal to those of native English speakers (Cummins, 1982), yet we test students who are new English learners. Ironically, teachers are forced to spend more time teaching to the test instead of offering linguistic opportunities. With such pressure and economic ramifications placed upon educators all over the country, the demand for elevated test scores must be met to maintain fiscal balance. Although authentic assessment is far more significant as an evaluation tool, schools that have high numbers of language minority students continue to be challenged, just as English-dominant schools are, to demonstrate that they are continuously improving academic achievement of all learners.

Using Authentic Assessments

Whenever possible, a range of authentic assessments should be implemented on an ongoing basis as the preferred method of measuring achievement of English language learners. According to Herrera, Murry, and Cabral (2007), what makes assessments authentic is their ability to directly assess what was learned from classroom instruction, group work, and activities. In other words, alternative assessments measure a student's genuine performance in class. In addition, authentic assessments involve students in the evaluation process, making them more reflective of their own learning. Additionally, authentic assessments are more aligned with real-life situations, emphasizing to students the connection of school activities to the wider world. Types of authentic assessment are many and varied and can include the following:

- Drawings
- Audio or video recordings
- Checklists
- Timelines
- Learning logs
- Reflection journals
- Anecdotal records
- Observation records
- Venn diagrams
- Projects
- Charts
- Informal assessments
- Self-evaluation
- Peer evaluation
- Teacher/student notes on progress
- Portfolios
- Holistic writing rubrics (a rubric that looks at the entire piece of writing as opposed to grading on individual parts of the assessment)
- KWL charts (what you know, what you want to know, and what you have learned, with the emphasis on what has been learned)
- Concept maps depicting what was learned, or any type of performance indicator that demonstrates the level of academic performance the student is doing

Students and teachers can choose artifacts collaboratively, and students can display their work in portfolios to reflect progress. Keep in mind that alternative assessments may show language and content mastery, and that must be accounted for. For example, when grading a writing piece, give two grades—one for the content and one for the mechanical mistakes. The student can be an excellent writer without being perfect, and should still be able to get a good grade regardless of mechanical mistakes. You must be sensitive to language acquisition processes and expect mistakes in the language. If students feel comfortable affectively, they will be more inclined to take changes and risk making mistakes.

The Importance of Questioning

Using comprehension questions during instruction is one way informal assessments manifest themselves in the classrooms. It is important that teachers must leave room for comprehension checks *as* they teach, not *after* they teach (Wiggins & McTighe, 2005). In a rushed effort to cover material, some teachers may feel tempted to leave off this informal assessment until they have extra time. However, by putting comprehension checks at the very end of the lesson, teachers lose an opportunity to get insights about students' learning of the material. A mastery of questioning techniques will provide teachers with important feedback on what students have or have not grasped. It is important to prepare questions that filter out nonessential matter and bring relevant understandings to the surface. Some basic guidelines for asking questions are summarized below:

- Ask one question at a time: If multiple questions are asked one after another, the student will not know which one to answer first.
- Try to keep the wording of the question aligned with the vocabulary of the lesson: Inadvertently substituting vocabulary with synonyms may confuse English learners.
- Give ample time for response: Second language learners may require extra time to process the question and formulate the response.
- If there is no response after ample wait time was provided, rephrase the question: Students may understand you better if you put the question in different terms.
- When you say, "Take some time to think about it," be sure to come back to the student and listen to his or her response, recognizing the effort.
- Be tolerant of mistakes: "Learners are going to mangle the language before they dominate it," and as long as they make themselves understood, it is something to celebrate. Instead of publicly "punishing" a student with explicit corrections, model structures and encourage students to repeat when appropriate.

Assessment Modifications for ELLs

Although creating assessments that are appropriate is a complex field in its own right, all teachers of linguistically diverse learners should remember this rule: If you adapted the content from the textbook, then you need to adapt available tests. If this rule is not followed, English learners will be at a disadvantage because they will be tested through wording to which they were not exposed. In other words, it is imperative that the language of the academic content and the language of tests remain consistent. Creating assessments that align with the adapted materials may take time, but teachers on the same grade level can collaborate in the process by spreading the objectives among each other and developing modified lessons and assessments that go together. In fact, the proponents of "design backwards" Wiggins and McTighe (2005) explain that teachers can guide students' learning better if they begin to design their curriculum with objectives and essential learning goals, followed by assessments. The actual planning of activities should be the final stage.

Assessments should be culturally responsive yet match the curricular goals of the classroom or school. Testing modifications for the English language learner can include the following:

- Extended wait time for processing questions
- Allowance for dictionaries, both English–English, and home-language-to-English
- The option of taking the test in a quiet environment with a bilingual or ESOL teacher present
- The choice to have the test directions translated into the native language

Assessing ELLs' Writing

When English learners' writing skills are being assessed, it is not fair to compare them to native English speakers. One helpful fact to acknowledge is that their cultural background and native language patterns will be reflected in their writing. After correcting thousands of papers throughout the years, it is easy for me to discern what native language a student speaks because I can see it in his or her writing. For example, a Spanish speaker will write run-on sentences and place commas where native English speakers will place periods. A Japanese or Polish writer will omit articles (*a, an,* and *the*) because articles do not exist in their languages. An overuse of commas is typical for Russian writers because punctuation rules are more abundant in their language. As for the format and style, it is equally easy to distinguish a paper by students with literacy in another language because the writing may not follow a predictable pattern. American students are trained to write according to a formula for paragraphs that includes a thesis statement and supporting details. Students are taught that every opinion should have support and that each reference to another author should be properly cited. Even an opinion piece is expected to have a certain structure, which must conclude in a summation of main points. American students are taught to "get to the point," not meander, and create writing that is linear. In other words, directness and clarity are valued both in essays and in writing for academic purposes.

To clarify expectations of students' writing, teachers can develop writing rubrics as a part of their assessment toolbox. A rubric that is truly authentic spells out the outcome(s) that both a teacher and student should be able to see in the end product. In other words, a rubric should reflect the skills that are of particular importance at a given stage of learning. Each requirement in the rubric should correspond to some aspect of students' learning while being quantifiable in case it is necessary to convert it to a percentage or a letter grade. Even though such complex activity as writing will involve skills that may not be mentioned in a given rubric (e.g., using quotes to allow characters to speak for themselves or using compound sentences), this is acceptable because these skills may be targeted in a future rubric. Teachers can seek students' input on creating elements of the rubric based on their self-evaluation of writing strengths and weaknesses. Another important step of using a rubric is demonstrating how a particular product meets or does not meet expectations for each criterion. A model, or high-quality product, should also be provided to set a certain standard for English language learners.

Table 11.1 is an example of a rubric that fourth-grade students may use for self-assessment:

TABLE 11.1   Rubric for Self-Assessment

Name _____	Focus	Organization	Sentence Vocabulary	Structure	Spelling
Very Good (2 pts)					
Good (1 pt)					
Needs Improvement (0 pts)					

To introduce the rubric, the teacher clarifies the meaning of *very good*, *good*, and *needs improvement*, giving ample examples of each level of quality for the specified criteria. Depending on the objectives of the lesson, this rubric may change its focus, in which case the teacher will rearrange and rename the columns according to the expectations.

As a conclusion, I encourage readers to remember that a lack of English fluency does not indicate a lack of knowledge or intelligence. Assessment should be interdependent, authentic, and designed to be done in conjunction with developmentally appropriate activities that reflect the English learner's true environment (Cummins, 1982; DeGeorge, 1988).

DISCUSSION QUESTIONS AND ACTIVITIES

1. Describe the differences between formative and summative evaluation processes. Think of a learning objective, an activity, and an assessment instrument you can use for the formative evaluation of learning gains. How will you use this instrument to guide your teaching?
2. Design a summative assessment instrument for the learning objective and activities. What determination could you make after giving students your summative evaluation? Discuss whether your summative instrument would be a true assessment of students' learning gains.
3. Imagine this scenario: After giving students an assignment, you realize that one student from Korea has plagiarized someone else's paper. With a group, discuss how you would handle this situation.
4. You notice that one of your English learners is looking at another student's paper during the assessment. Brainstorm possible reasons for this behavior, and discuss what action would be most appropriate on the part of the teacher.

PART FIVE

English Language Learners and the Wider Community

CHAPTER 12

How Teachers Can Help Parents of ELLs

Teachers in the American educational system know that parental involvement in the school is a cherished value, which may be contrary to school systems of other countries. American schools promote parent–teacher organizations, parents' volunteering in the classroom and helping out at school picnics and bake sales to raise money for the school, and parent–teacher conferences. From the American point of view, parental involvement is seen as the primary factor in the success of students (Comer, 1984; Lareau, 1987). Very often, American teachers assume that immigrant parents are not interested in their children's education when the parents do not participate in school interaction (Delgado-Gaitan, 1991). Nothing could be further from the truth, however. Parents from other countries usually revere the teacher and wouldn't dream of interfering with the educational process. Many valid reasons can account for noninvolvement in home–school interactions. Following are some possible circumstances that often impede parents from participating in school interaction (Ariza, 2000, 2002):

- Lack of English proficiency for communication with school personnel.
- Lack of knowledge of what school interaction is expected.
- Lack of literacy skills in the home language and/or English; parents cannot read the notices sent home.
- Parents defer to the teachers and do not want to interfere with their authority.
- Not enough time to attend school functions due to multiple jobs.
- No transportation.
- Lack of caregivers while parents attend school functions.
- Traditional gender roles prohibit the mother from leaving the house.
- Parents may fear authority figures due to their tenuous immigration status.
- Parents don't speak the language, so children have to interpret for the adults. This role switch may demean familial hierarchical status.
- Parents are uncomfortable with people not from their cultural group.
- Parents do not know they have power to make decisions about their children's education.

What Parents Need to Know

Schools must formulate outreach plans to educate immigrant parents about the educational and civil rights of their children. Teachers can play an important role in welcoming parents to the school and can provide the opportunities to teach them about their rights, such as (1) the right to a free and appropriate public education; (2) the right to receive information in a language they can understand; (3) the right to be informed, to understand, and offer consent or objection before any educational decisions are made about their children; (4) the right to be included in disciplinary discussions and actions that concern their children; (5) the right to understand and appeal any decisions with which they do not agree; (6) the right to actively participate in any informational meetings for parents, the public, and school personnel (Young & Helvie, 1996).

In an article I wrote for *Kappa Delta Pi Record* (Ariza, 2002), I describe a number of approaches that teachers and school personnel can implement to reach out to welcome immigrant families and make them feel comfortable about interacting with the schools. Educators who are familiar with the cultures of their student populations have the benefit of better understanding the protocol of behaviors and values that might seem unusual to the traditional American teacher.

Some school districts will be better equipped to address the needs of multicultural and multilingual populations than others. If school districts do not have personnel who speak the students' language or understand their cultures, look for bilingual individuals in the community, in ethnic food stores, churches, and native language newspapers, and parents and relatives (especially older siblings) of the student who will volunteer to interpret and translate, and invite them to help teach you about their culture and language. Be aware, however, that it is very possible that individuals can speak the language in question, yet have limited reading or writing ability.

Family and Community Outreach

Ways to begin outreach include the following:

- Translate school announcements, memos, newsletters, and correspondence with the parents. If you do not have an interpreter who is literate in the native language, look for someone who can call home to speak with the parents in their home language. Parents might not have received the literature or might not be able to read it, or perhaps the home language is not even one that has a written form, such as Hmong. Additionally, if a teacher calls home and tries to speak in English to family members who do not understand, even if it is to give a positive progress report, the child might get punished because in many other countries (such as Haiti) the teacher will only contact the parents if the child has misbehaved. This can happen also if the teacher leaves a message from the school. The parent might interpret the call from school as an indication that the child has done something wrong.
- An adult bilingual interpreter can be an excellent liaison between home and school. It is never a good idea to have a child interpret in a conference. In most countries, the familial structure is such that the parents have supreme power and the children are subordinate. When the positions are reversed in a new country, it is demeaning to the parents and can cause damage to the family structure. Also, be sure to keep eye contact with the adults instead of the interpreter during the session. You will show respect for the parents even though they might not understand the entire conversation. Adults are less apt to mislead or misconstrue the significance of what the teacher is trying to communicate to the family.
- In many cultures it is not uncommon for the teacher to visit the students' homes. A home visit, accompanied by an interpretor, can intitiate trust and goodwill, and it will give the teacher a glimpse of the child's homelife. Notice if there is a place where the student can study; if many family members live in a crowded apartment, for example, the student might not have space or quiet necessary for

homework or study. This fact should be considered if the teacher notices that the student is not doing homework or is scoring poorly on tests. If no one speaks English at home, it might be difficult for the student to complete homework because the student may need help but have no one to ask. Armed with this knowledge, the teacher can make modificiations by having the student start homework in class, be available to offer assistance, or have the student work with a buddy to explain difficult concepts.

- Through an interpreter, invite the parents to visit school during class time and attend school functions. Explain to them what they can expect to see, what clothing they can wear (many folks do not realize they can be more casual in the United States), and that it is customary for parents to be in the schools in this country.

- Through an interpreter, invite parents, grandparents, siblings, family members, and their neighbors to share their native culture in class through the use of songs, music, stories, pictures of their countries, special clothing or dances, giving a cooking lesson for a special dish, playing a game, or showing a video of their country. These ideas are a great way to enhance self-esteem, and students will be noticeably prouder of their heritage and family if the teacher celebrates their background.

- The teacher can plan a thematic unit of countries and ethnic backgrounds with all the students in the class. The focus can be on the countries people have emigrated from or the ethnic backgrounds of those who were born in the United States. A celebration of the entire class can be a wonderful teachable moment in which all students can learn to appreciate diversity from each other.

- Highlight the cultural backgrounds of your students all year by decorating the room with culturally representative items such as collages, posters, pictures, calendars in other languages, and momentos that represent the country (such as the coqui frog from Puerto Rico, a piñata from Mexico, a famous artist's picture from France, Haitian art or handcrafts, or the Chiva bus from Colombia). Have the children teach a mini-lesson on something from their country or background, and invite the family and other school members.

- Have the students create family histories, interview older family members or neighbors (in either language) by audio, video, or in writing. Have the students create questions they can ask to learn about the individual, and then invite him or her to visit the class.

- Invite the community to the school's cultural fair. Posters and invitations can be created and placed in the cultural neighborhood's stores, churches, or newspapers.

- Create a carpool for transportation for parents to visit the school for conferences, visiting or volunteering in the school, or just having lunch with their children.

- While parents are in the school, create an area for childcare so younger children can accompany the parents.

- Utilize the school library or media center for bilingual story time; invite families to enjoy story time with their children, or invite them to read the stories in their native language. In this case, younger students could translate the stories to their classmates. Use costumes and props to make the stories more creative.

- For a fun assignment, have the students do a Language Experience Approach activity with an older family member. The young student will write down everything the older person dictates, either in English or the native language. Later, the students can share the stories in class.

- Utilize school space to create and offer family literacy programs such as English to Speakers of Other Languages (ESOL), Adult Basic Educations (ABE), and adult high school equivalency (GED) classes.

- Try connecting individuals who want to get to know one another's languages and cultures, or create a program that offers a buddy to *adopt* a parent.

■ Offer intercultural classes for teachers, school personnel, and newcomers to get to know one another's habits, customs, and cultural values.

■ Be a community resource for parents; help them connect to community agencies, adult schools, and organizations that reach out to immigrants and/or newcomers to the community.

Brainstorm with other teachers, administrators, and PTA or PTO members to come up with ways to make the newcomers feel welcomed to the country and to the school, instead of intimidated by a new culture and educational system. School can become a nurturing, positive place to be when ideas and attitudes are congruous. By encouraging interaction within the schools and the community, newcomers will become empowered as they learn to function within the American system.

DISCUSSION QUESTIONS AND ACTIVITIES

1. In a group, create a plan that your school can implement to encourage parents to participate in school activities and functions. What steps would you take?
2. Think of ways you can promote community outreach that are not described in the chapter. What can you do to make the school more visible in the community?
3. You need to conference with parents but are having difficulty getting them to come to the school. Describe steps you can take to encourage them to meet with you.
4. Certain parents walk into your class at all hours and want to talk to you about their students. How will you handle this situation tactfully?

CHAPTER 13

Beyond the Classroom Walls: Suggestions for Noninstructional Staff

DIANA PETT, ELENA WEBB, AND EILEEN N. WHELAN ARIZA

Although the target audience of this text is mainstream teachers of English learners, noninstructional school personnel often plead for guidance, insight, and professional development in dealing with immigrant students more effectively. A cafeteria worker may wonder how to handle an anxiety-causing situation for a Russian kindergartener confused about the lunch choices. A monolingual school nurse may need to understand whether the tears of a non-English speaker signal an emergency or a minor ache. Considering the intricacy of our schools' nonacademic routines and the role of support professionals in maintaining them, it is essential that bus drivers, school police officers, custodians, clinic workers, and school volunteers feel prepared in helping newcomer immigrant students make a smoother transition to the realities of U.S. schools. In this chapter, Diana Pett, an ESOL/Spanish teacher, Elena Webb, a ESOL facilitator, and Eileen Ariza, teacher trainer, offer a comprehensive list of ideas that schools can adopt to improve communication and understanding among school personnel, English learners, and their families.

ESOL Teachers and Assistants

One of the first people to make contact with immigrant students and their families may be an ESL teacher, a bilingual facilitator, or an assistant acting as an ESL liaison. Although it is impossible to list all the ways in which an ESL professional could reach out to newcomers, some salient points and significant activities are highlighted here. First and foremost, an ESOL staff member should always be knowledgeable about and maintain a network of ESOL support services and information on county, state, and national levels, especially as they pertain to new ELL regulations. Checking in with the district ESOL coordinator (or the counterpart in your logistical area), logging on to a website of the board of education, and signing up for email updates about educational legislation are easy and effective ways of keeping your school informed about issues related to English learners. As a word of advice, one proven way to stay abreast of new developments in the field of teaching English as a second language is to become a member of an international, state, or a local association that promotes the interests of ELLs.

TESOL, Inc. is one major source of information, and your own state may have an affiliate organization. It is hard to overestimate the value of professional organizations in offering teachers opportunities to learn from each other.

In addition to disseminating information, an ESOL professional may also be the "pivot person" who connects all disparate school personnel in their efforts to assist English learners. It is often an ESOL teacher who is contacted by other staff members during their unexpected dealings with English learners. Experienced ESOL teachers have stated that maintaining an updated list of bilingual volunteers (and their schedules) can be of invaluable service for the school. Another way an ESOL professional can serve the immigrant population better is by providing office staff with files containing translated school applications, requesting ELL students' records from previous schools, and by making inquiries about new students' academic backgrounds. Although school personnel cannot question parents' legal status in the United States, they can and *should* learn as much as possible about students' academic histories to make informed decisions about assigning them to appropriate grade levels and programs. Because an ESOL teacher may be asked for an opinion on grade placement, it is important to learn about various educational systems in different countries and how they compare to schooling in America. An excellent resource on this topic is *Schooling Around the World: Debates, Challenges, and Practices* by Kas Mazurek and Margaret Winzer (2005).

In light of tremendous academic diversity within the growing ELL population, ESOL professionals need to be knowledgeable about effective instructional materials in order to help mainstream teachers select resources for English learners. They should also be competent in *differentiated instructional strategies* in content areas, as they may be asked to share pertinent information and classroom management tips with subject area teachers of linguistically and academically diverse groups.

Arranging and attending parent conferences may be yet another responsibility of ESOL/bilingual professionals. ESL teachers should use this opportunity to obtain emergency information from parents and explain sign-out procedures. Many parents are unaware that in case of an emergency, their children cannot be picked up by a relative whose information is not on file with the school. When ESL/bilingual teachers assist with interpretation, they should encourage all teachers in attendance to face the parents (not the interpreter) when discussing a student's academic progress. The parents will appreciate this gesture of respect and acknowledgment. Remember to avoid putting the child in the role of interpreter.

Administrators

Administrative personnel have the potential to benefit English language learners in their adjustment to school life. Usually, principals are well informed about the demographics of their communities because certain types of resources and even school funding may be tied to the percentage of the ESOL population. However, it is equally important for administrators to possess the deeper knowledge of students' cultures and use those insights to promote learning and cross-cultural communication in their schools. With this awareness in mind, administrators should plan multicultural sensitivity training and professional development for all staff, including, but not limited to, bus drivers, clinic workers, the school nurse, food service personnel, media specialists, paraprofessional assistants, and custodians. Table 13.1 lists important considerations for conducting sensitivity training and suggests some schoolwide projects that administrators could initiate to benefit their ELL population. As always, sharing ELL-related resources with other schools is essential in light of limited funding for linguistically diverse learners.

TABLE 13.1   Promoting Cultural Awareness: Suggestions for School Administrators

Recognizing Students' Backgrounds	Parent Communication	Safety/Emergency Procedures	Community Resources
▪ Help teachers and staff learn more about their students' cultures ▪ Establish a multi-cultural committee to identify and resolve ELL-related issues ▪ Consider the needs of ELLs when making purchasing decisions ▪ Plan multicultural events and encourage ELLs to participate ▪ Tailor professional development to the needs of teachers working with linguistically diverse students ▪ Invest in resources for differentiated instruction to help English learners master content as they acquire English	▪ Provide office staff with a file of templates for school announcements in different languages ▪ Organize ELL family nights and encourage parents to network with each other ▪ Maintain a bank of bilingual staff and outline their responsibilities in relation to parent communication ▪ Compensate staff for overtime translations or extra duties ▪ Consider investing in translation devices for unexpected dealings with non-English speaking parents ▪ Schedule book readings in the home languages of ELLs and invite parents to participate	▪ Keep students and parents informed about the upcoming safety drills and similar school routines ▪ Watch for signs of asthma attacks, seizures, fainting, or heart trouble in non-English speakers, as they may mistake drills for true emergencies; use a key phrase to let them know it is just a drill ▪ Go over emergency procedures with English learners (severe weather warning, lockdown, fire evacuation, etc.) before a situation occurs ▪ Place at least one bilingual staff member on the emergency response team and give him or her an electronic translator ▪ Brief students on what they must do if they get lost on their way to and from school; such safety information should be clear and unambiguous ▪ In case of an emergency, students should be reminded to stay with an adult in charge and not to wander off	▪ Translate information about community resources and make it available in the office and school library (library card application, homework hotline, etc.) ▪ Seek outside sponsorship from bookstores, electronics stores, etc. to benefit the ELL population ▪ Seek donations of bilingual books, learning CDs, tapes, and games ▪ Make CD and cassette players available for lending ▪ Train ELLs in using the Internet, and inform them about all places where Internet can be access without charge

In addition to including all support personnel in the sensitivity training, administrators should provide them with tips and insights relevant to their specific job assignments.

Bus Drivers

Because a bus driver is often the first adult to meet and greet a newcomer immigrant student, positive body language is essential in creating an atmosphere of trust (see Roger E. Axtell's *Gestures: The Do's and Taboos of Body Language Around the World* (1998). Drivers should seek help from bilingual personnel to translate bus rules and safety expectations for newcomers. During the year, drivers need to inform school personnel about upcoming drills and ensure that such announcements are translated into different languages. If that is not done, they risk confusing or scaring English learners, possibly causing them to run away from perceived danger. In addition to providing translated updates into the home language, bus drivers need to be aware of ways students of other cultures respond to adults. For example, Haitian students normally do not make eye contact when reprimanded by an authority figure, which is contrary to what a mainstream U.S. bus driver would expect. In other cultures, an adult raising his or her voice may be perceived as threatening, which may cause a student to shut down or start crying.

Crossing Guards

Crossing guards need to know that traffic and pedestrian laws are not universal; therefore, newcomer immigrant students may not act in a manner that is expected of pedestrians in our society. For instance, Russian children may not respond to the directions of crossing guards because they did not have them in their home countries. Since in certain cultures traffic lights are perceived as mere "suggestions" for drivers and pedestrians, students from those countries may try to cross the motorway running as long as there are no cars in sight. Crossing guards need to be patient and calm as they communicate pedestrian rules with the help of a bilingual teacher.

Food Service Personnel

Cafeteria workers need to understand that immigrant students may have different culinary customs. Breakfast items may not be the same for students from other countries. It is important to give those students more wait time as they make their food selections. They may not know if an item is sweet or salty just by looking at it, and previous expectations often confuse those who bite into a pastry expecting to taste meat instead of jelly. To help students chose items for breakfast and lunch, cafeteria workers should paste pictures and key words by the serving line. As in other situations, teachers can use the buddy system, pairing newcomers with helpful bilingual students who can explain unfamiliar items on the menu. Rewards, treats, and verbal praise should be used to encourage such interactions. Food service workers should also be aware of cultural and religious dietary restrictions. For example, students from the Middle East may not eat pork products or any foods containing gelatin (marshmallows, certain types of pastry, puddings, Jell-O, etc.). It is therefore important to indicate the use of pork on the menu with, for example, a picture of a pig's face, or the use of gelatin with a picture of a calf's hooves or bones. In addition to pork restrictions, students from Israel may not be allowed to combine dairy and meat during the same meal. Therefore, it would be culturally insensitive to insist that such students order pepperoni and cheese pizza or get a carton of milk with their beef burger.

Police Officers and Firefighters

Police officers and firefighters need to have knowledge of cultural groups living in their communities and learn more about their practices (e.g., rurally based Russian Pentecostal families attempted to smoke fish inside their homes). To assist nonspeakers of English, volunteers who can act as interpreters during emergencies might need to be called on. Police officers assigned to a particular school need to take time to introduce themselves to students. They need to smile and speak softly, keeping in mind that any adult in a uniform may be a menacing sight for ELLs who have lived under authoritarian rule. To explain emergency drills and the functions of safety devices in the building, police officers and firefighters should use pictures and demonstrations. Anti-drug information and safety updates should be distributed in multiple languages that are represented in the community.

Psychologists and Social Workers

Both psychologists and social workers need to work closely with ESL professionals to obtain background information about students prior to referring them to special education or counseling services. For school psychologists, it is critical to recognize and minimize cultural bias when using diagnostic or intelligence testing. Careful consideration should be given to the language, format, and setting of any evaluation. It is critical to remember that tests lose their validity once they are translated word for word from English into other languages. When trying to distinguish between a normal rate of second language acquisition and a learning disability, school psychologists need to use multiple quantitative data as well as anecdotal records. Social workers should tap into the linguistic resources of the community—seniors, grandparents, older siblings, or neighbors—to reach out to at-risk students. They should schedule home visits with ESOL staff to speak to parents who cannot attend conferences because of lack of transportation. Both psychologists and social workers should understand that some parents may be working multiple jobs and, therefore, cannot schedule meetings during regular school hours.

Coaches and P.E. Teachers

During multicultural training, it is important to inform P.E. teachers and coaches about the barriers that ELLs face when they consider participating in school athletics. Athletics teachers may be surprised to learn that upper-grade curricula in some countries consist solely of academic subjects and exclude physical activity. It is not surprising, therefore, that parents of English language learners may not recognize the value of P.E. or competitive sports in their children's school careers. Other barriers to participation include parents' financial constraints and their inability to equip an athlete or send him or her to a training camp. When ELLs do participate in school athletics, they may miss preseason or evening practices because they have to work. To secure participation of immigrant students in sports, coaches and P.E. teachers should seek input of ESOL professionals to ensure better communication between families and schools. As always, cultural sensitivity and being informed about students' backgrounds are crucial factors. For instance, opposite sex interactions in games or sports may be restricted in certain cultures, while certain religions (i.e., Islam) prohibit exposure of legs. Even group showers may conflict with some students' cultural values of modesty. Therefore, insisting on specific activities or penalizing students for not participating in a practice that their culture forbids is culturally insensitive.

School Nurses

In order to provide quality health assessments for all students, school nurses need to ensure the presence of bilingual staff during routine physical exams. Memos in native languages should be sent home to disseminate information about health concerns, vision screenings, community immunization clinics, and so forth. Follow up to make certain that parents are aware that information is being sent home. Health professionals should also be informed about the current health challenges in the immigrant communities (immunization gaps, tuberculosis, SARS, AIDS, etc.) and become proactive in meeting those challenges. Since school nurses are mandated to report any suspicion of child abuse and neglect, they must learn how such mistreatment manifests itself in different cultural groups. Health practices differ among cultural groups, and patients may choose to see a spiritualist (or whomever their particular culture believes) in addition to taking prescribed medicine as an added measure of security.

Technology Specialists

Technical support personnel must correctly spell ELLs' names since they are often entered as passwords for school computers. Hispanic students usually have two surnames, for example, Lucia Gomez Uribe. The student's last name is Gomez, while Uribe is the mother's last name. Many Asians put their surname first. For example, if a female student identifies herself as Hong Long, Hong will be her last name. Technology coordinators should communicate with the ESOL department about purchasing and loading English language learning software. They should also familiarize themselves with distance learning professional development programs (especially on cultural sensitivity) because that may encourage participation of teachers who function with crowded schedules. To help English learners supplement classroom learning, technology specialists need to maintain a pool of learning tools (e.g., science websites, English grammar on CD-ROM) and teach students how to utilize those resources. If possible, they should post important announcements on the school website in several languages.

Considering the scope of nonacademic challenges that newcomer ELLs encounter in our schools, it is hard to overestimate the crucial role of support personnel in helping those students to better navigate their new academic settings. As always, respect for cultural differences and patience are crucial for modeling cross-cultural communication and making our schools more welcoming for English learners and native speakers alike.

DISCUSSION QUESTIONS AND ACTIVITIES

1. Choose five cultures that interest you and research their health practices. Brainstorm what issues might arise if immigrants from those cultures continue to use healing methods that are not acceptable to the mainstream U.S. mindset.

2. Prior negative experiences of students can result in unexpected situations in the new environment. For instance, when uniformed firemen and their German shepherd appeared in the classroom during a career day, Russian students began to cry hysterically, insisting that they did not want to be taken away. An interpreter explained that the children feared the firemen because of their past encounters with border police in their homeland. Russian Pentecostal refugee families had suffered harrowing experiences during Gorbachev's changing government as they tried to cross the Russian borders, patrolled by armed officers and their hostile German shepherds. Research other conflicts that might arise as a result of previous negative experience in the home cultures. As a teacher of these students, how would you deal with these situations in a culturally sensitive, appropriate way?

3. In some Asian cultures, the rubbing of hot coins against the skin is used for curing sickness, releasing the "bad wind," and restoring a balance in the body. Haitians may use Voodoo, Hispanics may use Santeria, and Native Americans may appeal to the Great Spirit to heal ill health or pain, in addition to or instead of prescribed medication. These culture-specific health practices may appear to be mistreatment to the culturally untrained educator who is mandated to report any suspected child abuse or neglect. As a teacher, you might recognize that your students' families rely on practices of which a U.S. physician would not approve. How can you carry out your job responsibilities and ensure that your students are adequately cared for without disrespecting their home cultures?

PART SIX

Sampler of Cultural Groups: The Teacher as Cultural Observer

CHAPTER 14

Native Americans or American Indians

I have always believed that Native American people were the closest people to royalty that the United States could claim. In writing this chapter, my plan was to research Native Americans, or Indians, so I could generalize what mainstream teachers could expect from students of this culture. I discovered that this was almost impossible, as I found over 500 indigenous tribal groups with distinctive cultural traits and over 2,200 languages spoken among them. Much mystery and misunderstanding surrounds the nation's first inhabitants. Interestingly, even Mormons have their own theories about Native Americans, believing that they are the ten lost tribes of Israel.

Sherrin Watkins (1992), of Shawnee and Cherokee blood, from the Cherokee Nation, offers a rich description of tribal nations in the introduction to her book *Native American History*. She writes:

> United States' history has largely ignored the fact that every tribe has its own government and societal rules providing for the common good, punishment for violation of the public peace, safety, health and morals of their people. These governments provided rules for determining who made civil and military decisions, enforced the rules, provided for the children, and cared for widows, orphans, the sick and the indigent.
>
> Every tribe had its own language, sometimes related and mutually intelligible to other tribes, but usually not. Every tribe had its own traditions, culture, mythology, and religion. Indian people were free citizens of their tribes when the people who would one day form the United States were the subjects of tyranny in lands far from here. Each tribe had citizens loyal and devoted to their nation, religion, language, society and culture.
>
> United States' history has largely ignored, until recently, the Indian patriots' struggle to maintain their national identity while surrounded by the occupation force of an alien government, in favor of a focus on property issues. (p. 9)

Accordingly, it is not easy to measure English language proficiency or the extent of mainstream acculturation found within the Native American tribes across North America (Baruth & Manning, 1992). I had read that members of Native American cultures were offended by being called Indians; however, according to my research, books written by Native Americans claim this is not always true, and it truly depends on the individual's preference as to which is the more courteous and politically correct name (Axtell, 1988). Axtell suggests that reservation and urban Indians prefer the term

Diane Talley-Strike contributed material for this chapter.

"Indian" over Native American, but the term "Native American" is found on federal grants and college applications. Technically, all people who are born in the United States could refer to themselves as "Native American." The ideal situation is to study individual tribes and to refer to the individuals according to their tribes in this manner. "This semester we are going to study the Navaho and Hopi Indians (or whatever individual tribe is chosen as a topic of study)," as opposed to consolidating all Indians together.

Another point I will add is that I kept finding different spellings for a certain tribe or word to describe an Indian object. I attribute this to many incorrect interpretations of pronunciation made by English speakers. Additionally, many words used in English today come from Indian origins or are a misconstruction of original Indian words. Table 14.1 shows examples from Watkins's book (1992).

What greatly offends are racial stereotypes (*Redman* or *Redskins*; the sidekick *Tonto*, for the Lone Ranger; the requisite Indian statue outside of a store indicating that it is a trading post, etc.); Indians portrayed as sports mascots; trivialized spiritual ceremonies and inappropriate use of sacred items such as pipes, feathers, and body paint designs; and myths that are innocently passed on by teachers who read inaccurate history books. I suggest that all teachers read books such as *Lies My Teacher Told Me, Everything Your American History Textbook Got Wrong* by James W. Loewen (1995) and *Tribes and Tribulations, Misconceptions About American Indians and Their Histories* by Laurence M. Hauptman (1995).

Individuals of all cultures mirror the influence of community norms and values; imagine the miscommunication that can take place in the mainstream classroom when Indian children behave according to the rules and values of their home culture. Philips (1983) studied the community norms and socialization practices of tribal groups and found that they indeed do determine the behaviors of Native American students in the

TABLE 14.1   Words of Native American Origin

Athabaska is also *Athapasca*.

Chippewa, another pronunciation of *Ojibwa*, means "roasted until puckered."

Crazy Horse, a Dakota warrior, was so named by English speakers because of a misinterpretation of his Indian name, which meant that he was so great that just the sight of his horses made people crazy with fear.

Eskimos call themselves *Inuit* (the people). Eskimo means *raw meat eaters* in Eastern Canadian Algonquin. Some Inuit prefer *Eskimo* not be used (Damas, 1984).

Goyathlay is the Apache name for *Geronimo*, which means *yawning* or *sleepy*.

Hopi means *Hopitu* (peaceful ones) or *Hopitu-shinumu* (peaceful all people).

Igloo (*igdler*) means "snow and ice house."

Iroquois is Algonquin for *I'inakhoiw*, which means "real adders."

Kayak is an Inuit man's boat.

Klondike is Athapascan for *chendik* or *deer*.

Maize (corn) originates from the Arawak, *marise*.

Manhattan means "hilly island."

Missouri is Algonquin for "Big Muddy."

Ojibaway is also *Ojibway*, or *Ojibwa*.

Potlatch means *giving* or *gift* and relates to the Chinook (Nootka Indian language) ceremony: the custom of giving away things, gifts of blankets, at the end of a ceremony, or the giving of valuable gifts so a man can increase his social prestige and standing (Pierre, 1971).

Wampum originates from the word *wampampiak*, which approximates a meaning of a string of white shells used as money by Indians and early white settlers (Pierre, 1971).

Wigwam is Algonquin for *wegiwa*.

classroom. Although not all tribal nations are the same, often we can find overarching tendencies that might baffle the teacher who judges all students by cultural norms practiced by mainstream North Americans. The focus of this chapter is to examine some fundamental beliefs shared by many Indian tribes and to see how we can modify our classrooms to accommodate the different cultural, behavioral, and learning styles of Native American students.

Tharp (1989) posits that two salient learning styles that contrast with each other are visual/verbal and holistic/analytic. Often schools value and reward the student who is verbal/analytical, as opposed to the student who has a more visual learning style and prefers to learn through observation and practice. Typically, the Native American student demonstrates a more holistic thought process and may find the mainstream classroom incongruent with his or her cognitive learning style.

The Traditional Native American Classroom

Ms. Diane Y. Talley-Strike, a full-blooded Ojibwa Indian and member of the Sault Saint Marie Chippewa Indian nation, is a teacher who writes the following narrative about teaching Native American students. Her rendition of what being a Native American means illuminates the ideals, cultural characteristics, and learning styles of the Native American student. After reading her illustrious description, a mainstream teacher will be better prepared to teach the Native American in the classroom and will be able to adapt learning strategies to successfully reach students from Native American cultures.

I have had the fortune to see several of the classrooms on many reservations. Except for the different languages, each classroom is alike in its expectations with obvious similarities. On one of the reservations, the school is set up to house approximately 10 to 20 students. The school is circular with all the rooms leading to an atrium or a fire circle, and each room exits to a patio where group projects have a natural entrance to nature and the playground. There were ten rooms that started at the fire circle along the hall to each classroom and bathrooms were set between each classroom.

Each classroom has a different theme, depending on the age of the students who will inhabit the room. The younger ones have mats and pillows, and a rug in the middle of the room. A loom rests on one of the patios attached to the classroom; during the third-grade year, students learn how to weave in many different methods. A fire pit with the rules for fire makers is located on another patio. In this world, a fourth-grade class will boil the colors that are needed for the rug.

Once the students get to the fourth grade, they start to experience the different jobs within the complex system of the reservation and tribe. Some classroom patios have plants where students are learning medicine man ways from traditional old ways. Some of the patios had homes built from natural resources, for example, a tipi from skins, a hut from leaves and willow branches, and so forth. Each classroom focused on a different skill that the students would be learning for that year.

Today's society operates with computers, as they do on the reservations; they have one room complete with computers and a media center attached that even has a studio for television productions. The school has been equipped with all the latest conveniences. It is not the normal reservation school, but this tribe has seven casinos and a leader who has reinvested the profits in the tribe with acreage, schools, houses, and has promoted tribal support. This particular school goes to the ninth grade, but they recently learned that the ninth grade will be relocated to the high school the following year to make room for two new kindergarten classes.

Teachers carefully watch the students to see what their interests are, so they can start teaching the students an occupation within the tribe. Once the students' natural interests are determined, this is the work they will be dedicated to performing in the tribe. The students will begin to work with an elder who does the job the student wants to learn. These apprenticeships will last for the duration of the individual's membership with the tribe. When the person becomes an elder, he or she will take over the position at the time that it is needed. The older students also start teaching the younger students about the job they are doing. All students help the reservation out by picking up trash and building with the elders to make the reservation buildings better. Part of the day is spent with the elders; this is the highlight of the day for the children. The students are part of the community and are taught very early that they are responsible for the world around them.

The school day starts out the same; all the students get together at the fire circle with the elders, teachers, and staff. They watch announcements and discuss the day's assignments. They talk out problems and note the successes in a council fire setting. They do have fire pits so some of the students can learn to be keepers of the fire.

The students have mock council fires so that children can learn what position is right for them in the celebration setting of the circle of life. When the elders have a council fire, students are invited to learn how the elders reach agreements; the students are able to look on, but say nothing during an elders' council. Sometimes the elder council fires are at the school and other times they are held at the reservation council fire where the important tribal decisions are made.

Throughout the school, the most important concept the teachers try to promote is that of good manners so the students learn appropriate behavior from examples. The teachers talk to all the students, no matter what age or class that the student is in. This school is like a community with all eyes watching all the community members; no one can get away with bad behavior very easily. When an adult starts talking to the student, the young child's eyes move to the ground and you can actually see the child thinking about what is being said.

These are the children of the earth. They like to be outside with nature. The classroom is confining with four walls when one is used to being able to feel and touch nature. These are students who embrace the world around them. They believe everything has a spirit and every day, 24 hours a day, seven days a week, and 365 days a year, they are in God's country, being the keepers of the earth and skies. Every person is responsible for his or her own actions, rather than placing blame on good or evil, and the earth's force is all giving and loving to all. This goodness of earth will lead one in the straight path of life, if the choices for the good life are made.

These students will be the ones who learn by doing and experiencing the world around them. They may not sit in the chairs, but may choose to sit on the floor. They may be the ones who choose not to write, but will tell tales of the past and forecast the happenings of the future. Storytelling is an important skill that is taught to students so that the oral traditions are kept alive. The use of the hands to explain what is going on designates whether the student will be the researcher, a listener, or speaker. They will learn to listen and express their feelings and learn when it is their time to listen or be the talker. This is what you will see and feel with a Native American child in your classroom.

Cultural Beliefs

Native American culture and spirituality teach the group the value of living in harmony with the earth, honoring each other, and respecting the interdependence of all life. By looking back and rediscovering "The Old Ways," we can look forward to applying these constant truths to our modern dilemmas of today. Native American spirituality is based on an understanding of the fundamental organization of religion, for this is the basis of the culture. The spiritual approach gives the participant a chance for growth and to experience life.

Native American cultures look at life as a pathway that will lead them back to the whole life and to oneness with the creator. They are here to experience the love of life and to accept the great mystery of the seasons of maturity throughout the universe.

Throughout time, mankind has asked questions and has sought answers to the questions of existence, mortality and immortality, what direction to follow, or how to find the answers that justify existence. Humans cling to the belief that there is a greater force in the universe and that there is a greater power than us. This belief system gives people comfort, logic, and order to the world they live in. In the Native American life, there is no death, only a passing that is celebrated for one year after what is considered to be the passing of the body to the pathway to the next world. Each individual tries to find a path to balance and understanding, to find his or her center and the meaning of life. The first lesson that was taught the Native Americans when the Europeans stepped foot on the land was that religion is a manmade institution, but the Creator gives spirituality to us. The Native Americans do not practice their way of life just on Sundays; they practice it every minute of the day, seven days a week, year in and year out.

Native Americans believe that we all possess the same spirit and energy. We may all have different qualities, gifts, and powers, but overall, we are all one. We are connected to the circle of life. Once these beliefs are understood, the mainstream teacher will connect with and understand the Native American; the child is taught to see the Creator in all living things: animals, birds, insects, plants, herbs, trees, rocks, air, water, fire, and earth. These are all part of the creation and life; they are their grandfathers, grandmothers, brothers, and sisters.

Cross-Cultural Communication Problems

The cross-cultural communication problems may not be apparent if the teacher does not realize he or she has Native American students, since many of these children have been Europeanized. Some tribes have returned to the old ways with the old languages. These students have been given their education on the reservations in both the old ways in the language of the tribe and in English with the new methods.

The tribes that have been able to survive and relish the culture they had previously have retained the past as much as possible in the new culture of today. The children may not be talkers but may be listeners, and they are concerned about nature and other fellow beings and spirits. These students live in a household where there is no yelling. If wrong decisions are made, they are asked to think about what was done right or wrong and to talk it over to correct a problem or to seek the wisdom that is needed to point one in the right direction. It is a different way that many people don't include in today's society.

Problems to Expect in the Classroom

The major problems that teachers can expect to see from the indigenous child is that of introverted feelings. At home, the indigenous children listen and learn, and they are not expected to talk back, to be rude, or to be belligerent. The tribal customs may not include talk about a God; however, they may talk about spirits, so the student might be confused if the teacher talks about the history of different cultures. Also, many of the tribes have a custom that the younger person looks down at the ground to show respect when an adult is speaking to him or her.

The teacher might be from the mainstream culture that expects the child to look at the person talking, which conflicts with the indigenous culture. The tribal elders use a talking stick, and the person talking holds the stick; he or she passes the stick when the next person is to talk. As the person with the stick is talking, the others listen and look down, showing respect for the stick and person talking; they are listening, and the speaker's thoughts come easier. Therefore, if the teachers like the students to look at them, it might not happen, even though the students will be listening.

Teachers will also have trouble communicating the methods of learning if they are trying to obtain answers without using the hands-on method of instruction. These students learn from discovery and are taught that the world moves in a circle of life; thus, touching is a major learning experience.

Their Language

The student's English language literacy and proficiency will vary, depending upon the acculturation of their tribe. The origins of each tribe's language can be traced back to about twelve original linguistic families of languages that have been identified. These languages are Eskimo-Aleut, Athapaskan, Algonquian, Iroquoian, Siouan, Muskogean, Caddoan, Shoshonean, Hokan, Shahaptian-Penutian, Salishan, and Wakashan. Languages are subdivided under the twelve larger language families. The languages have numerous derivatives, and each smaller tribal unit has defined itself over time by its own linguistic identity. Therefore, depending on the geographical location, the language will vary according to the individual tribe.

Indigenous people feel that language is a valuable, living thing that is another special way of looking at the world. The Native American Indian languages are rich with connotation of man's natural relationship with the universe. Concepts and shades of meaning that cannot be expressed in English relate naturalistic and humanistic behavior. Although English may be the language of instruction and communication, the indigenous child should also be given the opportunity to study and learn his or her own language. When native language is recognized as an important part of the school curriculum, the student feels a sense of pride and security in his or her culture and in being a member of the tribe.

The indigenous languages are primarily oral, with an introduction of the written language in a simplified form. It names objects and builds simple sentence patterns. No grammar rules are stressed, but rather the emphasis is placed on learning the language through pattern and repetition. The general Indian language is a living symbol of the cultural heritage. Children must be given the opportunity to preserve the language both orally and in its written form; otherwise, in a few generations from now, language will be part of the past and irreplaceable. Too much of the knowledge of the customs and life values of the ancestors have already been lost.

Implications for the Classroom

The indigenous child will be a challenge if a teacher has a classroom that is not moving, up and around, adventurous and challenging. The indigenous child is always mannerly but needs to be in motion, not hyperactive but touching the surrounding world, exploring and asking questions after thinking about what is happening with the situation. The classroom has to be challenging, and everything learned is going to help the tribe in the future. The child being groomed as a chief will be learning different skills than the child that who will be a medicine man or hunter for the tribe. Each job in the tribe has different skills that need to be learned. The incongruity of the mainstream classroom with the Indian child's reality will be a challenge for a teacher.

The spiritual center of the indigenous student can be discovered in meditation and healing, as he or she seeks to "walk in balance" of spirit, mind, and body. The numbers four and seven are important in Native American cultures. Spiritual guidelines are given to the children of the tribe as the healing power from within. The children are taught to find their own pace, to be conscious of each breath, and to shed anything that might be hindering their journey. They are taught to stay tuned in to themselves and let experience be the guide to find the center of their being. Students are taught to ponder their experiences, and to show gratitude and reverence to the God who has walked with them. When the child is picking up an object and moving it to other places, he or she will tell Mother Earth his or her plans for the object, and thank her for producing the object to be used.

Students are taught to love tobacco, a product abhorrent to mainstream America. Tobacco may also be left as a thank you for something good in life happening, like a mother giving birth. Tobacco is revered as having high spiritual value and is thought to refurbish the earth. Many tribes have a giving tree where one ties a pouch of tobacco for thanks. These customs, although beautifully spiritual, may be contrary to what is found in the mainstream American classroom where days are organized, a schedule is fixed, and moments of silence or prayer are outlawed by the government.

What the Teacher Should Know

The first step is for the teacher to know the spiritualism of the tribe or nation the students come from in order to understand what values have been taught. Most students know the magic of an immediate, intimate, personal connection with the natural world; they usually will learn better with hands-on experiences. Animals are important to the tribes, and care must be taken not to be offensive or discourteous when talking about or studying animals. Each tribe has its own beliefs about the sacredness of animals. Therefore, teachers should know which nations the students come from to educate themselves about rituals and spirituality of the individual cultures.

Indigenous people believe in forbearance, charity, and helping one another; students are generous and giving. They are the ones who will give away their last supplies, which may be contrary to the American values that foster individualism and competition. When looking at the lifestyles of students, we see that they socialize in colorful gatherings where many different tribes came together, forming vast towns of other nations, where members wear different ceremonial outfits, and celebrate with dancing and singing, racing and playing, gambling games, trading stories, and bartering for goods. These meetings or events give the young men and women of different tribes the chance to meet, court, and fall in love. A person is held in high esteem not for his or her wealth but for the generosity the person has extended. Giving is an act of sacrifice; to give in any other way is not deemed as honorable.

In these nations, it is often surmised that men see more in the physical world and women see more in the spiritual or inner world. Native American culture in general has a great respect for age. Children are brought up more by their grandparents than their parents, who are busy being the providers for the clan. The elders, having lived long, full lives, are believed to have many lessons in survival to teach the youngsters. The elders are the guardians of wisdom, and they pass this wisdom down through the line of ancestors. Modern problems of inexperienced, heavily stressed parents rearing children in isolation do not exist, as these people enjoy an extended, supportive familial community. Children are not scolded and are allowed to be children; for example, children with imaginary play friends are not told to grow up, but are seen as potentially having the gift of vision. Teachers need to look at these qualities of life in the Native American culture to understand where the child is coming from, to understand how to help the student cross over into mainstream society and into the culture of learning in the non-native classroom.

The idea of the Native American warrior is a source of pride in this culture, and a child being raised in this light is learning compassion and tolerance along with the skill and courage of coping with the enemy upon whom he is advancing. He is taught that disputes are settled not by war but by sporting competitions that are often dangerous and require physical prowess and freedom from fear. These students accept life as fragile and short, as a transitory journey with the purpose of which is returning to the spirit world. One wonders how these teachings affect the interactions in a classroom of mainstream students. Does it create more tolerance for individuality?

These indigenous people are raised to sit in council, which is the tribe's organized body of government, where they prove their ability to think, act, and speak in the best interest of all. Balance and harmony are important to the community. The process of listening, thinking, and then talking when holding the stick is evident in the classroom as the teacher questions the student who does not answer immediately. This child will be the thinker first, then will react to the situation that is presented. Allowing extra wait time is crucial, and being comfortable in silence is a positive, explicit message that says it is acceptable to think before speaking. Many teachers might say, "Susie, can you help Johnny with the answer?" before Johnny has had a chance to formulate an answer.

The child who is slated to be the medicine man will be the entertainer, to show another side of life to the members of the community. This student acts with mythological vision. He shows the courage to plunge into the situation and get his feet wet, while being able to see the green of the world, the remedies of the world, and become the healer of the community.

The people of this culture realize that each individual brings a unique experience to the tribe or clan that all are expected to share, so each person is taught a different part of life. One mold is not for all people; the traditional teacher has to discover what mold that child comes from and encourage that student to move down the path of his or her individual destiny. Ideally, with a small class, the teacher can foster this individual growth. However, in reality, the teacher may have more than thirty students in the class, with a specified curriculum to follow within a given time, which makes individual attention very difficult.

More Effective Classrooms

It is easy to see why communication difficulties arise in the mainstream classroom. Native Americans are more comfortable with silence and longer periods of time without interaction, whereas typically mainstream American teachers expect quicker responses. High verbal activity is not necessarily a positive value in the Native American culture; in the traditional mainstream classroom, talking and participating are encouraged. In fact, teachers often base a grade on how often students respond in conversation. Native Americans usually speak more softly and are overall less verbally responsive.

Students are expected to be analytical and verbal, in the style of the mainstream American student; these cognitive styles are preferred to the visual, symbolic, and holistic thinking, which typically represent the Native American student (Tharp, 1989). After learning about the tribal values, the teacher can weave the preferred style of learning into the class; for example, have students read the story through to the end before discussion, instead of taking it piece by piece (Tharp & Yamaguchi, 1994). Try to utilize materials that will be culturally relevant to the Native Americans. For more effective teaching, exploit the social organization preferences of Native learners, and use cooperative learning, hands-on activities, and group work with peer-oriented direction instead of adult supervision. Individual or group activities replicate the tribal circle of interaction. Manipulatives, group productions, and mental images are other strategies that the teacher can incorporate to create a more realistic learning experience for Native American students.

The Native American child needs to be looked at as a naturalist who loves the environment and everything in the natural world. If the teacher makes the learning environment feel like a real-world atmosphere, Native American students are bound to achieve.

The guidelines in Table 14.2 for teaching Native Americans were taken from the Ableza Institute website (1998) and were written by Native Americans (www.ableza.org/dodont.html). This website is one of the useful resources you can turn to for comprehensive information about the indigenous students in your classes.

TABLE 14.2   Appropriate Methods for Teaching Native Americans

Understand that the term "Native American" includes all peoples indigenous to the Western Hemisphere.

Present Native Americans as appropriate role models for children.

Native American students should not be singled out and asked to describe their families' traditions or their peoples' culture(s).

Avoid the assumption that there are no Native American students in your class.

Use books and materials that are written and illustrated by Native American people as primary source materials, such as speeches, songs, poems, and writings that show the linguistic skill of a people who have come from an oral tradition.

When teaching ABCs, avoid "I is for Indian" and "E is for Eskimo."

Avoid rhymes or songs that use Native Americans as counting devices, e.g., "One little, two little, three little Indians . . ."

Research the traditions and histories, oral and written, of Native Americans before attempting to teach them. Know the significance animals play in each nation. (Certain tribes may ascribe to complex cleansing or religious rituals after seeing animals, such as a bear.)

Avoid referring to or using materials that depict Native Americans as "savages," "primitives," "The Noble Savage," "Red Man," "Red Race," "simple," or "extinct."

Present Native Americans as having unique, separate, and distinct cultures, languages, beliefs, traditions, and customs.

Avoid materials that use non–Native Americans or other characters dressed as "Indians."

Avoid craft activities that trivialize Native American dress, dance, and beliefs (e.g., toilet-paper-roll kachinas or "Indian dolls," paper bag and construction paper costumes and headdresses). Research authentic methods and have the proper materials. Realize that many songs, dances, legends, and ceremonies of Native Americans are considered sacred and should not be "invented" or portrayed as an activity.

If your educational institution employs images or references to Native American peoples as mascots (e.g., "Redskins," "Indians," "Chiefs," "Braves," etc.), urge your administration to abandon these offensive names.

Correct and guide children when they "war whoop," use "jaw-breaker" jargon, or employ any other stereotypical mannerisms.

Depict Native Americans, past and present, as heroes who are defending their people, rights, and lands.

Avoid manipulative phrases and wording such as "massacre," "victory," and "conquest" that distort facts and history.

Teach Native American history as a regular part of American History and discuss what went wrong or right.

Avoid materials and texts that illustrate Native American heroes as only those who helped Europeans and Euro-Americans (e.g., Thanksgiving).

Use materials and texts that outline the continuity of Native American societies from past to present.

Use materials that show respect and understanding of the sophistication and complexities of Native American societies. Understand and impart that the spiritual beliefs of Native Americans are integral to the structure of our societies and are not "superstitions" or "heathen."

(continued)

TABLE 14.2   Continued

Invite a Native American guest speaker/presenter to your class or for a school assembly. Contact a local Native American organization or your library for a list of these resources. Offer an honorarium or gift to those who visit your school.

Avoid the assumption that a Native American person knows everything about all Native Americans.

Use materials that show the value Native Americans place on our elders, children, and women. Avoid offensive terms such as "papoose" and "squaw." Use respectful language.

Understand that not all Native Americans have "Indian" surnames, but many have familiar European and Hispanic names as well.

Help children understand that Native Americans have a wide variety of physical features, attributes, and values, as do people of ALL cultures and races.

Most of all, teach children about Native Americans in a manner that you would like used to depict YOUR culture and racial/ethnic origin.

Source: Ableza Native American Arts and Media Instiute (1998).

DISCUSSION QUESTIONS AND ACTIVITIES

1. What steps can you take to determine whether you have Native American students in your classroom?
2. Understanding Native American cultural beliefs, describe what steps you would take to ensure that your students feel comfortable in the learning situations you create in your classrooms.
3. List ten cultural values of Native Americans, and discuss what teachers can do to make these values congruent with the values of the mainstream teacher.
4. What are some negative or incorrect stereotypes often associated with Native Americans? How do you think these misconceptions came to be so prevalent?

CHAPTER 15

Asian Americans/Indians

We need to clarify what we mean when we use the term "Asian" or "Asian American" in this book. According to the *Asian American Almanac* (1995), Asia and the Pacific Islands have at least thirty different ethnic groups with their own religions, cultures, and national heritages. Four major groups of Asian Americans are East Asian (Chinese, Japanese, and Korean), Pacific Islander (such as Hawaiian, Samoan, Tongan, Tahitian, and Guamanian), Southeast Asian (Thai, Cambodian, Laotian, Burmese, Filipino, and Vietnamese), and South Asian (Indian and Pakistani). Groups of immigrants will often settle in ethnic clusters, such as the Samoans in California or the Hmong in Massachusetts.

Asian groups that include Chinese (mainland China, Taiwan, and Hong Kong), Japanese, Korean, and Vietnamese have settled throughout the entire United States, and teachers will quite likely find representatives of these groups of students in their classrooms. Additionally, numerous South Asian students from India are studying and living in the United States. They are usually multilingual and speak English as a native language. English is a global language, however, and speakers from different cultures converse through diverse dialects, with distinct stress, pitch, and intonation patterns in their spoken language. These deviations from standard American dialects can interfere with the American English speaker's understanding and can cause miscommunication. Later in this chapter, I will discuss factors that will help mainstream teachers understand this cultural group.

Asian Americans

Some Asian students come to America from stable countries, with excellent educational backgrounds and monetary resources, but others come as refugees from war-torn countries with interrupted studies (Brand, 1987). Many U.S. born Asians have lived in this country for generations. Because of these differences, we will see much disparity between Asians new to the country and those who are born in the United States. Additionally, some newcomers come from literate societies (such as the Vietnamese) with skills and abilities that aid in adaptation to the American work force. Yet others, such as the Hmong, who have no written language, are not likely to bring skills that are easily transferable to the American labor market (Trueba & Cheng, 1993).

Trueba explains that Chinese Confucianism and tradition, coupled with Indian Buddhism, have greatly influenced East Asians. Confucian principles focus on ideals

Susan Hobson and Jini Heller contributed material for this chapter.

such as respect for elders, deferred gratification, respect for authority, the value of discipline and educational achievement, self-control, and familial responsibility. When a student does poorly in school, it is more likely to be seen as a lack of will or motivation than of educational ability. In response, parents may react punitively and increase restrictions on the child. Disorders such as learning disabilities or depression are interpreted as a lack of motivation or as being sick and are seen as shameful. Therefore, great care must be taken to explain these problems to Asian parents so they will realize that professionals can help solve the problem, along with parents' cooperation (Kleinman & Good, 1985).

Family welfare is considered more important than individual welfare, so failing in school will reflect on the family as a unit. Formal education is valued, and academic success is related to family integrity. Success brings honor and prestige, whereas failure incurs shame (Lee, 1989; Shen & Mo, 1990).

Asian American students tend to conform to the ideals of the authority figure, and they are usually more dependent than American children. Asians will be more responsive to reinforcement from teachers and will expect a well-organized, quiet, and well-structured educational environment (Baruth & Manning, 1992). Schools are seen as an institution where educators are highly respected and where parents should not interfere. For this reason, Asian parents might believe that educators who expect parental involvement in their children's education are incompetent (National School Public Relations Association, 1993).

Frequently, Asians are stereotyped as the "model minority" or as "whiz kids" and are seen as having special family and educational values, based on Confucian ideas, that lend to their success. However, Siu (1992) maintains that the high level of educational achievement of Asian Americans is more likely due to the interaction of cultural and family values with social factors than to natural superiority or being a "whiz kid." The problem with being labeled a "whiz kid" or "model minority" is that real problems are masked and individual problems may be overlooked. If we assume these students are automatically going to be high achievers, we may unintentionally neglect them and later encounter delinquent behavior and inadequate academic preparation. Learning disabilities that are overlooked (Shen & Mo, 1990), language barriers, and misunderstandings of the U.S. school system may impede success.

In the United States, we appear to be informal; this misconception can be confusing to others who understand clear lines of formality between teacher and student. Some teachers expect the students to interact with the class, and students are graded according to their class participation. Asian students are not usually comfortable with speaking out or drawing attention to themselves, and they may be hesitant and shy about speaking in class. Standing out or being chastised can be particularly distressing to the Asian child. Listening rather than speaking, speaking softly, and behaving modestly are valued by Asian societies. A teacher cannot accurately judge the student's knowledge by how often the student raises his or her hand to participate in class (Baruth & Manning, 1992).

To help the teacher understand Asian Americans, Baruth and Manning (1992) suggest that the best way is to become familiar with the Asian cultural values, traditions, customs, home life, and support system of their students. Showing interest in their native languages and encouraging parents to maintain the use of the native language in the home will help the students in several ways. Students will realize that the teacher values their native heritage; at the same time, using the native language at home will give English learners a rich foundation of language that they can later translate into English. Classroom teachers can collaborate with ESOL teachers and use interpreters with limited English speaking parents (Trueba & Cheng, 1993).

American school values reflect the culture at large, which espouses traits such as independence, individuality, competition, and self-actualization. Trueba and Cheng (1993) explain that Asians often see their self-identity in relation to the group, family, or society, which is a direct contradiction to American values. Self-esteem and confidence are undermined when cultural values clash. As with students from every culture, the disparity between home beliefs and school beliefs may be great. For example, unlike the Asian student, it is not unusual for an American student to challenge authority and question teachers. Teachers can mitigate these types of conflicts by creating classroom activities that do not force the students to behave in ways contrary to their upbringing. Peer tutoring and group work will promote natural conversational interaction with native English speakers. Involve the students' family and community support system in the educational experience to provide assistance in language and cultural learning. Finally, teachers must not assume that all students have the same background knowledge that American students have. Not everyone has experienced birthday parties, dressing up for Halloween, Easter bunnies, or even fire drills.

Cross-Cultural Communication Problems

Miscommunication between Asians and Americans can easily occur, regardless of how much each culture has in common. All cultures have hidden dimensions that are not evident until they clash with one another. It is difficult for educators to know every culture, but it is important to make an effort to at least try to get to know the beliefs of your students. For example, conceptions of time may differ. Although Americans typically operate in a linear schedule, other cultural groups may not. This disparity may be manifested in broken appointments, tardiness, or an apparent disregard for the teacher's time. Additionally, Asians are often polite, or even seemingly submissive, so it may come as a shock when a dispute results in sudden hostility. This may happen as a result of misunderstanding body language or nonverbal clues. Asians often try to avoid appearing offensive and will not make critical remarks. They often favor ambiguity and will repeatedly nod their heads during conversation and refrain from making eye contact (Kim, 1985; Matsuda, 1989). The conversation partner might believe that the head nodding indicates agreement, when the listener is only indicating that he or she is listening. A smile might only be confusion or embarrassment, instead of pleasure (Coker, 1988). To determine what the enigmatic smile really means, the teacher can observe the student in different situations and note the behaviors that indicate consent and disagreement.

Spiritual practices may be a factor in misunderstanding certain behaviors or practices foreign to the American culture. Blessing the grounds in certain areas, unfamiliar religious practices (e.g., performing a ritual cleansing where crimes took place before students return to school), and respecting rites that are important to each cultural group are ways to validate the importance of the individual's beliefs and to mitigate potential friction.

An important issue that teachers are often unaware of is that of the hierarchical imbalance the immigrant family suffers in the United States. Most families recognize the traditional role of the father or the parents as being the head of the household. Families suffer when the youngsters learn English and the parents do not, thus causing great tension as the children become the interpreters and decision makers for the adults.

Educators must realize and understand the issues and cultural values of their English learners. Gathering as much information as possible about the student will help the teacher to determine the best teaching practices to employ. Realizing that many immigrants are accustomed to living in societies where self-disclosure is avoided due to ineffective or tyrannical governments, truthful answers may be withheld from the school. Ages or immigration documents may be falsified, and educational history may be unattainable. In that case, the teacher must try to ascertain English language proficiency, to determine previous educational experience, and to evaluate the student for correct placement. Difficulty in communication can mask health or other problems.

Effective Communication

English learners may have difficulty with the subtleties of English modals. For example, English speakers use "You must" judiciously; we know how to get the point across without using the imperative form. English learners cannot discern when they sound rude, and they may unintentionally offend the native speaker. Matsuda (1989) offers suggestions for educators to follow in trying to communicate effectively with the Asian American:

1. Do not hesitate in assuming the role of the authority. The teacher will be more respected.
2. Respect the beliefs of the Asian family.
3. Do not rush communication. Be patient and respect the silence of the parent.
4. Be very clear and provide step-by-step information, with details of each point. Make sure the parents know what you will do, what they will do, and what the family will do. Give comprehensible advice.
5. Compromise with the family.
6. Note body language. Nodding of the head does not mean agreement with what you are saying. The family may be saying no without verbalizing their disagreement.

Ms. Susan Hobgood, a teacher in Korea, writes about the Korean culture from her perspective. Although all Asian cultures are not the same, many similarities are discernable, especially if the individuals live under the guidance of Confucian or Buddhist principles. Additionally, many of the Asian languages have similarities; as a result, students of English display similar language interferences as learners transfer (positively or negatively) concepts from the native language to English. Therefore, although Ms. Hobgood refers to Korea, many of the idiosyncrasies she writes about can be related to Chinese, Japanese, and other Asian cultures.

Ms. Hobgood begins her rendition by describing a scenario that took place in her second-grade language arts class in the United States, which consisted of twenty students. One little girl from Seoul, Korea, Soo-Min Park, had been in the United States for six months. The following scenario shows how easily linguistic misunderstandings can occur when learning a new language.

TEACHER:	Everyone take out your reading books and turn to page 60. Sally, would you please read for the class?

(Sally begins to read. Soo Min looks confused.)

TEACHER:	Soo Min, what's wrong?
SOO MIN:	What page?
TEACHER:	Page 60. Let me see. Soo Min, that's the wrong page; that is page 16. We are on 60.
SOO MIN:	Oh, sorry.

(Class finishes reading the story.)

TEACHER:	Let's talk about the story. Johnny, why was the boy in the story so sad?
JOHNNY:	He was sad because his dog ran away.
TEACHER:	Who helped him find his dog, Rosa?
ROSA:	His mother, father, and his friend, Billy.
TEACHER:	Who has a dog?

(Students raise hands.)

TEACHER:	Soo Min, what is your dog's name?
SOO MIN:	Nabi, but not my home. Older home.

TEACHER:	Oh, so you had a dog in Korea?
SOO MIN:	Yes.
TEACHER:	But you don't have a dog here?
SOO MIN:	Yes.
TEACHER:	You do have a dog here?
SOO MIN:	No, in Korea.
TEACHER (sounding frustrated):	I'm confused; you don't have a dog here?
SOO MIN (looking down):	Yes, my dog in Korea.
TEACHER:	Soo Min, please look at me when I talk to you.

(Later at recess, three other girls are talking to Soo Min.)

YA CHEN:	Soo Min, we are going skating today after school. Do you want to come?
SOO MIN:	I can't. I am go to math academy.
FATIMA:	You mean you have to go to school again?
SOO MIN:	Yes, Monday and Wednesday, I go math academy.
SARA:	How terrible to have to go to school twice.

In this scenario, it is clear the teacher has little information about Korean culture. Obviously, the scene is exaggerated, as most teachers would be more sensitive, even without knowledge of Soo Min's culture. This incident, however, demonstrates some possible communication misunderstandings that can occur.

The United States has always been a place that receives many immigrants each year. According to the Census Bureau, in 2002 the foreign-born population was around 32.5 million people, which is 11.5 percent of the population. Of these 32.5 million people, 25.5 percent were Asians. In 2000, there were 1,228,427 Korean-born residents in the United States. This is an increase of 54 percent since 1990 (Logan, Stowell, & Vesselinov, 2001). Koreans come to the United States for a variety of reasons. They come to reunite with family, to work, and to learn English. One of the biggest motives for coming to the United States is for education. Since South Korea began allowing its students to study abroad, tens of thousands of students have come to the United States to study. Many parents feel that the educational system in Korea, as well as in some other Asian countries, does not meet the needs of a society that is trying to compete with other countries economically. Classes in many Asian countries are large, rote learning is the primary method of instruction, and the curriculum is rigid (Moon, 2001). Teachers in the United States often find that their Asian students come to study in the United States because they did not get accepted to a university in the home country.

Since Koreans, as well as other Asians, place a high value on education, they will spare no expense to make sure their students get the best education possible. They are even willing to go into debt to make sure their children go to a good school, attend after-school academies, or have private tutors (Lee, 2003). According to an article in the *Korea Times*, South Korea is ranked first in the world in private spending on education (Seo, 2002).

Confucianism influences Korean society profoundly, as it does other Asian countries. The values taught by Confucianism include harmony with the family and community, hard work, and a strong emphasis on education (Kim-Rupnow, 2001). Additionally, it promotes respect for elders and those in authority. Koreans and most Asians are taught to respect the hierarchy in their families, in school or work, and among the people with whom they interact (Lee, 1996). For example, when seated at the dinner table, the younger ones may not eat until the oldest person at the table begins. When handing something to an older person, two hands are always used. Older people, or those in power, are never called by name; instead, they are addressed by a title. Teachers in Korea are called *Sonsaengnim*, or Teacher. An older brother, or any older male, is called *oppa* (for girls) or *hyeong* (for boys), which simply means older brother. Asian languages, especially Korean, demonstrate this hierarchy. Different forms of a word are used, depending on whether the speaker is talking to well-known peer or an older person. Everyone in the family has his or her own roles. After the parents, the person with the most responsibility and power is the oldest brother. He is the one who is responsible for taking care of his parents as they grow older. He also becomes the head of the family, should anything happen to his father.

The value of harmony within community and family is practiced in everyday life. In the workplace people are not addressed by name but by their title, which denotes their standing within the bigger system. Grown children often live at home, even when they finish university. Sometimes after marriage the wife goes to live with her husband's parents. Decisions are not made alone. Parents are consulted even if the children are not living at home. To make a decision alone, without consulting others in the family, would be considered selfish (Kim-Rupnow, 2001).

Religion is an important part of Asian society. Many of the holidays and customs come from Buddhism. Although Christianity is widely practiced, most families still follow the Buddhist rituals on holidays. Buddha's birthday is celebrated in May every year with a festival and a procession of lanterns. During Chusok, or the Korean Thanksgiving, many Koreans travel to ancestors' graves where they bring ceremonial food, gather with family, and bow to their ancestors (J. E. Shim, personal communication, November 1, 2003). Many events in Korea are based on different calendars, including the lunar calendar, but all traditional holidays are based on the lunar year. Some Koreans celebrate two birthdays a year, a solar birthday and a lunar birthday.

Regarding familial relationships, at one time divorce was considered taboo, and many couples would stay together despite infidelity and other marital problems. Now the divorce rate is on the rise, growing 250 percent in the last ten years. In 2002, the Korean divorce rate was 3 cases for every 1,000 people (Onishi, 2003). Although the divorce rate is lower than in the United States, it would not be uncommon to find a student in a one-parent household. Many mothers will take their child to the United States for an education while the father stays behind to work. Many fathers in Korea have joined groups to share information about their children's education abroad (Moon, 2001).

Asian students in the United States may find the educational system unchallenging because in most Asian countries, in addition to English academies, children also attend math, art, music, science, Chinese character, tae kwon do, and countless other after-school classes. It is not uncommon for a middle school student to attend as many as six academies. Students are assigned homework from their regular schools as well as from their additional academies. Students may go to bed at midnight or later because of studying. School vacations, both in the winter and summer, can be a time of increasing the number of academies. Therefore, the American school systems may appear to be very simplistic. If Asian students apply the same rigor to their studies in the United States, academic achievement is easily explained.

Implications for the Classroom

Cross-cultural miscommunication can easily occur between the Korean or Asian student and the mainstream American. It can start when a teacher asks a student's age. For example, Koreans follow a different system than the Western way of tracking ages. Koreans believe you are 1 year old when you are born. You also become the next age on January first of every year. So, if a Korean student tells you he or she is 10 years old, that could mean 8 or 9, depending on the actual date of the student's birthday (Lee, 1996). If school or grade placement is determined according to age, a problem can start from the moment a Korean child enters the American school.

According to Lee (1996), indirectness is a big part of Korean culture, as well as Asian cultures in general, and that can affect students in the classroom. Koreans are taught to practice *nunchi* before speaking and to modify their answers accordingly. *Nunchi* is the ability to grasp the unspoken word or intention of others (Kim, 2001). Therefore, responses to the teacher or to other children may be based on what they think the other person wants to hear, based on their observation and interpretation of body language and facial expression. Hall (1990) explained this type of culture as being high context as opposed to the low context of American culture.

In Korea, when a teacher or a person of power or respect is speaking to a student, the student is not supposed to make eye contact. So, typically, when a student is being scolded, he or she looks down. This is contrary to the American expectation that children look at us when we are speaking to them. In speaking with several Koreans who have studied in the United States, they have all said that at some point they got in trouble for not looking the teacher in the eye.

Koreans also may use a smile or laughter in a difficult situation. When a child is in trouble, he or she may smile. A U.S. teacher may perceive that as disrespect or not taking the problem seriously. That is probably not the case. The student is most likely just feeling confused or embarrassed (Huang, 1993). Often East Asians, Koreans included, will remain calm and polite during a conversation or disagreement. As Westerners, we may take that to mean everything is in accord; we may not see any warning signs of impending trouble. Then suddenly, they will become very hostile seemingly without reason. This is a perfect example of anthropologist Edward Hall's (1983) description of **high-context** culture, which means that individuals do not verbally transmit information. The rules of the cultural expectations are implicit. As previously mentioned, this behavior is contrary to that which is found in the United States, which is a **low-context** culture. Procedures, thoughts, ideas, and feelings are explicitly verbalized in U.S. culture. The United States is comprised of individuals from many cultures with a variety of dissimilar behaviors, whereas most of the population of Korea is comprised of Koreans who behave within a similar cultural paradigm. The same can be said of other Asian countries and cultures.

The concept of *nunchi* goes both ways. Asian people may assume that Westerners are reading their nonverbal signals, so they perceive that we are being insensitive (Huang, 1993). In not paying attention to the nonverbal signs, the Korean custom of *chaemyon* is being violated. Loosely translated, this means "dignity" or "face." Koreans are supposed to practice *nunchi* so they do not embarrass the other person or cause him or her to lose *chaemyon* (Lee, 1996). Koreans have an indirect nonconfrontational approach to problem solving, so that all parties involved can save face.

Korean students, as well as many other Asian students, place high pressure on themselves to achieve superior grades to avoid bringing shame to the family. A Korean student may receive a 90 on a test and get very upset. A 90 is a good grade, so an American teacher may not understand the implication of receiving a less-than-perfect score. As previously mentioned, a fundamental value of the Confucian society is the importance of formal education. The Korean parent sacrifices much for the student's education. A good grade or a less-than-desirable grade reflects on the whole family's integrity. Anything less than perfect may be perceived as undesirable. Therefore, much pressure is placed on the child to succeed, which can cause stress and conflict within the family (Huang, 1993).

Language Difficulties

One difficulty in learning the English language occurs when Koreans agree in a negative form within **tag questions** (Choi, 1991). This is also called a false negative. For example, when you say to an American child, "What's the matter, you don't want to play?" The American child will respond by saying no, meaning, "No, I don't want to play." When asking a Korean child that same question, the response might be "yes."

This means, "Yes, you're right, I don't want to play." Needless to say, this phenomenon can be a confusing exchange if the teacher is not aware of the differences in the language context.

A great source of pride in Korean history is the invention of the Korean language, or *Hangul*. In 1446, King Sejong created the Korean alphabet. Chinese was used by scholars, but many of the common people could not read or write because of the time and effort needed to learn Chinese (Korean Overseas Information Service, 1997). He created an alphabet of twenty-eight letters, but only twenty-four are used today. It is a simple alphabet that is easy to learn to read, and children learn it at an early age. Because of the simplicity of Hangul, illiteracy is virtually nonexistent (Korean Overseas Information Service, 1997).

Hangul is very different from the Roman alphabet, which can cause the Korean student some problems when learning English. Each syllable has three parts: the initial consonant (*ch'osong*), the peak vowel (*chungsong*), and the final consonant (*chongsong*). Korean used to be read from top to bottom, but now most Korean is written from left to right.

There are certain sounds in English that do not exist in the Korean language. For example there is no /f/ or /z/ sound. You may hear students saying "pish" instead of fish and "joo" instead of zoo. There is also not a distinction between /l/ and /r/, which also causes some pronunciation problems. I saw an English textbook, written in Korea, that attempted to demonstrate the sounds of the English alphabet with Korean characters. Since not every English letter has a Korean counterpart, this can create pronunciation problems.

As a teacher, I have discovered there are sounds that are difficult for the Korean student to hear. The difference between short /a/ and short /e/ are hard to distinguish. When I say the word *bad*, many times the student will write down the word *bed*, or vice versa. The short /i/ sound and the long /e/ sound also cause some difficulty. The /th/ sound, which doesn't exist in Korean, is mispronounced in several ways. *Think* may be pronounced "tink," "sink," or "shink." Pronouncing /th/ seems to be almost impossible for most ELLs, and it is important to remember that language learners cannot reproduce sounds they cannot distinguish or "hear." Visualizing sounds can be helpful, so have students touch their lips, feel vibrations, look at the placement of tongue against teeth, or touch their throats when uttering a sound. A small mirror can be used to have the students watch their mouths as they copy the sounds the teacher is making.

There are a number of Korean words that have been borrowed from the English language. They are not always used or pronounced correctly, which can be problematic. This is often called "Konglish." An example of Konglish is the word *cunning*. In English it is an adjective meaning tricky or devious. In Konglish it is a verb meaning to cheat. Often students will say, "Teacher, he cunning" (translation: "Teacher, he is cheating"). Because the Korean language does not have some of the English sounds, as in Japanese as well, often other sounds are substituted. During the World Cup in 2002, I would often hear Koreans yelling, "Korea team hiting." I had no idea what that meant until I really paid attention. They were saying *fighting*, and lacking the /f/ sound in the Korean language, they substituted the /h/ sound.

A noticeable contrast exists between the grammatical structure of Hangul and that of English. Verbs almost always come at the end of a sentence in Korean (Goodman, 1997). For example, in English I say, "I am Susan." In Korean I would say, "Nanun Susan Imnida" or "I Susan am." This can be difficult for the English learner in terms of sentence structure. Articles and prepositions are used in a totally different way in Korean. Using them correctly can be a challenge. Even very good Korean speakers of English tend to drop their articles every now and then.

I can imagine any ELL would have problems with English grammar. English has rules, exceptions to rules, and irregular verbs. English speakers add an /s/ to the third person singular in the simple present verb tense. I have often been at a loss to explain to a student why English speakers say, "in the morning," "in the evening," but "at night." Park (1995) reports a study that found most Korean American students happy about their life in America, but one-third of them experience difficulty learning English. I am surprised it is not greater, as English is a very complex language to learn for non-native speakers.

The Korean student may have a number of problems in a mainstream English situation. If Korean students live in a city with many other Koreans, such as Los Angeles or New York, they may speak English only in the classroom. In talking to a Korean student who lived in the United States, she said that even at school between classes she spoke Korean with the other Korean students. She said that made it harder to progress quickly in learning English (C. Shim, personal communication, November 4, 2003).

Korean students, as well as other newcomers to American classrooms, can expect to face many new hurdles, from cultural differences to language, even to the difference in the way the class is taught. Many teachers in the United States have very little knowledge about Korean culture (Lee, 2003). As a result, miscommunication between the teacher and the Korean student is prevalent. As previously mentioned, the teacher may get irritated when the student does not make eye contact. A teacher may get frustrated when a child who is being scolded smiles and appears to be unconcerned. Sometimes for the purpose of teaching a concept, American teachers may encourage students to debate or discuss issues with them. As in most other countries in the world, this is not the style of teaching that is used in Korea. Additionally, this apparent disregard for boundaries between teacher and student can confuse the child who has been taught not to argue with those in authority. The American educational system often encourages students to share their thoughts and ideas and will grade students on active participation in class. The Korean student may feel uncomfortable with this approach because at home the teacher is always right and is not questioned.

Koreans may experience high levels of stress in the classroom. They are learning in a different way and in a language that is very different from their own. Their parents have high expectations for them, and the children may even feel that acceptance is contingent on their school success (Lee, 2003). Students also feel the pressure to become "American" while still maintaining their cultural identity. One research study showed that, although becoming acculturated to American culture may decrease stress, the participant may feel as if he or she has abandoned Korean traditions and culture, which can cause depression (Oh, Koeske, & Sales, 2002). The pressure to conform to the classroom culture can cause the student to feel torn. Other class members, who may not understand or may not be sensitive to cultural differences, may cause the Korean student to feel ashamed or to feel like an outcast.

Although Korean students tend to do very well in math algorithms, they may have some challenges when dealing with numbers verbally. The unit of numbers in Korea is based on four digits instead of three, as it is in the United States (Wong & Teuben-Rowe, 1997). For example, 235,000 is said "two hundred thirty-five thousand," in English. In Korean it is "i-ship sam man o chun" or twenty-three ten thousands five thousand (23,5000).

An American teacher may notice the Korean students have difficulty interacting with their classmates because in Korea a peer is only someone who was born in the same year. Anyone else is either his or her senior or junior (Lee, 1996). Koreans will only use a person's name if that person is the same age or younger. The oldest person in the group is the one who "calls the shots" and can tell others what to do. In America, although age has some importance, the "leader" tends to be the one with the most outgoing and assertive personality. Korean students may be offended by a younger student treating them like equals or may be frustrated when a younger student does not follow their direction. In a group project, the Korean student may assume that the oldest child will be taking the lead in the project, where in actuality that may not be the case. Obviously, this trend may cause a problem in the U.S. school where a more egalitarian outlook is observed. The older Korean students may have the younger students carry their books or do their homework, which is contrary to American expectations. Thus, these students are wedged between the old culture and the new culture's value system.

A student may not want a parent to attend a school function or a teacher conference. This may be because of embarrassment about the differences in culture. It is more likely that the student is worried about the limited English proficiency of his or her parents (Park, 1995). In Park's study, 80 percent of the students participating wished that their parents could speak English well.

Students who are in a mainstream class and are pulled out for an ESOL class may experience some shame. If a student is in a class for exceptional students with learning disabilities, the shame is even greater. Many Koreans do not understand or recognize disabilities of any kinds. Although being in an ESOL class is certainly not a disability, the child may perceive it as such. Parents may just ask that the child remain in the mainstream class, and they will get a tutor at home. Koreans tend to see a disability as a failure or a curse upon the family (Kim-Rupnow, 2001). Parents may deal with the disability without help and hope that the child will grow out of it. Children frequently use the Korean word for handicapped as an insult to tease others. After viewing the movie, *I Am Sam*, about a mentally handicapped father, I discussed it with a Korean friend. He said, "When I was watching the movie, I was so frustrated." When I asked why, he said it was because Sam did not try to get better. This is an educated, well-spoken man who did not understand mental disabilities at all.

A student may not volunteer to speak in the classroom due to the influence of Confucianism's concept of **formalism** (Lee, 1996). Formalism emphasizes accuracy, rather than fluency. In Korea, as in most Asian cultures, being talkative is not valued. Unless students can say the sentence correctly, and know beyond a doubt that the answer is correct, they may refuse to say anything, especially when surrounded by native speakers. I have seen this firsthand in the classroom. Or if the student does not understand, he or she will not admit it, but will go home and try to learn it alone. Very bright students will not answer a question unless they are positive they can say the answer perfectly. Therefore, when a Korean student, or any ELL for that matter, volunteers to answer a question and forgets the English word or answers in the native language, the teacher should compliment the child for participating, rather than reject the answer (Lee, 2003).

Although Korean culture emphasizes studying and being disciplined in schoolwork, that does not imply that school comes easy to every Korean student. The American stereotype of the "Asian whiz kid" can put an added burden on the child, which can cause emotional distress and school failure (Huang, 1993). Teachers and other students may just assume that this child will do very well with little struggle, when in fact that may not be the case. Many teachers who are accustomed to the overachieving Asian student suffer from this illusion.

Although Korean students are taught to respect their elders and those in authority by age or position, they still have a strong sense of right and wrong. Korean culture emphasizes the deference to authority and the priority of the group over the individual (Kim, 1998). In Kim's study, Korean students gave priority to the authority figures who gave directions based on correct moral judgments. Therefore, Korean students probably have a strong enough foundation to resist orders from older children who encourage them to do the wrong thing. This can cause conflict as they struggle with wanting to do the right thing yet violating their own sense of respecting authority.

Rather than hinder the progress of the mainstream class, I believe that having a Korean student, or any foreign-born student, can be a benefit to the class. Other students get a chance to learn firsthand about another country and culture. Korean students are taught to be diligent, and this could inspire others in the classroom to invoke the same study habits. Although the Korean student may need to get accustomed to the lack of hierarchy when working on a group project, he or she is already familiar with the idea of community and may work well with others and encourage others to do the same.

Using examples of the student's culture and language in the classroom can be beneficial to the entire class and can put the immigrant students at ease. "When home languages and cultures are included in the classroom, students feel they do not have to 'give up' their identity and background to learn English" (Edelsky, 1996, as cited in Wong & Teuben-Rowe 1997, p. 1). As teachers, we can help students feel included rather than excluded from the class. It is the responsibility of the teacher to help the students develop language and social skills, without making the students feel they have to give up their own cultural and personal identification with their native culture (Oh et al., 2002).

One way to encourage understanding of the intricacies of language and writing would be to showcase different writing systems in the classroom (Wong & Teuben-Rowe, 1997). Students can become aware of the various writing systems that exist and compare them to English. Native English speakers might feel the thrill of having the Korean student write their English names in Hangul. The teacher can spend some time discussing the different systems and how they are read (right to left, left to right, etc.).

A classroom could have some decorations from the students' native countries, material published in the students' home language, and some resources or activities about their home country. This can help the Korean, or any newcomer, to feel more at ease and respected (Lee, 2003) while inspiring the English speakers to find interest in other cultures. Also, a teacher can occasionally mention the other countries' events and compare them with American holidays and so forth. For example, U.S. Thanksgiving and Chusok could be discussed, or students could compare the Korean representative system and the U.S. Congress. Common Asian customs can be demonstrated, such as bowing to greet one another, as the students explain the different types of bowing. Students from other cultures are fascinated as they watch the different Asians demonstrate how they bow to their parents as a measure of their degree of respect (e.g., the bow may find the person prostrate on the floor). Let the student share about a Korean game such as **Yut Nori**, a game involving four sticks. Teachers need to understand that when the home and school behaviors share congruity, children maintain respect for their home heritage (Lee, 2003).

Students from other countries usually bring their native foods to eat in school. For example, even those students who have been in America for quite a while eat Korean food for lunch. Different smells and tastes will be evident in the lunchroom. Instead of having a situation where other students ridicule the student for eating something different, the teacher can set the mood by showing curiosity about the food (Lee, 2003). It can become a learning experience where students can compare Korean and American diets. The teacher can exploit this great opportunity to share multicultural customs by highlighting different foods people eat, as well as expectations we have about what constitutes certain meals. For example, Americans eat bacon and eggs, cereal, pancakes, and waffles for breakfast, whereas many other people eat rice and soup.

Korean and other Asian names may seem like unusual tongue twisters to the native English speaker. As in Chinese and Vietnamese cultures, the family name is usually first, so a child may tell a teacher he is Kim, Chang Soo, Kim being the family name. The given name of a Korean has two parts. One part of the name is generational. It was determined many generations ago and is now a part of their family history. All the children born in the same generation have the same name (Choi, 1991). The other part of the name is usually given by the paternal grandfather or the oldest male relative on the father's side. Many Korean and other Asian children take on Western names for their English classes. They may choose a name from a TV show or just pick a name that they like. One of my kindergarten students insisted we call her Cinderella. As an interesting interchange, the class could let the Korean student give Korean names to the others to help the children become more at ease with the difference in names. To correctly pronounce a student's name, no matter how foreign sounding it is to the teacher, is a great gift of acknowledgment that builds a student's self-esteem.

Teachers should also keep in mind that it is important not to inadvertently embarrass or humiliate any child but to pay careful attention to the student's struggle. Words or actions that may not be a problem for a native-English-speaking student could cause problems for the Asian student. It is necessary to remember the concept of *chaemyon*, or self-respect. Teachers should use appropriate words and indirect expressions when correcting or admonishing the student (Lee, 1996). The teacher should also not insist that the Korean child look him or her in the eye.

Of crucial importance in working with English learners is the concept of "wait time" when asking questions. Language learners may not respond right away, as they need time to put together the answer in English and to reflect on what is said. For this reason, feel comfortable in allowing an extended period of time for the ELL to think; don't expect an answer right away. Consider periods of silence an opportunity for reflection (Huang, 1993). Ask one question at a time, provide clear information as to exactly what is being asked, and give clear guidelines as to what is expected. Try to encourage Korean students to voluntarily participate in discussion, and then be sure to acknowledge their efforts and willingness to share.

The behavior of Korean parents might frustrate the teacher in the United States. It is not uncommon for a parent to be late or not show up for a meeting. Korean time is polychronic (i.e., they perform multiple tasks simultaneously). Whereas Americans will attend to one person at a time, Koreans do not. Koreans perceive time and events as an "unfolding process" (Lee, 2003), as compared to the Western way of looking at events independently and scheduling them that way. In other words, events happen as they happen, instead of at an appointed time. Teachers need to be patient when a parent is late or misses a meeting, as no offense is intended toward the teacher. Do not confront them (again, the concept of *chaemyon*), as they must save face. When scheduling meetings, indicate the importance of appointment times and explain that there are other appointments scheduled after theirs. When a parent misses a meeting, it may be because of work. Working long hours is typical of a Korean worker.

As with all parents, when meeting to discuss their child, a teacher needs to be careful not to criticize the child (Lee, 2003). Discuss the child's strengths before looking at problems. Give specific guidelines for improvement, and ask for help from the parent. Make it very clear that any academic problems are not a source of shame. Rather than having the parent feel that an ESOL class or extra tutoring means the child is slow, the teacher can help the parent to see that it is an opportunity for the student to progress. It is also a great time for the teacher to ask about the student's cultural and family background. This will help the parent feel that the teacher is open and interested in the child. Additionally, assure the parent that speaking the native language at home is important and that it won't interfere with learning English (Lee, 2003). When talking to students who have lived abroad, I have discovered that many of them had to relearn their own language when they returned to Korea. In addition, it is now commonly believed that the richer the language and literacy foundation the child has in the native language, the easier it is to transfer knowledge to the second language.

Parents may have trouble speaking English, but don't automatically assume that they are not proficient in English (Lee, 2003). Many people in Korea are learning English independently. Koreans tend to be well educated, so a parent may very well have high English language skills. Chances are they have some English foundation, as English is so prevalent in Korea. Koreans may know more written English than verbal, as they all learn it in middle school and high school. When communicating with parents, it is a good idea to use written communication rather than the telephone (Lee, 2003). If you should visit a Korean student's home, as in almost any Asian home, make sure to take off your shoes at the door, as this is part of the Korean culture.

Korean parents are very serious about wanting their children to succeed academically. Don't be surprised to receive gifts from your Korean students. My older students have explained to me that extravagant gifts are frequently given to the teacher in hopes that the teacher will bestow a more favorable grade on the student. This is described in a Korean expression that loosely translated means *the swish of the mother's skirt*.

TABLE 15.1 Tips for the Classroom

Encourage children to continue speaking their native language at home. Explain that it is exciting to know two languages (Lee, 2003), and they will transfer knowledge easier.

Not only should a teacher learn about the child's cultural background, but knowledge should be gained about personal and family background also. This is crucial to making the classroom a culturally sensitive environment (Lee, 2003).

If possible, find a Korean parent volunteer who can spend time interpreting and helping the student (Lee, 2003).

Use music in the classroom. Children love to sing, and it helps the Korean student to become more comfortable with the English language. Group singing will help the Korean student feel less inhibited about pronouncing words. Maybe even ask the student to share a recording of a Korean song or, if the student is outgoing, to sing a song for the class.

Don't write a student's name in red ink. This is the same as writing it in blood in Korean. Some believe that they or a family member will die (Wong & Teuben-Rowe, 1997).

Use some stories and textbooks that have Korean characters or stories in them. The Literacy Place series by Scholastic uses a variety of stories from different countries.

Have students write and illustrate a fairy tale. Encourage the Korean student to use Korean folktales such as "Hongbu and Nolbu," or the story of how Korea came to be.

Be careful how you pronounce your words, and speak slowly. Remember to stress sounds such as the short /a/ sound. Be aware of the sounds that may cause the student trouble.

Use pairs and small groups to work on assignments. The student will take a little while to get used to it but eventually will be comfortable. The student may feel more comfortable speaking to one or two other people, than to the whole class.

If the student goes to an ELL class, be in constant communication with that teacher, and continually assess the student's progress.

Table 15.1 provides tips for the classroom gathered from various sources, as well as my own teaching experience.

As the Korean and other Asian populations in the United States grow, it becomes increasingly necessary that educators learn about the cultures, which can be very distinct. No longer can we assume that all students fit under the title of "American" or "Asian" and can just learn things in the same way. Students need to learn academics, but they also need to learn about new ways of adjusting without losing their own cultural identity. We as teachers play a significant role in helping the students to develop biculturally. We need to relate to Korean and other Asian students, as they come to us: following a hierarchical structure, needing silence at times, and going home to an environment which may be traditional in practice. We need to reach out to the parents and invite them to be a part of their child's educational life. We need to educate other students in the ways of Koreans and other Asian groups, so they in turn can reach out to the Asian student as an individual. If we are going to help these students succeed, we must be proactive in ensuring that success will take place.

Indians

I called upon Ms. Jini Heller, originally from India, to offer her insights regarding Indian students. Ms. Heller is one of those individuals who has had the experience of being able to step outside her culture and compare how she was raised with her life and environment today. Married to a Swiss man who speaks English, German, and French, Ms. Heller speaks English, Hindi, French, and several dialects from her native India. Her 4-year-old daughter, who has spent most of her life in Switzerland, speaks English, German, and Hindi. A master's student in education, Ms. Heller returns to India for several months every year. She is living in the United States because of her husband's job. I asked her to tell me about the Indian student in the classroom and to explain what mainstream teachers should know. She researched the topic and shared her insight with me.

I am grateful to have the opportunity to share my thoughts with teachers in the United States. This presentation gave me the opportunity to research facts about my home country, as well as share my in-depth knowledge as an Indian woman who has experienced life in many countries and in the classrooms of the United States. India is a multifaceted country with intricate issues. What is perfectly understandable in my country often becomes a complex mystery to Americans. I hope to be able to shed some light on the complexities that teachers may encounter in the classroom situations.

The Federal Republic of India possesses a population of 1.04 billion people, 72 percent of whom are Indo-Aryan, 25 percent Dravidian, and about 3 percent of other lesser-known ethnic groups. We are multilingual and speak Hindi, Urdu, Tamil, Bengali, Kashmiri, and, of course, English. The core of our culture consists of historically traditional ideas and accompanying values that emphasize the intangible and symbolic aspects of group life. As Banks explains, India consists of a macroculture, the national or shared culture of the nation-state, or the big culture, as well as the smaller cultures within that constitute the microculture (Banks, 2001, p. 72). Banks's categorization is perfect for a vast, diverse, and multicultural nation like India. As Banks depicts, India's macroculture is traditionalist, with freedom of religion and spirituality and belief in the family as an institution. The microcultures within would be the work ethic, literacy, material progress, and behavioral patterns influenced by cultural values, and so forth, including intense social issues like women's rights; *sati*, or bride-burning; and dowry systems (Banks, 2001, p. 73).

In my attempt to provide teachers with insights into the culture of immigrant student from India, it is important to note that "religion" permeates every single aspect of Indian culture—surface or deep, tangible or intangible. You see religion in art, devotional music, fashion, housing and decor (**Vaastu Shastra**, a type of Indian architecture), festivals, death, celebrations, marriage, birth, business, growth and development, material progress, ecology and environment, and so forth. Culture in India is a function of race, religion, region (urban or rural), and socioeconomic level. Respect for all elders is sacred, and the student will feel discordance in the classroom if other students disrespect the teacher. Additionally, the male child is favored, and being shy and reticent is considered a positive trait, especially for the female child. This should not be regarded as maladjustment.

Language in India

There's no "Indian" language per se, which is partly why English is still widely spoken almost half a century after the British departed India. Eighteen languages are officially recognized by the constitution, but over 1,600 minor languages and dialects were listed in the 1991 census. Major efforts have been made to promote Hindi as the national language and to gradually phase out English. But while Hindi is the predominant language in the north, it bears little relation to the Dravidian languages of the south. In the south, very few people speak Hindi.

The Indian upper class clings to English as the shared language of the educated elite, championing it as both a badge of their status and as a passport to the world of international business. In truth, only about 3 percent of Indians have a firm grasp of the language.

Education in India

Traditionally, Indian culture regarded education as a holy duty that was linked to religion. **Mullahs**, **sadhus**, **gurus**, and saints taught the holy scriptures, languages, and sciences to the people in their community. The Hindu goddess Saraswati is the goddess of knowledge, widely revered and worshipped by the Hindus. Education was seen as a means to attain higher social status and spiritual well-being and was not available to all classes of society. Women of nobility and higher class had access to education through their priests. Today, education is available to all in Indian society in the form of public schools, private schools, and religious schools. Convent and Muslim schools are attached to temples for Hindus and Buddhists, and all schools use English as the medium of education. Indian school schedules are based on a British format, that is, ten years of elementary and high school, two years for junior college, and three years of senior college, and postgraduation is another two or more years. Higher education is important, since professions such as medicine, engineering, and higher education are most sought after and augment the person's status in the marriage market. Literacy of females in India is over 50 percent, whereas literacy of males is 73 percent. Therefore, education is a vital factor in life positions, as arranged marriages are still prevalent, both in India and among Indians in the United States.

Currently, India is making headlines internationally for taking jobs from the West, rather than for its teeming slums and rural poor. At the same time, the burgeoning middle class in India of 250 to 300 million scampers to acquire education in the United States. The United States is by far the number-one choice for an Indian for migration and education. The typical Indian student in the United States is usually from a middle- to upper-class urban Indian family, has migrated to the United States at a young age with professional parents, was born in the United States, or was sent to the United States as an adult for higher education. The student will be totally dedicated to the pursuit of education, as the family will have spent much money and will have made a huge investment for the student to succeed. Meanwhile, the student will be strongly attached to an extended family back home in India or here within the United States.

Indian Immigrant Students

The Indian immigrant students will most likely possess common characteristics noticeable to the mainstream teacher. Students will have a good level of English literacy unless they are from the rural or urban poor society. Unlike in many other immigrant groups in the United States, parental involvement in education is the norm. Teachers work hard, along with the parents, to ensure academic success. Students are accustomed to rote and memorization strategies, and they are taught at a young age ways and means to enhance memory and concentration powers. Young students are not encouraged to ask questions. Instruction methods are traditional with no audiovisual techniques; reading, writing, and memorization are the preferred strategies. Finally, teachers will note that poverty or socioeconomic level is not an indicator of intellect and academic success in Indian society. Students of all socioeconomic levels will demonstrate the same commitment to educational attainment.

- The Indian immigrant student:
  1. Shows deep respect for teachers of any race, sex, or culture.
  2. Believes that obedience and humility are the norm.
  3. Is usually well adjusted socially and psychologically.
  4. Interacts with fellow students without much reserve, as he or she is used to diversity.
  5. Will show respect for an older student, and it is customary for the older ones to look out for the younger ones and to act as their mentors.
- The mainstream teacher can expect:
  1. To see a generally well-behaved, respectful, and academically focused Indian student.
  2. To encourage the Indian student to work more independently and to ask questions.

3. To empower the Indian students by teaching them to become more responsible for their own learning, as the Indian student is used to following instructions and orders and does not voluntarily or proactively initiate learning.

4. To make the most of the Indian student's innate sense of "looking out for the younger ones," encouraging the student's natural empathy to form friendships with other students who have greater problems adjusting to a new cultural environment.

■ Impact on multicultural classrooms:

1. Family and parental participation in the child's academic life should be expected.

2. An Indian student would almost never assimilate or merge in the "melting pot," by losing his or her sense of identity and cultural belonging. He or she would acculturate relatively smoothly, and hence the multicultural educator would not have to grapple with "cultural and psychological interventions" in order to prepare the child for academic success (Igoa, 1995, p. 44).

3. Nonverbal communication such as not meeting the eye of the teacher should not be regarded as disrespectful. The educator needs to instruct the child that it is important to look the teacher in the eye when speaking.

For Indians, deep culture seems to have a tendency to change more slowly than surface culture. It would be easier for a modern Indian to change his or her dress style or food habits than other entrenched family values, social beliefs, and religion. Economic development, materialism, and consumerism lead to changes in values, culture, and social outlook. Although change is inevitably taking place as modern technology reaches further and further into the fabric of society, essentially rural India remains and will remain much the same as it has for thousands of years. So resilient are its social and religious institutions that it has absorbed, ignored, and eschewed all attempts to radically change or destroy them. This reluctance to change has been somewhat modified as more immigrants come to the United States; however, the basic tenets of Indian culture remain fixed. I hope that I have clarified these cultural values to an extent that is helpful to the mainstream teacher in understanding the actions of the Indian student in the classroom.

DISCUSSION QUESTIONS AND ACTIVITIES

1. Your new student, Jin Wu, focuses intently as you are giving instructions for the writing test. Students have 45 minutes to complete the exam. Students begin to work, and Jin Wu puts his head down and starts reading. Complete silence fills the room as students write furiously. After 30 minutes have elapsed, Jin Wu raises his hand to ask a question. You go to him, and he points to the first writing prompt and asks what it means. It reads, "Mr. Wagner's gross expenses far exceed his net salary and he can barely break even. Describe some ways for him to improve his lot." What do you think happened here?

2. Choi Soon Lee is a new Korean student in your class. He makes friends with other Koreans in class; soon you learn that he is carrying books, buying lunch, and doing homework for others who are a bit older. What do you think is happening, and how would you approach this sensitive cultural issue?

3. Akemi Matsuno listens to her teacher talk and nods her head affirmatively. When asked if she understands, she says yes and leaves to do her homework. The next day she shows up with her assignment in hand. When her teacher corrects the paper, she discovers that the assignment is totally wrong. She talks to Akemi about being sure to ask questions when she doesn't understand. Akemi nods her head affirmatively, but the next day the same thing happens. What is the reason for this behavior?

4. Idris and Sabera are students in your class. Every time you ask Sabera a question, she lowers her eyes and puts her head down while Idris answers for her. You need to talk to Idris to tell him that he has to let Sabera answer her own questions. What is happening, and how will you approach this topic?

16

Muslims, Followers of Islam, and Speakers of Arabic

Semitic is the word that is used to describe cultures and languages of the Middle East. Middle Eastern students may be Arab, non-Arab, Muslim, Christian, or Jewish. Israel is considered the Middle East, but Israeli students reflect a more European outlook.

Semitic people are descendents of ancient tribes that originated in the southwestern part of Asia and northern Africa. They speak Arabic, Hebrew, Aramaic, and Amharic languages and are often from countries such as Palestine, Israel, Jordan, Syria, Iraq, Oman, Yemen, Eritrea, Ethiopia, Sudan, Egypt, Libya, Algeria, and Morocco. The primary Semitic population is comprised of two groups, Jews and Arabs. In Israel, English is taught along with Hebrew, but this is not necessarily the case where Arabic-speaking students study. Language learning is accompanied by cultural learning; therefore, since Israelis have more in common with Europeans, they might appear to be more culturally congruent with English-speaking cultures than with Arabs.

Islam, practiced by Muslims, is one of the fastest growing religions in the United States and around the world; however, it may be one of most maligned and least understood. Being Muslim really has nothing to do with speaking English; many Americans are Muslims with English as their native language. Followers of Islam can be from any racial or ethnic background, including African Americans who belong to the Nation of Islam, although they may not be Muslim. Many speakers of Arabic follow Islam and many Muslims speak Arabic, but all Islamic followers pray in Arabic. In the American schools, you may find students from Algeria, Djibouti, Egypt, Iraq, Jordan, Kuwait, Lebanon, Libya, Mauritania, Morocco, North and South Yemen, Palestine, United Arab Emirates, Oman, Qatar, Saudi Arabia, Somalia, Sudan, Syria, Chad, and Tunisia (and other African countries) who are usually Arabic speakers. Arabic is used in the Koran (Qur'an, which is Islam's book of scripture), so all followers are influenced by Arabic, possess a certain level of understanding of Arabic, or are able to recite Arabic. However, most Muslims are not Arabic and come from diverse countries such as Indonesia, Malaysia, Pakistan, China, Fiji, and Barbados, where they do not usually speak Arabic.

At this point in time, it is especially crucial to try to understand values of Middle Eastern cultures because they are so misunderstood and face additional challenges from negative stereotyping, racism, and discrimination. Vilification and heightened distrust of Arabs can be seen in movies, in personal encounters, at the airport, and in the media. Widespread misinformation about their history, religious practices, and culture abounds. Islamic Middle Easterners face the difficulty of trying to practice their religion in a primarily Judeo-Christian environment. The Islamic religion might supersede cultural traits of the Muslim's ethnic and cultural traditions.

It is tragic that some individuals condemn an entire population of people of Arab heritage or Islamic faith for crimes that are committed by terrorists. True Islamic followers explain: "Nothing in the Arab culture or the Islamic faith preaches or condones this kind of terror. It is never justifiable to punish an entire community or ethnicity or religious group for the actions of a few." As one of my students pointed out, "We don't punish the brother of a serial killer. Why do I have to be afraid to go do my student teaching because I have Arab features?" The irony is that this young man was of Indian descent. The most heart-wrenching story I heard was from a third-grade teacher whose student passed in his assignment with a different name. When asked why he put a different name on his paper, he said, "I don't want to be called Mohammed any more because people think I am bad."

Because the diverse classroom is a microcosm of the world at large, teachers have an ideal opportunity to mold the belief system of their students by promoting understanding and tolerance of all. In the classroom, everyone should be equal; it is the perfect place and opportunity for teachers to mitigate differences and to encourage recognition of parallel values.

Middle Eastern Cultural Values

Although distinctive characteristics can be seen throughout Middle Eastern cultures, we need to remember that there will be individual differences, as in any group of people. Society dictates appropriate behavior; family, friends, religion, and the environment prevail upon the individuals to behave according to social norms as opposed to individual beliefs. My Arab students have explained to me that formality is the rule in daily routines, social customs, and interrelationships. Members of this culture are always polite, even with people they dislike, which is reflective of the Koran's teaching. Respect and consideration for one another include never criticizing an individual in public, thus saving face (Adeed & Smith, 1997, p. 505). Teachers must keep the Arab's sensitivity to public criticism in mind; therefore, it is prudent to try to avoid embarrassment when addressing problems stemming from the variety of levels of language proficiency, stages of acculturation, or maintenance of cultural heritage in a foreign, and perhaps alien, society. In the U.S. culture, we make a habit of commenting on others' negative traits, which appears immoral to the Arab.

Harmony in the nuclear and extended families is of primary importance in this paternalistic society. Elders play an important role in this culture, and parents must always be obeyed. Students will study what their parents want them to study, instead of what interests them. Intergenerational differences might cause problems when students are in the American culture, so it is helpful to try to involve the family when students are having problems.

Personal relationships are extremely important to Arabs. Compared to shallow-appearing friendships we make in the fast-moving United States, the Middle Easterner's relationships are deep and committed. Same-sex relationships are very close, and opposite-sex relationships are not permitted. When students come to the United States, they may have opposite-sex friends for the first time, which may cause problems due to mismatches of cultural and social expectations.

Schooling in the Middle Eastern countries often reflects the paternalistic, authoritative culture. The students imitate the teacher, memorize, and study by rote. Respect for the teacher is as prominent as respect for the parents. When students arrive in the United States, they may be confused by the U.S. teacher's insistence that students learn by self-investigation and that they are expected to verbally participate and to express their opinions. The student might wonder when the real teaching is going to begin. A teacher who admits to not knowing an answer to a question will be seen as a failure. The teacher is supposed to be all knowing. My Arab students have told me that teachers in their countries will invent an answer if they do not know the correct answer. As a teacher in the United States, I have often replied to a question: "I don't know; let's look it up."

As a result of historical occurrences, Middle Eastern students might display a distrust or suspicion of "outsiders." Consequently, they may not readily divulge personal information to others without knowing why the information is needed. Americans often ask one another how the family is doing. An Arab may not appreciate being asked about the family. Be aware of this propensity when asking Arab students to complete questionnaires or to write about themselves or their families. They may be reluctant to divulge information.

Many differences between Arabic and English are obvious; one salient distinction is Arabic writing, which is similar to an art form (as in calligraphy), as it is an interpretation of Arabic and Islamic tradition. As with Hebrew, the direction of the writing goes from right to left. Writing is always a reflection of a language and culture, and Arabic and Arabic speakers are expressive, poetic, and indirect. Comparatively, English is direct and to the point. Consequently, Americans may appear curt and rude to many non-English speakers.

The teacher will notice problems with students who are learning to write English because English is linear; for example, we write a thesis statement, then supporting facts, and do not include superfluous personal opinions. We do not "beat around the bush" but get right to the point. Arabic is more circular, poetic, descriptive, and does not get right to the point.

The Arabic alphabet is a complex, cursive-based system fashioned from other Semitic languages. Written letters curve and twine around each other artistically; they take on different meaning, depending on whether they appear at the beginning, in the middle, or at the end of the word. As in Hebrew, no letters exist for vowels; instead, diacritical marks appear above or below the letters they define. In the Arabic language, the /p/ sound does not exist, so speakers usually approximate it with the /b/ sound. The /r/ is rolled, which might transfer negatively to English words.

Communicating with the Middle Eastern Student

All students who are new to a country suffer varying degrees of culture shock. If students have recently arrived in the country, culture shock and feelings of estrangement may be severe. Long-time residents of the United States will be more comfortable than recent arrivals, and second generation Arab Americans may feel right at home. Middle Eastern students have additional issues they have to deal with if they feel alienated because of perceived prejudice and ridicule of their rituals; as a result, negative feelings or behaviors might be conveyed as a defense mechanism (Jackson, 1997). Arabs come from a collectivist culture where the group is more important than individual preferences. Students may stand closer to one another or to the teacher, which might make non-Arabs feel uncomfortable. If you have students in a group, make sure it is not a mixed-gender group.

Many family members will be involved when the teacher asks to confer about the students. Teachers should know as much as possible about the individual's family and culture, so they can build a rapport that will be more conducive to true communication with the student and family. In spite of the overarching cultural traits, teachers should recognize that each family has its own way of interaction. Let the family take the lead when you need to approach issues concerning school, behavior, and academic performance (Adeed & Smith, 1997). It is best to start out in a positive manner; find the good in the student and word your concerns very carefully. The family may not feel comfortable sharing feelings with someone who is not well known to them. Helping families cope with varying levels of acculturation, language differences, and conformity to tradition can enable students to develop a positive identity that is both personally satisfying and respectful of their heritage.

Incorporating Arab Culture in the Classroom

An ideal way to promote understanding of Middle Easterners is to provide opportunities for inclusion of Arab culture in the classroom. Ideas such as visiting Arab community institutions; showcasing Arab films or newscasts; inviting Arab American leaders to speak at assemblies or in the classrooms; featuring Arabic music, language, art, words with Arabic roots, food, customs, and clothing at a school festival; celebrating Arabic history and customs; and explaining the tenets and practices of Islam and the Koran will familiarize students with Arab American tradition and beliefs (American-Arab Anti-Discrimination Committee [ADC], 1993a, 1997). Anti-racism training and religious tolerance education will help to demystify the culture and to eliminate prejudice and discrimination.

Many controversial concerns may arise in the public school setting, and educators should be familiar with the fundamental beliefs of Muslims. The First Amendment of the U.S. Constitution protects religious rights of individuals. Students will need a tolerant, nonthreatening atmosphere where they feel free to observe mandatory religious practices during the day. This is not to imply that the school system must espouse any particular religion, only that modifications must be made for students who live by certain daily rituals.

Instructors can take advantage of "teachable moments" that arise when they have Muslim students in their classes. Demonstrating tolerance and showing a true interest and respect for other cultures models multicultural understanding. Classroom teachers should know as much as possible about all students' religions and cultures so they can promote understanding toward the nonmainstream student.

The Council on American-Islamic Relations published a booklet called *An Educator's Guide to Islamic Religious Practices* (1997) that helps teachers relate to Islamic followers. The Educational Service Staff of AFME (American Friends of the Middle East, or AMIDEAS) describes cultural characteristics in their chapter "Cultural Clues to the Middle Eastern Student." Muslims from different countries all over the world may worship the same, but they have distinctly different cultural practices. Remember, however, one does not have to be Arab to be Islamic, and not all Islamic followers are Arab. Not all Arabs are Muslims—they could be Christians, Jews, or atheists.

Another excellent source that offers information on Arab Americans is the Detroit Free Press, which has produced a publication that seeks to explain issues and practices found in the Arab culture. Its website (www.freep.com/legacy/jobspage/arabs/index.htm) offers 100 questions and answers that describe who Arabs are, their origins, language, history, demographics, family, stereotypes, customs, and media coverage. Some of the information listed here is derived from the site, as well as the previously mentioned booklet published by the Council on American-Islamic Relations (CAIR; 1997).

Following are important points that will help teachers understand the issues that can produce conflict for Muslim students in public schools.

Clothing and Modesty

Some females cover their head with a scarf, which is called *hijab* or *chador*. Covering the head is a religious practice that reflects modesty, but covering the head is not a universal practice. Not all Muslims wear the *hijab*, but girls who do cover their heads in a school setting must be respected and be allowed the freedom to practice. Never allow other students to remove, bother, or play with the young lady's head covering. This type of behavior can be prevented before it occurs by allowing the student to explain the significance of her *hijab*. Use the opportunity as a multicultural teachable moment.

Robes that cover the entire body, except the face and feet, are also worn by many Muslims. Regular clothing is worn underneath the robe. As in other cultures, black may be worn for those in mourning for a short time, for a long time, or simply because it is fashionable. Men might wear a traditional checked headpiece called a **kafiyyeh**, but it does not have religious significance. Wearing the *kafiyyeh* demonstrates pride in one's cultural identity.

Modesty in dress is expected for males and females. Features of the body should not show, and clothing should cover all parts of the body. This requirement might cause a problem in the physical education class, as shorts, tank tops, bathing suits, or other brief clothing might be the P.E. uniform. Even males must wear pants down to their knees. Allow Muslim students to wear long sleeves, long pants, and modest swimwear.

Undressing in front of others, even the same sex, is not permitted. Therefore, showering or undressing in a closed area would have to be arranged. Mixed-sex swimming or interaction is unfavorable, and students should not be penalized for abstaining from such types of cross-gender classes on religious grounds.

Touch and Socialization

In U.S. public schools, it is normal for boys and girls to interact with one another. They may be partners in projects, act in plays together, dance with each other at dances and proms, sit with each other in clusters at their desks, share the computers as partners, and so on. Muslim children may not interact with each other in this way; Islamic law prefers segregation by gender. Dating, dancing with members of the opposite sex, and premarital intimacy are discouraged. It is not the normal conduct for followers of Islam. Additionally, cross-gender touching is not appropriate in most Muslim societies. When greeting a member of the opposite sex, do not automatically offer your hand. It is better to offer a verbal greeting until you know the proper protocol to practice. Males may hug or touch one another, and females may hug or touch each other, but males and females will not touch each other. School personnel should not encourage this behavior or assume that students are acting in an antisocial way.

Personal feelings will probably be well guarded, and students are not likely to be confrontational. Politeness, humility, family privacy, and not embarrassing or shaming one another are characteristics the teacher will probably notice about the Muslim student. Islam prohibits the practice of receiving or paying interest, so Muslims might not own a house or a credit card.

Traditional family roles reflect the father as the head of the household, while the mother cares for the home and children. Elders are respected, and children are expected to obey unquestioningly in a paternalistic and authoritative culture. Parents often determine what their children's careers will be, and in some cases, parents still play an important role in choosing the children's spouses.

Religious Obligations

Muslims follow the scripture of Islam and behave according to the Koran, or Qur'an. The principal tenets of Islam are called the **Five Pillars** and consist of acceptance of the creed, prayer, almsgiving, fasting during Ramadan, and pilgrimage to Makkah, Saudi Arabia.

Prayer and fasting are the two practices that warrant concessions, as they will usually occur during school hours. Muslims pray five times a day, and the midday and midafternoon prayers can be said in school. The student will need a place to wash and cleanse before prayer, and a quiet place to go to pray for about 15 minutes. Fridays are a day for congregational worship at the mosque (*masjid*) for the midday prayer. Students may ask to leave the campus for approximately 30 to 45 minutes, and schools routinely grant the request for observance of religious observation. If this presents a hardship, a private place at school can be provided. During prayer time, the student will need to stand, bow, and touch the forehead to the ground. Worshipers may have a prayer rug for this purpose.

Fasting from dawn to sunset is observed during holy days and festivals, such as during the month of **Ramadan**. Dates of these special days change yearly as they follow the lunar calendar. It is kind to show special sensitivity during this time. Teachers can excuse students from strenuous activity, and alternate tasks can be assigned. Additionally, Muslim students should not be forced to go to the cafeteria when fasting. Perhaps they can spend the allotted lunch time in the library or in the computer lab.

Dietary Considerations

Halal is food that is permissible to consume. Special preparation of food is necessary to observe Islamic law. Food such as pork or pork derivatives (gelatin, lard), bacon, pepperoni, certain candies, marshmallow, alcoholic beverages, and foods prepared with animal shortening or that use trace alcohol, such as vanilla or Dijon mustard, are banned from consumption. Parents can be consulted to determine what foods or treats can be offered in the classroom. During parties or class events such as picnics, invite the Muslim parents to prepare a dish or baked goods that are permissible to eat. Cafeteria staff can be made aware of dietary restrictions of their students, and vegetarian dishes can be offered as a replacement.

Conflicting School Practices

Everyday rituals mainstream U.S. students practice may be troublesome to the Muslim student. For instance, saluting the flag or saying the Pledge of Allegiance might be offensive to observers of Islam because it may appear to be irreverent to God. Although the Muslim student may mean no disrespect to the U.S. government, it may appear to be insubordinate to the U.S. onlooker. Having the student stand with the class but not recite the pledge can mitigate this misunderstanding.

Birthday or Halloween parties may be objectionable to individuals from other religions as well. The students who do not wish to celebrate in the customary way should be given other options at the time the class is scheduled to enjoy these traditions. Again, it is important that educators be sensitive to the feelings of the students. The mainstream student may feel that the absent student is being penalized or punished. This would be an excellent opportunity to present a class discussion—the objective of this lesson would be to promote cross-cultural understanding with all parties involved sharing their cultural and religious beliefs. In my experience, typically the other students are excited about expressing their opinions, questions, and learning answers from one another. Once they understand each other's viewpoints, very often the younger students become great advocates for their classmates.

DISCUSSION QUESTIONS AND ACTIVITIES

1. Every day at the same time, Maha takes a small rug to the restroom and stays there for about 20 minutes. She washes her face, hands, arms, and feet. What do you think she is doing and why? How can you work around this daily routine so that Maha does not miss instructional time?
2. What elements of Arab/Islamic beliefs will probably clash with American cultural beliefs? Can you see similarities or differences among Semitic/Middle Eastern groups? How might they be different from American philosophies or values?
3. Explain what miscommunications might occur as a result of our misunderstanding one another. How could you address these issues in your classroom?

17

Haitians

Being an educator in South Florida has given me the opportunity to learn much about Haitians and Haitian culture. The more my students from Haiti share about themselves, their beliefs, and their culture, the better I comprehend that Haiti is a historically rich, complex, fascinating country with citizens who are rightfully proud of their heritage. Ms. Rose Ethel Saint-Claire, Ms. Claude Gabriel, Mr. Joey Bautista, and Ms. Sheila Santiague have shared their perspectives on Haitian life and culture with me. Many mainstream teachers may not ever have the opportunity to know Haitians; therefore, I would like to share the delightful aspects of this culture, as well as clarify some unwarranted negative assumptions. People with whom we are culturally distant and have virtually no interaction often appear "mysterious" to mainstream Americans. Understanding a culture helps educators to provide a more amenable climate for instruction. However, realizing that research is not always current, may be inaccurate, and anecdotal experiences may appear to be hearsay, I will do my best to illuminate the richness and depth of this most fascinating society.

Haitians proudly proclaim that they were the first blacks to gain freedom from slavery when they fought against France in 1804. As descendents of African slaves, Haitians are predominately black, with a small number of mulattos (a mix of black and white) who often compose the more elite, privileged ruling class.

Haiti has two national languages, French and Haitian Creole, but the higher status language is French. Schooling has typically been through French. Although virtually everyone can speak or understand Haitian Creole, until recently it was easy to determine the educational status of individuals because anyone who had been to school spoke French. With the shift from teaching only French to the inclusion of Haitian Creole in the schools, it is now more difficult to determine educational backgrounds. Because of its lower status, many Haitians deny their ability to speak Creole. On the other hand, because of its prestigious status, some individuals falsely claim to speak French.

Haiti's culture and society are complex, and they struggle with issues that are dualist in nature. Dualist characteristics include the following areas:

1. French language versus Haitian Creole.
2. European (or White) ethnic background versus African (Black) ethnic background.
3. Socioeconomic class differences between the mulatto elite and the majority population of poorer Blacks.
4. The wealthier urban versus the poorer rural population.
5. Christianity versus the Voodoo religions.
6. The inequity of the extremely wealthy versus the abject poorer masses.
7. Educational access of the rich versus the poor, who may be illiterate. (Civan, 1995)

As in many less advantaged countries, unskilled rural peasants have migrated into the cities in search of work, thus overpopulating the cities and contributing to urban problems and significant social changes. A prominent class system was typically marked by the distinction of the highly educated Haitians, who are extremely wealthy, and the very poor Haitians, who are illiterate or undereducated.

In the United States school systems, we see all types of Haitian students who reflect their educational and economic class, including a recently emerging middle class. As an educator, I am in awe when I meet Haitians from rural areas who could not afford to send their children to public schools (because they could not afford uniforms or books), yet they have triumphed over incredible odds to get to the United States. As I have learned from my students, many parents who have made it to the United States have found jobs and have sent money home to pay for their children's education, only to learn later that it was misused and the children never attended school. It is not uncommon for teachers in the American schools to have a new Haitian student, in any grade, who has never attended school. Or, in the case of one teacher, she found that the child in her class was obviously not the age the "birth certificate" states. False papers used to enter the country were shown when the student was registered in school; consequently, the student was incorrectly placed according to the stated age on the passport. Conversely, the reverse happens as well, when a student is placed in a class of age-related peers, yet is far more academically advanced than his or her American counterparts.

Religion and Vodou (or Voodoo)

Misconceptions about the Haitian religious practices abound and are as complex as they are distinct. One of the most salient and negative stereotypes about Haitians concerns the practice of **Vodou** (also known as Voodoo, Voudou, Bodoun, or Vodun) (Brown, 1998). Although traditionally the population has been predominantly Roman Catholic, a small minority are Protestants, and many Haitians are converting to fundamentalist Christianity due to the proliferation of Protestant missionaries feeding and providing healthcare to the poor in Haiti. Some Haitians are exclusively Vodouists. This is not "black magic," but is a religion that combines African religious beliefs with rituals blended from Roman Catholic symbols, pictures of saints, and prayers and is similar to the Santeria beliefs of Cuba and Brazil. The amulets that are used in Catholicism may really represent saints or spirits in Vodou. Others observe a mixture of religious practices or practice no religion at all.

In actuality, this tradition of blending spiritualism with a traditional religion, such as Catholicism, is not limited to Haitians. I have seen this phenomenon in many Latin American countries. My own Colombian mother-in-law, a devout Roman Catholic, placed a glass of water and a votive candle in front of my deceased father-in-law's picture. She explained that his soul might return and be thirsty. Incorporated within the blend of rituals of traditional religion are beliefs in family spirits that may be ancestors of the living, intermediaries of God, human emotion, or natural forces. *Loas* (spirits) or *iwas*, can be called upon to help families, to bring fortune, to protect the family or loved ones, or to attack enemies in return for gifts of food, drink, or flowers. Drumming, dancing, and drinking near the family altar are usual components of Vodou ceremonies. Vodou beliefs do not encourage individual accountability for personal actions; therefore, the Roman Catholic clergy is more accepting of vodou practices than Protestant clergy, who think that the practices are diabolical (Civan, 1995).

During illness or crisis, religion plays a major role in Haitian life. Vodou beliefs may include the ideas of the "living dead" (zombies) that bring misfortune. Craan (1988) explains that zombification (catalepsy) results when an individual is poisoned with a neurotoxin (like that of a puffer fish) and is apparently dead. My students have explained to me that this is really a hoax to control the population. The person who appears dead has a funeral, and the family and friends mourn for the loved one. The apparent "deceased" is buried in a coffin that has holes or some way to let the individual continue breathing. Later the person is aroused, only to frighten the others into believing that he or she is a zombie. Uneducated individuals who are unaware of this scam are controlled by folk beliefs and superstitions. Practitioners of Vodou (Coriel, 1983; Cosgray, 1995) may be the following:

- Readers or diviners
- *Hungan* (male priests), *mambo* (female priests), or *bokors* (black magic practitioners)
- *Docte fey* (folk healers)
- *Matronn* or *fam saj* (midwives)
- *Docte zo* (bonesetters)
- *Pikirist* (injectionists)

Health Practices

After looking at the Haitian perspectives of religion, it is easy to understand the connection between religion and health practices. Undereducated Haitians are likely to attribute illness to reasons that are not based on scientific sources. Cold, heat, winds, bodily imbalance, punishment from God, or bad spirits (Colin & Paperwalla, 1996; Martin, Rissmiller, & Beal, 1995) may be blamed for disease and afflictions. To a population whose beliefs and daily practices are shaped by a lack of basic healthcare (clean water, prenatal care, antibiotics, etc.), folk or spiritual healing may be the only options that have ever been available for treating disease. By learning about and understanding living conditions and the environment in Haiti, it is easier to understand why we might see Haitians who go to a doctor and also seek treatment from the herbalist, *docte fe*, and use magic/religious measures to prevent illness or harm (DeSantis & Thomas, 1990). In fact, this occurs in many other societies, including the United States.

As in many cultures (Italian and Jamaican, for example), Haitians recognize culture-bound illnesses such as **maldyok** (the evil eye, which is brought on as a result of an envious glance from another). Disease prevention (Colin & Paperwalla, 1996) may include being plump (as a result of eating well), sleeping well, keeping warm, exercising, and keeping clean to avoid weakness (*febles*). A balance between "hot" and "cold" factors such as hot and cold foods is believed to prevent illness. Enemas (**lavman**) for children and pregnant women are used to purify the inner body. Herbal teas, massage, and spiritual practice (including Catholic ritual and Vodou practices) are other ways to prevent illness. It may be frustrating to the U.S. educator when the Haitian does not comply with traditional doctors' prescribed medicine or treatment (Preston, Materson, Yoham, & Anapol, 1996). Noncompliance with conventional prescribed medicine may be a consequence of many causes, such as difficulty understanding the illness, difficulty maintaining ongoing relationship with the care providers, self-medication, or because the patient is listening to the spiritual healer instead of the doctor. In the case of a minor, this type of situation becomes delicate because U.S. educators, who are mandated to report child abuse, might misinterpret the actions of the Haitian parent and report the incident to the child welfare authorities.

According to my Haitian students, the most devastating prejudice they have experienced was the misconception that they all had AIDS. When they went to donate blood, they were denied and told it was because they were Haitian. In 1982 the U.S. Centers for Disease Control mistakenly assumed that AIDS began in Haiti. Later, in 1985 the classification was abandoned, but the damage was already done; Haitians everywhere have been ostracized and have felt like pariahs in U.S. society (Rose St. Clair, personal communication November, 24, 2004). This fallacy is slowly losing ground, but many Haitians recall the mortification of living through this travesty.

Social Relations

Haitians usually live with the extended family, but this may not be possible after leaving their country. Although a matriarchal family structure is the norm, common law marriages (**plasaj**) are considered acceptable, and an individual might have more than one common law marriage in life (Coreil, Barnes-Josiah, & Cayemittes, 1996). The extended family includes half-brothers and half-sisters that are born to either the mother or father. They will live harmoniously in the same household. The man of the family is controlling and the highest authority, but both parents are authoritative, and discipline is corporal. When Haitians live in the United States, this attitude presents a problem because corporal punishment is considered child abuse. Haitian parents face true crises in the United States. Because they fear governmental authorities, they often lose control of their children to the negative influences of the U.S. culture. Without a strong ethnic enclave to support one another, Haitian families may not survive in the United States (Colin & Paperwalla, 1996).

Implications for the U.S. Educator

Before beginning this section on education, I want to point out that in any teaching or learning situation the most difficult goal to achieve is trying to teach a concept that is nonexistent to the students. You are asking them to imagine something they have never seen. For example, most U.S. children know what a zoo is. But if they have never visited a zoo, how can you explain what it is? Some students do not know what I mean when I talk about an escalator. Why not? Well, think about where you would find an escalator—in a modern mall, maybe? If the parents shop only at a swap meet where tables are laden with goods or spread out on a blanket on the ground, you can see why they would not understand the concept of an escalator. This is true for Floridian students who have never seen a New York fire escape, a basement, an attic, a fireplace, or snow. By the same token, a child from Massachusetts may not know about central air conditioning or a Florida room. Even the most educated students may not know what culturally bound concepts are. Many Americans do not know what a bidet is. My own child made me realize this simple yet profound truth. One day when my daughter was 5, I was ironing a blouse. Pointing to the iron, she said, "Mommy, what is that?" I was incredulous, and a little embarrassed. Had I not taught her what an iron was? It occurred to me that I ironed only at night when the children were asleep. But what would her teacher have thought if she had asked my daughter to label or describe an iron?

Haitian culture is vibrant and rich in oral tradition. Jokes, riddles, proverbs, folktales, games, and stories reflect their clever use of oral expression. Storytelling is an art and is performed for an appreciative audience. This expressive ability is quite a contrast to the literacy statistics; about 50 percent of Haitians can read and write (*The World Factbook*). Although the dropout rate is high, there is no age limit on returning to school. Therefore, an adult could be in a class of young children.

In U.S. schools and school supply stores, resources are unlimited and are governed only by the teacher's budget. The Haitian teacher, like many teachers all over the world, becomes adept at creating something out of nothing. However, what Americans recycle (such as a tire), might hold a different meaning for someone from another culture. Two students in my graduate class demonstrated this point vividly when we were examining a picture of an U.S. recycling center that showed used tires used as a planter for flowers and for a children's swing hanging on a tree. My Venezuelan student shared with the class that a tire would never be recycled as trash; they use tires to make shoes. However, my Haitian student said that in her country, in times of political unrest, the tire could be used as a burning barricade or a mode of execution known as **"Pe Lebren"** or **"Pere Lebrun,"** named after a man who owned a tire store. We were all shocked to learn that tires were put around someone's neck and lit on fire as a deadly warning to others.

The educational system in Haiti is very different from that of the United States. The school system was modeled after the traditional French system with a rigorous, classical curriculum; in spite of recent reforms, receiving an education in Haiti remains an elusive goal for most citizens. A limited number of Haitians receive formal education. In 1987, the educational system was changed to include instruction through Haitian Creole, the prominent language originally shunned by the elite. Education remains a class privilege only afforded to the wealthy and the middle class.

Official transcripts might belie the amount or quantity of educational content the student from Haiti might possesses. Huge academic gaps may exist, and often the student must first learn to read or write. Or on the other hand, the student might be further advanced than his or her counterpart in the American school. Previous educational and life experiences will vary greatly; it is up to us as educators to determine, to the best of our ability, the individual needs of our students.

DISCUSSION QUESTIONS AND ACTIVITIES

1. In Mrs. Brown's class, Pierre Frank, a student from Haiti, is having difficulty in a number of areas. He will not look at Mrs. Brown when she speaks to him, and she thinks he is very rude. What is the reason for Pierre's behavior, and how can Mrs. Brown learn about his culture?

2. Mrs. Brown needs to have a conference with Pierre's family; she has called his house several times, but she has gotten nowhere. She sends letters home only to find them in Pierre's book bag months later. He is having a difficult time taking multiple-choice tests. Describe ways that Mrs. Brown can help Pierre become more successful in school.

3. Pierre has been sick, and Mrs. Brown has noticed strange smells emanating from his clothes. He went to the doctor, who prescribed antibiotics, but he went to see a folk healer as well. What might be the reasons for this behavior?

Hispanics, Latinos/as, and Spanish Speakers

Understanding Spanish-Speaking Cultures

Ms. Rivera, an ESOL teacher in a community college, asked her new students to introduce themselves to one another as an icebreaker activity in the classroom. One by one, the students talked about where they were from. "I am Denis, from Kazakhstan," said one. "I am Ya-Chien, from Taiwan," said another. "I am Marlen, and I am Spanish," said the pretty young lady. Ms. Marefka said, "Oh, what part of Spain are you from?" Marlen answered that she was from Puerto Rico, not Spain. "Well then," said Ms. Rivera, "wouldn't you say that you were Puerto Rican, but you speak Spanish?" "Yes," Marlen agreed, "but here on the mainland, everybody call [sic] me Spanish because I speak Spanish. I am tired to correct [sic]."

Hispanics in the United States hail from Cuba, Mexico, Puerto Rico, the Dominican Republic, Central America, South America, and Spain, but the majority are born in this country. Other Latinos, or Hispanics, trace their roots to the Africans who were brought as slaves to the New World and are designated as black Hispanics (Fitz-Gibbon & Garcia, 2003). To the outsider, it may appear that all Spanish speakers are the same. However, each area of the world is distinct, with individual customs, music, clothing, and idiosyncratic practices. The Spanish language is spoken by all, but foods, dialects, ways of interaction, and attitudes may differ throughout most Spanish-speaking countries. Many researchers (Perez, Pinzon, & Garza, 1997; Valdez, 1996) have determined that most Hispanic cultures share certain universal values including importance of family; religion and spirituality; love and importance of children; formalities of etiquette; interdependence of family and fictive kin (McDade, 1995), which is called *compadrazgo* (godparents or coparents); hope and faith in a better future; and the idea of *respeto*, or respect, in conforming to expected roles (de Paula, Lagana, & Gonzalez-Ramirez, 1996; Kayser, 1998; Valdez, 1996). Independence is not seen as a positive value; family obligations and interdependence are prized ideals, and members support one another. It is not uncommon for families to host members of the family, the extended family, friends, or friends of friends for long periods of time in the home.

Traditionally, Hispanics are conscious of etiquette; manners are important if one wants to be considered *bien educado*, or polite. In addressing elders or professionals,

Carol Chursenoff and Wilma Diaz contributed material for this chapter.

the protocol is to use family names and titles such as *Señor* (Mr.) and *Señora* (Mrs.) or *Señorita* (Miss). **Don** and **Doña** are used with first names to show respect.

Upon meeting someone and when saying goodbye, a handshake, an embrace, a kiss on one cheek or two cheeks is offered, even if the encounter lasts for a few minutes. Physical proximity to one another may make the mainstream American uncomfortable. Spanish speakers maintain physical closeness to one another during conversation (about 18 inches). English speakers stand about 36 to 48 inches apart. For Hispanics, physical distance is interpreted as being cold, uninvolved, and emotionally distant. This is relevant to a classroom teacher's awareness about avoiding the inadvertent nonverbal message "move away," through body language (Pajewski & Enriquez, 1996).

Affection is displayed openly, and hands or arms are used for gesturing in a conversation. Unlike the typical North American gesture of wiggling a crooked finger to beckon someone to come to you, the entire hand slapped downward is a more polite way of asking someone to come. Sneezes oblige another to say, "salud," and a yawn or belch will be stifled, as these are impolite. Additionally, the art of *tirando piropos* (making flattering remarks to women) is not impolite and is an accepted common occurrence.

According to *Culturegrams* (2001), some of the general overall attitudes of Hispanic societies are the concepts of individualism, personal pride, and attention to a person's appearance. It is essential to project an impression of affluence and social position, which may be reflected by the quality of clothing or possessions one owns (especially if they are made in the United States or other affluent countries) and by political power. People often correct each other's mistakes, point out errors or flaws they see in someone else, or comment on someone's physical appearance (e.g., you have gained a lot of weight). This practice is considered rude by English speakers.

One of the most disconcerting first impressions I had as a native English speaker in a Spanish-speaking country was being called "*gordita*," which I immediately translated to "little fat one." It did not matter to me that it was supposed to be a name of tenderness and affection. To me it meant I was being called fat. I was also surprised to hear people being called *viejito* (little old man), *feita* (little ugly girl), and *flaco* (skinny one, but not necessarily in a complimentary sense).

As mentioned earlier, the concept of time is seen differently in every culture. Problems only occur when individuals do not know the significance of time to the cultural participants. If the entire country knows that parties do not start until several hours after the indicated time, no problem exists. If the host country functions on the premise that a dinner invitation for 7:00 P.M. truly begins at 7:00, a problem occurs only if the individual arrives late. In many cultures, Hispanic included, the individual is more important than the schedule; in fact, the idea that a party invitation may say the function starts at 4:00 P.M. and ends at 6:00 P.M. is unfathomable to an individual who lives in a society that does not place great importance on time. They ask, "How do you know what time it ends if the party hasn't even started yet?" In this society, punctuality is never expected at a social affair, and time is not fixed. Visitors to countries with the idea that time is a valuable commodity are frustrated because they expect *mañana*, to mean "tomorrow morning," not "some tomorrow in the future." The present time is more important than the scheduled appointment (e.g., a doctor may keep you waiting for a very long time for your appointment, but when you are in your consultation, he or she takes all the time necessary and does not rush). The individual at hand is more important than a previously arranged appointment. Teachers may have difficulty with parents or students who have appointments but do not appear at the appointed hour. They must explain that a schedule of appointments is necessary to make sure everyone has ample time with the teacher.

Ramirez and Casteneda (1974) list the following classroom strategies to be congruent with the learning styles of Hispanic students:

- Cooperative learning
- Personalized rewards
- Modeling
- Informal class discussion
- Concepts presented globally, rather than in detail oriented way
- Explicit classroom rules
- Personal interaction such as hugs and pats
- Humanizing the curriculum using humor, fantasy, or drama

In recognition of the cooperative structure of their home culture, Hispanic children often are more successful doing group projects. Students are accustomed to being touched frequently and to having a more one-to-one relationship with adults. Therefore, teaching strategies will be more congruent with learning styles of the student if the teacher offers individual recognition, hands papers directly to students instead of passing them from student to student, and affords students more physical interaction, such as a pat on the arm or a quick hug. For many students, short-term daily projects are more likely to be completed and to enhance interpersonal understanding than are long-term projects.

Hispanics are predominantly Catholic, although other religions are quickly being adopted. Spiritualism is practiced alongside traditional Catholic and other recognized religious rituals. In many Hispanic countries, religion and religious holidays permeate daily life and often interfere with school attendance. In the home country, religious observations are linked to education, and a religious ceremony usually is an adjunct to political events. Although no political functions are connected with religion in the United States, individual religious ceremonies, practices, or beliefs might also interfere with school attendance.

In the home country, students might be accustomed to a more authoritative school system, and whether public or private, all students wear uniforms. Issues such as mixed-gender classes might become problematic because Hispanic students are often segregated by gender in their home schools. The concept of a mixed-sex physical education class might be frowned upon, and even in the same-sex locker room, modesty issues might prohibit a student from changing clothes in front of peers.

In the classroom setting, students from other countries are often accustomed to a different classroom setup or desk configurations. Many schools in Latin America do not have traditional American-style windows in the classroom. In Spain, the climate was chillier; therefore, the school structure reflected the climatic needs. In Colombia, Puerto Rico, or the warmer places in Mexico, the classroom might have a solid wall, except for the top few feet, which is open to the air. Perhaps a window opening exists but will not contain glass. Screens are not typical window dressings. I always enjoyed the airiness of these classrooms but found it difficult to concentrate as the outside noise entered the class and seemed to reverberate off the walls. However, the students and other teachers were not affected the same way. Perhaps they were accustomed to the **polychronic** cacophony of sounds, whereas, being from the **monochronic** U.S. culture, I needed total silence to function as a teacher. Additionally, I found that the accepted noise levels differed in each Spanish-speaking country as well.

Student configurations are also different in each country. Students might have worked with partners, studied in groups, or sat with others in a row of attached desks. In the United States, desk configurations and classroom decorations might change weekly to control student interaction. Instruction is often conducted in a more democratic manner than what the students are accustomed to in their home countries. An egalitarian classroom can be confusing to those who are used to a more authoritarian approach to teaching and learning. Teachers who quickly mete out corporal punishment for transgressions and improper behavior are often the norm in other countries. Additionally, teaching by rote memorization with less emphasis on critical thinking might cause more difficulty for students from foreign countries. In the United States, teachers use a more Socratic method of instruction, audiovisual aids, and manipulatives, and have access to well-stocked laboratories. Students from other countries often claim U.S. schools are easier because of these differences. Additionally, U.S. teachers push students along, believing in the adage that if the student fails, it is the teacher's fault. From what I have witnessed, most other countries expect the student to conform to the teacher, good or bad. This is especially evident in public universities; a certain number of slots are available, and the students across the country compete by taking national exams, for which they study for years. Maybe the top 30 percent of the country's student population can score high enough to be accepted to the public university. Those who do not make the grade will not get the chance to study that year. If the student comes from a family with financial stability, then he or she may attend a private university with less academic rigor.

Learners who are socialized with this competitive academic attitude may prove to be extraordinary students in U.S. settings. I have heard comments from overseas students about how different the school system is in the United States because teachers often give students a "break," allow them to use calculators instead of being obliged to memorize formulas and rules, and offer many second chances if students fail. Trying to help students succeed in the classroom is the primary goal of U.S. school systems; millions of dollars are spent on compensatory or remedial programs as well as accommodations for exceptional students, gifted students, and financially disadvantaged students. Families from other countries might look upon special education or ESOL programs negatively because "afflictions" or inability to keep up with the class are often thought of as weaknesses due to the person not trying hard enough to overcome the "disability." Participation in these programs might also be seen as an insult or retribution for wrong behavior.

Teachers and students might miscommunicate due to misunderstanding nonverbal communication. Appropriate body language and use of personal space differs among cultural groups. Hispanic students might be expected to lower their eyes when communicating with elders, especially when being reprimanded. I noticed this while interacting with students from Puerto Rico and the Dominican Republic. Throughout my travels, the prevailing attitudes I found were that the teacher is the ultimate authority, is given total respect, is the main contact for the student, and is expected to provide for the needs of the student in all educational capacities. Unlike in the United States, where parents are expected to volunteer in the classroom and attend meetings, parents from many other cultures are not involved in the school operation. The school will not have guidance counselors, special education teachers, or the PTA. When parents do not interact with schools, they should not be judged as uncaring simply because they do not adhere to U.S. cultural values. They may not know or feel comfortable with these expectations.

Fifth-grade teacher Ms. Carol moves in two different worlds in her classroom as she works with students on a reading and writing assignment. In one world are her students whose native language is English, and in the other are the Hispanic immigrant children who are in various stages of acquiring language proficiency. Although Ms. Carol has a very limited knowledge of Spanish, she is expected to meet the grade-level needs of her students, including content area academics for the immigrant children who struggle just to understand the enormous complexities of a second language. The students themselves have a great disparity in their educational backgrounds and academic ability, including one girl who has just arrived from El Salvador and does not know letter sounds or words in either English or Spanish. Another Hispanic student has just been tested as "gifted." Not surprisingly, his academic work is on grade level as well, yet the school records still have him designated as limited English proficient. He may remain inappropriately tagged by an educational system that does not have the time or resources to update his status as he moves further along in his academic career.

The Hispanic children in this class are quiet, attentive, and very well mannered while listening to their teacher give directions. They begin the assignment, many working in pairs. A student's hand goes up as an indication that he needs help with a concept, and Ms. Carol is at his side discussing the student's work in English. A quizzical look tells her that the student still doesn't fully understand. Another Spanish-speaking student sitting nearby explains the concept again, this time in Spanish, and a smile spreads across the face of the boy who had not understood his teacher's first effort. Other Hispanic children try to help the nonliterate girl from El Salvador with letter sounds and picture cards she is making, but they have their own assignments to complete. The teacher has no classroom aide or adequate school assistance to help work with this new girl.

Ms. Carol is not alone in her frustration in meeting the complex needs of her students, both academically and culturally, in this diverse classroom. This same scenario plays out in schools throughout the United States. Teachers find themselves under increasing pressure to address the near-impossible task of teaching English learners while also attempting to meet the unrealistic demands of high-stakes accountability and misguided legislative agendas generated in the present U.S. political climate. Often classrooms are comprised of students from a number of different countries and cultural backgrounds. The teacher struggles not only to understand these children but also to address their very diverse academic and emotional issues.

DISCUSSION QUESTIONS AND ACTIVITIES

1. Students from Spanish-speaking cultures are called a variety of names such as Hispanic, Latino/Latina, Chicano/Chicana, and so on. If someone is from Guatemala, he or she might be called Guatemalan and may not even speak Spanish. If you were to ask the individuals what ethnic group they are from, they might answer "Mayan." If a student is from Paraguay, he or she might be Guaraní. What are some ways to determine what your students prefer to be called? If you were from the United States, what would you call yourself?

2. You are planning to have a conference with some of the parents of your Spanish-speaking students. Describe some strategies you would use to make the family feel comfortable. How would you greet them? If they didn't speak English well, how would you make your points clear? If you have an interpreter, what protocol would you follow to make the family feel at ease?

3. Discuss multicultural strategies you could implement to show your Spanish-speaking students that you value their heritage. How could you get involved or show interest in their community functions and activities?

ESOL Methods and Strategies

A. Methodologies/Approaches:
  - **A1.** Total Physical Response (TPR)
  - **A2.** Natural Approach
  - **A3.** Cognitive Academic Language Learning (CALLA)
  - **A4.** Whole Language Approach
  - **A5.** Language Experience Approach (LEA)
  - **A6.** Retelling a Story
  - **A7.** Activating Peer Knowledge

B. Visuals/Graphic Organizers/Other Audiovisuals:
  - **B1.** Flow Charts
  - **B2.** Maps
  - **B3.** Charts
  - **B4.** Graphs
  - **B5.** Pictures
  - **B6.** Semantic Webbing/Mapping
  - **B7.** T-Charts
  - **B8.** Venn Diagrams
  - **B9.** Story Maps
  - **B10.** Timelines
  - **B11.** Computer/Software
  - **B12.** Realia
  - **B13.** Videos/Films/CD ROM
  - **B14.** Demonstrations
  - **B15.** Captioning
  - **B16.** Labeling
  - **B17.** Music/Songs
  - **B18.** Jazz Chants/Raps
  - **B19.** Cassettes–Music/Books
  - **B20.** Language Master

C. Interactive Strategies/Cooperative Learning Activities:
  - **C1.** Peer Buddy
  - **C2.** Small Group Activities
  - **C3.** Pairs and Threes
  - **C4.** Jigsaw
  - **C5.** "Corners"

From the School Board of Broward County, Florida Multicultural/Foreign Language/ESOL Education Department ESOL Instructional Strategies Matrix.

      C6. Think/Pair/Share
      C7. Group Reports, Projects
      C8. Panel Discussion/Debate
      C9. Choral Reading/Read Around Groups

D. Other Interactive Strategies:
      D1. Field Trips
      D2. KWL (Know/Wants to Know/Learned)
      D3. Role Play
      D4. Games
      D5. Dialogue Journals

E. Modified Class Work (Based on Level of English Proficiency):
      E1. Vary Complexity on Assignment
      E2. One-on-One Instruction with Teacher or Aide
      E3. Modify Nature of Assignment
      E4. Substitute Diagram for Paragraph
      E5. Use of Home Language for Instruction
      E6. Explain Key Concepts
      E7. Repeat/Paraphrase/Slow Down
      E8. Vocabulary with Context Clues
      E9. Reading with a Specific Purpose
      E10. Use Simple, Direct Language (Limit Idioms)
      E11. Use All Modalities/Learning Styles
      E12. Provide Meaningful Language Practice
      E13. Drills (Substitution, Expansion, Paraphrase, Repetition)
      E14. Matching with Visuals
      E15. Unscramble Sentences, Words, Visuals
      E16. Categorize Vocabulary
      E17. Context Clues
      E18. Outline Notes
      E19. Directed Reading/Thinking Activity (DRTA)
      E20. Semantic Feature Analysis
      E21. SQ3R (Survey, Question, Read, Recite, Review)
      E22. Summarizing
      E23. Note Taking
      E24. Word Banks
      E25. Repetition
      E26. Question–Answer Relationship (QAR)

F. Multicultural Resources:
      F1. Guest Speakers
      F2. Use of Community Resources
      F3. Cultural Sharing
      F4. Varied Holiday Activities

G. Alternative Assessment Instruments:
      G1. Interview
      G2. Content Retelling
      G3. Content Dictation
      G4. Cloze Procedure
      G5. Graphic Representation
      G6. Student Self-Rating and Evaluation
      G7. Teacher Rating Checklist
      G8. Writing Sample
      G9. Group Testing
      G10. Observation/Anectodal
      G11. Portfolio

Language-Level Classifications and Descriptions

A¹ Non-English Speaker (NES) or minimal knowledge of English:

Demonstrates very little understanding.

Cannot communicate meaning orally.

Unable to participate in regular classroom instruction.

A² Limited English Speaker (LES):

Demonstrates limited understanding.

Communicates orally in English with one- or two-word responses.

B¹ Intermediate English Speaker:

Communicates orally in English, mostly with simple phrases and/or sentence responses.

Makes significant grammatical errors that interfere with understanding.

B² Intermediate English Speaker:

Communicates in English about everyday situations with little difficulty but lacks the academic language terminology.

Experiences some difficulty in following grade-level subject matter assignments.

C¹ Advanced English Speaker:

Understands and speaks English fairly well.

Makes occasional grammatical errors.

May read and write English with variant degrees of proficiency.

From the School Board of Broward County, Florida, Multicultural/Foreign Language/ESOL Education Department.

*C² Full English Speaker (FES):

Understands and speaks English with near fluency.

Reads and writes English at a comparable level with native-English-speaking counterparts.

May read and write the native language with variant degrees of proficiency.

D Full English Speaker:

Speaks English fluently.

Reads and writes English at a comparable level with English-speaking counterparts.

E Monolingual English Speaker

No services required.

---

*When students achieve C² status, they can be exited from the ESOL program. State guidelines require that all ELLs' progress be monitored for two years after exiting the program.

APPENDIX C

Websites: Standards for English Language Learners

Florida Department of Education. (n.d.). Office of Academic Achievement Through Language Acquisition, consent decree www.fldoe.org/aala/cdpage2.asp

Florida Department of Education. (1996). *Language arts through ESOL: A guide for ESOL teachers and administrators*. Retrieved August 7, 2004, from www.firn.edu/doe/bin00011/egtoc.htm and www.firn.edu/doe/nav/images/banner/1.gif

National Council of Teachers of English. (n.d.). *Standards for the English language arts*. Retrieved August 7, 2004, from www.ncate.org/standard/new%20program%20standards/tesol.pdf

Teachers of English to Speakers of Other Languages. (1997). *The ESL standards for pre-K–12 students*. Retrieved August 7, 2002, from www.tesol.org/s_tesol/sec_document.asp?

More Resources at the TESOL Website (www.tesol.org)

Implementing the ESL Standards for Pre-K-12 Students Through Teacher Education

Program Evaluation: English as a Second Language: A Comprehensive Guide for Standards-based Program Evaluation for Schools Committed to Continuous Improvement

Integrating the ESL Standards Into Classroom Practice: Grades Pre–K–2

Integrating the ESL Standards Into Classroom Practice: Grades 6–8

See Appendix H for additional website resources.

Social Studies Adaptation: U.S. Government

This appendix shows a PowerPoint presentation that Honey Smith created based on authentic text from a book on U.S. government. She demonstrates how to modify the content for learners with beginning, intermediate, and advanced language proficiency. Visuals should be added to provide clarity and illustrate concepts: Magazine pictures, clip art, pictures from the Internet, old text, or any other sources should be integrated into the written text. Content integrity must be preserved while language is simplified for comprehension. Remember not to "water down" the material.

This presentation is based on the excerpted passage; the adaptations can be used with language learners with beginning, intermediate, and advanced English proficiency. Pictures were compiled from various images on the Internet. Pictures can be cut from magazines, ads, newspapers, old texts, clip art, or any other available source.

Another example of adaptation can be found in Appendix E, which shows adapted science material.

Honey Smith developed material in this appendix.

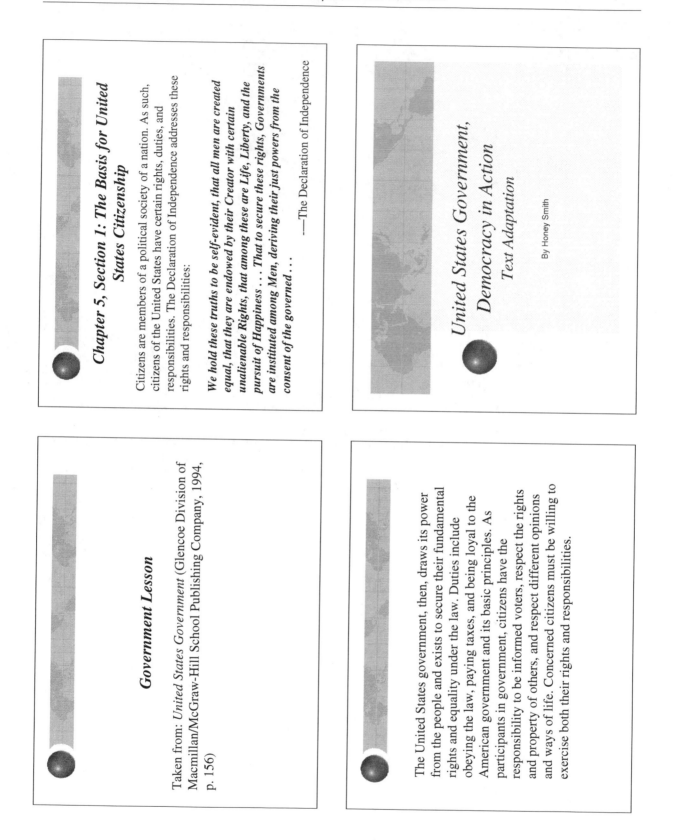

United States Government, Democracy in Action
Text Adaptation

By Honey Smith

Chapter 5, Section 1: The Basis for United States Citizenship

Citizens are members of a political society of a nation. As such, citizens of the United States have certain rights, duties, and responsibilities. The Declaration of Independence addresses these rights and responsibilities:

We hold these truths to be self-evident, that all men are created equal, that they are endowed by their Creator with certain unalienable Rights, that among these are Life, Liberty, and the pursuit of Happiness . . . That to secure these rights, Governments are instituted among Men, deriving their just powers from the consent of the governed . . .

—The Declaration of Independence

Government Lesson

Taken from: *United States Government* (Glencoe Division of Macmillan/McGraw-Hill School Publishing Company, 1994, p. 156)

The United States government, then, draws its power from the people and exists to secure their fundamental rights and equality under the law. Duties include obeying the law, paying taxes, and being loyal to the American government and its basic principles. As participants in government, citizens have the responsibility to be informed voters, respect the rights and property of others, and respect different opinions and ways of life. Concerned citizens must be willing to exercise both their rights and responsibilities.

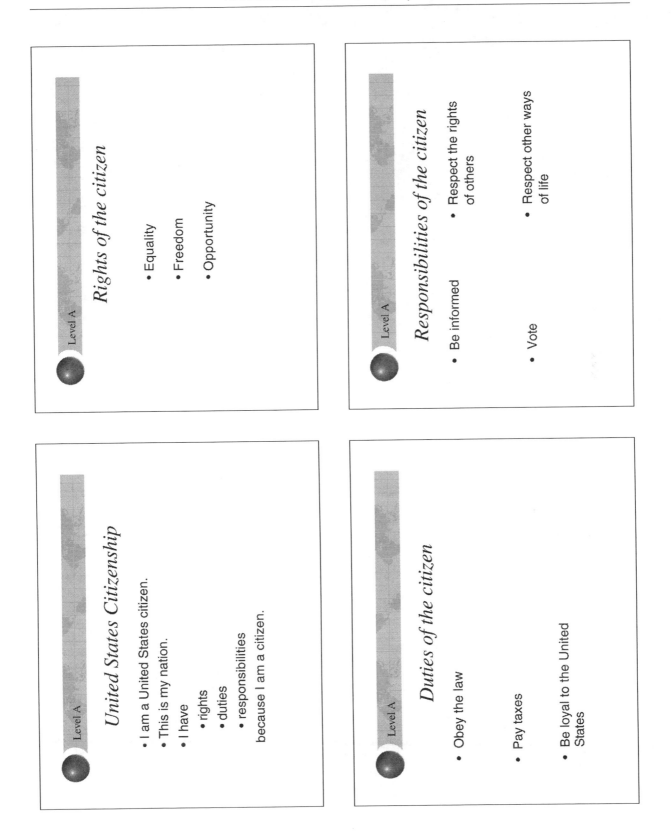

Level A

Rights of the citizen

- Equality
- Freedom
- Opportunity

Level A

Responsibilities of the citizen

- Be informed
- Respect the rights of others

- Vote
- Respect other ways of life

Level A

United States Citizenship

- I am a United States citizen.
- This is my nation.
- I have
  - rights
  - duties
  - responsibilities
  because I am a citizen.

Level A

Duties of the citizen

- Obey the law

- Pay taxes

- Be loyal to the United States

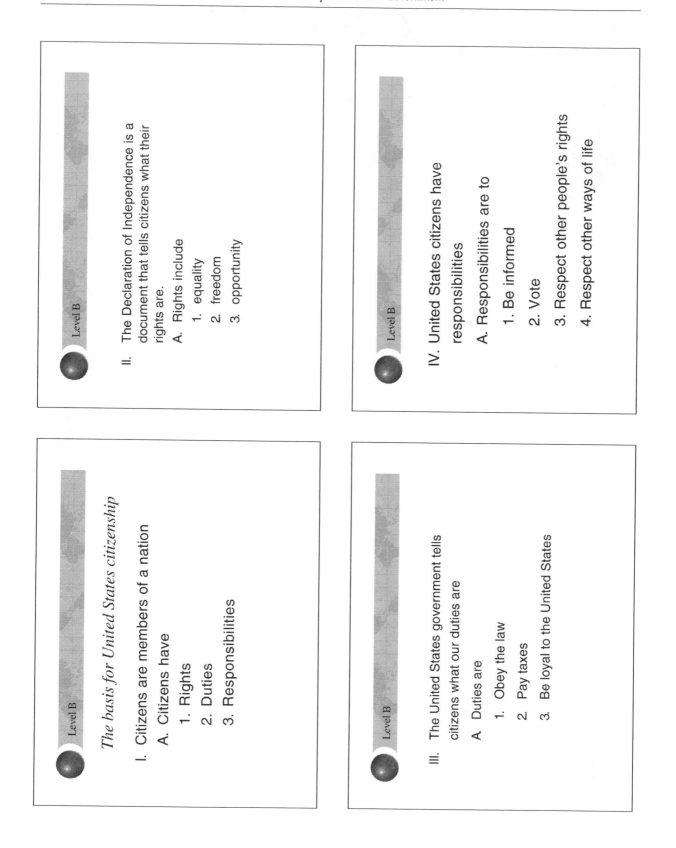

Level B

The basis for United States citizenship

I. Citizens are members of a nation
   A. Citizens have
      1. Rights
      2. Duties
      3. Responsibilities

Level B

II. The Declaration of Independence is a document that tells citizens what their rights are.
   A. Rights include
      1. equality
      2. freedom
      3. opportunity

Level B

III. The United States government tells citizens what our duties are
   A. Duties are
      1. Obey the law
      2. Pay taxes
      3. Be loyal to the United States

Level B

IV. United States citizens have responsibilities
   A. Responsibilities are to
      1. Be informed
      2. Vote
      3. Respect other people's rights
      4. Respect other ways of life

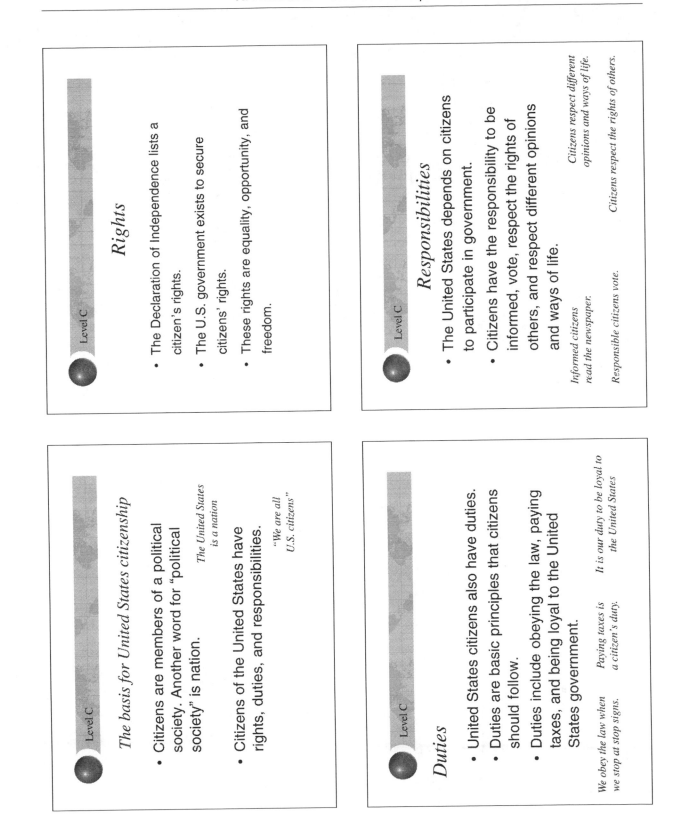

Level C

Rights

- The Declaration of Independence lists a citizen's rights.
- The U.S. government exists to secure citizens' rights.
- These rights are equality, opportunity, and freedom.

Level C

Responsibilities

- The United States depends on citizens to participate in government.
- Citizens have the responsibility to be informed, vote, respect the rights of others, and respect different opinions and ways of life.

Informed citizens read the newspaper.

Responsible citizens vote.

Citizens respect different opinions and ways of life.

Citizens respect the rights of others.

Level C

The basis for United States citizenship

- Citizens are members of a political society. Another word for "political society" is nation.
- Citizens of the United States have rights, duties, and responsibilities.

The United States is a nation

"We are all U.S. citizens"

Level C

Duties

- United States citizens also have duties.
- Duties are basic principles that citizens should follow.
- Duties include obeying the law, paying taxes, and being loyal to the United States government.

We obey the law when we stop at stop signs.

Paying taxes is a citizen's duty.

It is our duty to be loyal to the United States

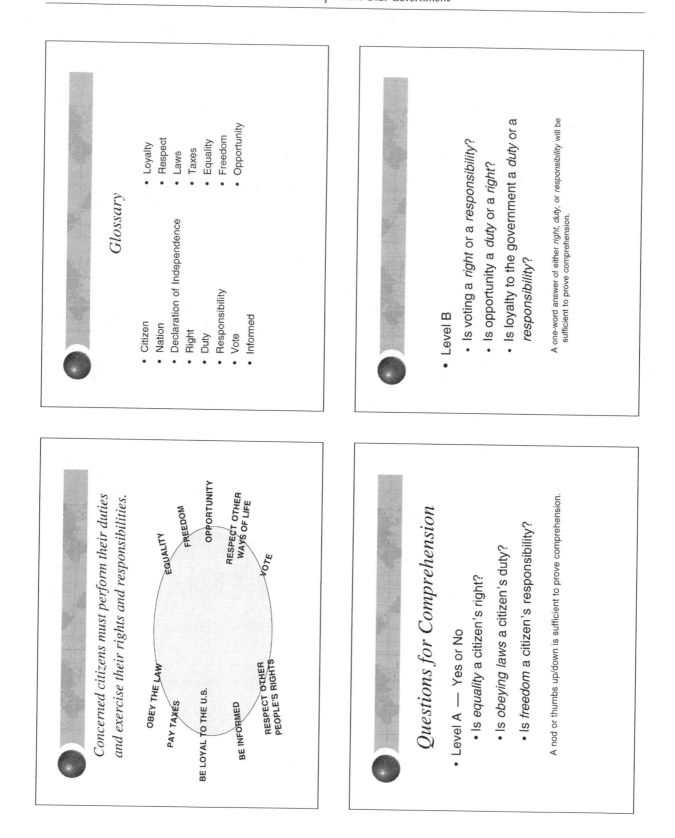

Glossary

- Citizen
- Nation
- Declaration of Independence
- Right
- Duty
- Responsibility
- Vote
- Informed

- Loyalty
- Respect
- Laws
- Taxes
- Equality
- Freedom
- Opportunity

Concerned citizens must perform their duties and exercise their rights and responsibilities.

OBEY THE LAW

PAY TAXES

BE LOYAL TO THE U.S.

BE INFORMED

RESPECT OTHER PEOPLE'S RIGHTS

EQUALITY

FREEDOM

OPPORTUNITY

RESPECT OTHER WAYS OF LIFE

VOTE

• Level B

- Is voting a *right* or a *responsibility?*
- Is opportunity a *duty* or a *right?*
- Is loyalty to the government a *duty* or a *responsibility?*

A one-word answer of either *right, duty,* or *responsibility* will be sufficient to prove comprehension.

Questions for Comprehension

• Level A — Yes or No

- Is *equality* a citizen's right?
- Is *obeying laws* a citizen's duty?
- Is *freedom* a citizen's responsibility?

A nod or thumbs up/down is sufficient to prove comprehension.

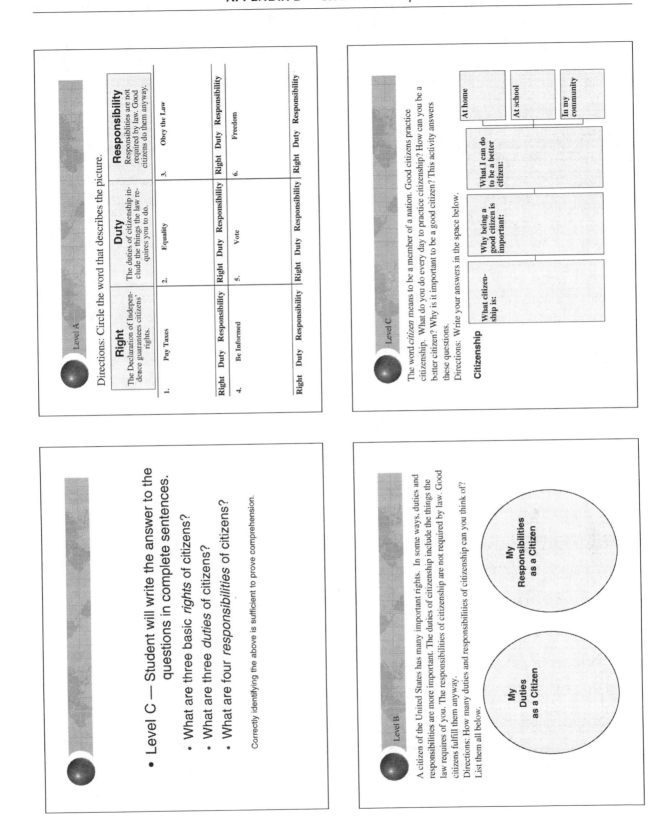

Level A

Directions: Circle the word that describes the picture.

Right	Duty	Responsibility
The Declaration of Independence guarantees citizens' rights.	The duties of citizenship include the things the law requires you to do.	Responsibilities are not required by law. Good citizens do them anyway.
1. Pay Taxes	2. Equality	3. Obey the Law
Right Duty Responsibility	Right Duty Responsibility	Right Duty Responsibility
4. Be Informed	5. Vote	6. Freedom
Right Duty Responsibility	Right Duty Responsibility	Right Duty Responsibility

Level C

The word *citizen* means to be a member of a nation. Good citizens practice citizenship. What do you do every day to practice citizenship? How can you be a better citizen? Why is it important to be a good citizen? This activity answers these questions.
Directions: Write your answers in the space below.

Citizenship

What citizenship is:

Why being a good citizen is important:

What I can do to be a better citizen:

At home

At school

In my community

Level C — Student will write the answer to the questions in complete sentences.

• What are three basic *rights* of citizens?

• What are three *duties* of citizens?

• What are four *responsibilities* of citizens?

Correctly identifying the above is sufficient to prove comprehension.

Level B

A citizen of the United States has many important rights. In some ways, duties and responsibilities are more important. The duties of citizenship include the things the law requires of you. The responsibilities of citizenship are not required by law. Good citizens fulfill them anyway.
Directions: How many duties and responsibilities of citizenship can you think of? List them all below.

My Duties as a Citizen

My Responsibilities as a Citizen

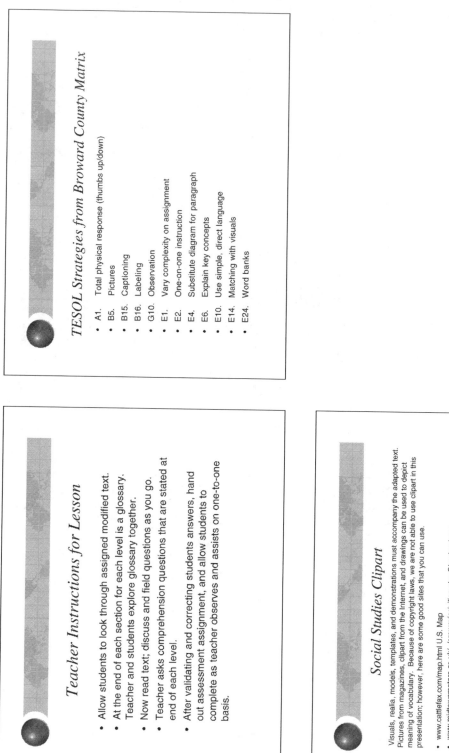

TESOL Strategies from Broward County Matrix

- A1.   Total physical response (thumbs up/down)
- B5.   Pictures
- B15.   Captioning
- B16.   Labeling
- G10. Observation
- E1.   Vary complexity on assignment
- E2.   One-on-one instruction
- E4.   Substitute diagram for paragraph
- E6.   Explain key concepts
- E10.   Use simple, direct language
- E14.   Matching with visuals
- E24.   Word banks

Teacher Instructions for Lesson

- Allow students to look through assigned modified text.
- At the end of each section for each level is a glossary. Teacher and students explore glossary together.
- Now read text; discuss and field questions as you go.
- Teacher asks comprehension questions that are stated at end of each level.
- After validating and correcting students answers, hand out assessment assignment, and allow students to complete as teacher observes and assists on one-to-one basis.

Social Studies Clipart

Visuals, realia, models, templates, and demonstrations must accompany the adapted text. Pictures from magazines, clipart from the Internet, and drawings can be used to depict meaning of vocabulary. Because of copyright laws, we are not able to use clipart in this presentation; however, here are some good sites that you can use.

- www.cattlefax.com/map.html U.S. Map
- www.midtownmotors.co.uk/.../crownviccivilian.php Obeying Law
- www.streetupdate.com/tax/ Pay Taxes
- www.pirg.org/highered/ Pay Taxes
- www.lifelongaidsalliance.org/advocacy/voter.html Vote
- www.nlbts.org/images/equality.jpg Respect the Rights of Others
- www.whitehouse.gov/.../vpphotoessay/part2/03.htm Respect Other Ways of Life

Science Adaptation

Cheryl Quinn developed the material in this appendix.

Original text from:

Harcourt Science

- Grade levels 1–5
- Unit: Different Kinds of Animals
- Chapter 3
- Pages A49–A53

Adapted Text for Level A

- MAMMAL
- Milk from mom
- Hair or fur

Science
Textbook Adaptation
Different Kinds of Animals

By Cheryl Quinn

Adapted Text Level B

- MAMMAL
- Feeds its young milk
- Has hair or fur

Adapted Text Level A

- AMPHIBIAN
- Smooth, wet skin
- Live in water and on land
- Frogs, toads, salamanders

Adapted Text Level B

- MAMMAL
- Feeds its young milk
- Has hair or fur

Adapted Text Level A

- REPTILE
- Rough, dry skin
- Scales or hard plates
- Alligators or turtles

Adapted Text Level A

- FISH
- Live in water
- Gills
- Scales

Adapted Text Level B

- REPTILES

- Have rough, dry skin

- May have scales or hard plates

- Alligators and turtles

Adapted Text Level B

- FISH
- Live in water
- Gills help them breathe
- Bodies have scales

Adapted Text Level B

- BIRDS

- Have 2 wings and 2 feet

- Have feathers

- Some fly, run, or swim

Adapted Text Level B

- AMPHIBIANS

- Have smooth, wet skin

- Frogs, toads, and salamanders

Adapted Text Level C

- MAMMAL
- Feeds milk to its young
- Has hair or fur on its body

Adapted Text Level C

- BIRDS
- Have 2 legs and 2 feet
- The only animals with feathers
- Some fly, run, or swim

Adapted Text Level C

- REPTILES
- Animals with rough, dry skin
- May have scales or hard plates
- Alligators, turtles, and snakes are reptiles

Adapted Text Level C

- AMPHIBIANS
- Animals with smooth, wet skin
- Live part of life in water and part on land
- Frogs, toads, and salamanders are amphibians

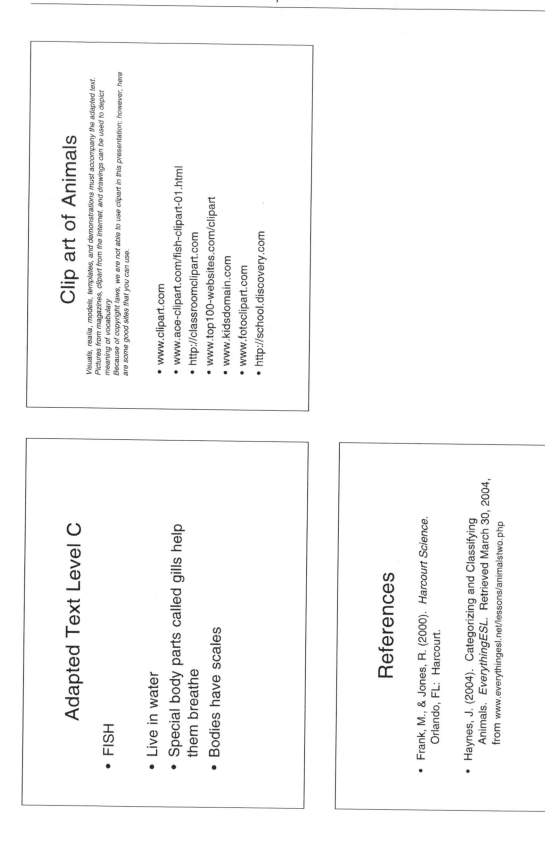

Clip art of Animals

Visuals, realia, models, templates, and demonstrations must accompany the adapted text. Pictures from magazines, clipart from the Internet, and drawings can be used to depict meaning of vocabulary

Because of copyright laws, we are not able to use clipart in this presentation; however, here are some good sites that you can use.

- www.clipart.com
- www.ace-clipart.com/fish-clipart-01.html
- http://classroomclipart.com
- www.top100-websites.com/clipart
- www.kidsdomain.com
- www.fotoclipart.com
- http://school.discovery.com

Adapted Text Level C

- FISH

- Live in water
- Special body parts called gills help them breathe
- Bodies have scales

References

- Frank, M., & Jones, R. (2000). *Harcourt Science.* Orlando, FL: Harcourt.

- Haynes, J. (2004). Categorizing and Classifying Animals. *EverythingESL.* Retrieved March 30, 2004, from www.everythingesl.net/lessons/animalstwo.php

Class Assignment: Content Area Textbook Analysis Form

Name of Textbook:

Publisher:

Publication Date:

Content Area:

Grade Level:

1. Content Objectives of Entire Book—Scope and Sequence (Describe)
2. Unfamiliar Cultural Assumptions (Think beyond the box: Try to look at the text from the perspective of a non-native English speaker, as well as someone from another country. Look hard: There is always something.)
3. Higher Order Thinking Skills (Look at Bloom's taxonomy. Find and list exercises that call for higher order thinking skills and relate them to the skill.)

Example	Skill
Suppose the height of a right prism is doubled. What effect does it have on the surface area?	Predict, draw conclusions; Relate knowledge from several areas; Use previous knowledge to create new ideas . . .

4. Evaluation of Overall Text
   (In three or four paragraphs, tell why you would or would not recommend this text, why, how it could be improved, and if you would use it to teach ELLs.)

Project Rubric for Modification of Textbook

Name/s _____ Subject modified _____ Grade level___

Choose a chapter from a textbook. Please attach original chapter in hard copy. You may also submit the chapter on disk. Do not forget to cite your references using APA 5th edition style.

Modification of text for ELLs with language levels A (beginner), B (intermediate), and C (advanced). Using the language levels (see Appendix B) as your guide to the proficiency levels of your students, modify text for beginner, intermediate, and advanced speakers.

10 points possible _____   Attach a copy of the original text you are adapting.

10 points possible _____   Make three separate sections with dividers so it is
                                 clear which section is for each level.

                                 For beginning speakers . . .

                                 For intermediate speakers . . .

                                 For advanced speakers . . .

25 points possible _____   Modify the chapter in your chosen content area.
                                 See Appendices D and E for examples of
                                 modifications of a text.

Modify the content for A, B, and C language proficiency levels of project. Include questions for comprehension (at least one question for each level) for each level of proficiency. Try to use higher order thinking skills (see Bloom's Taxonomy.)

10 points possible _____   Include Visual Representations (pictures/pictorial)

10 points possible _____   Outline Formats (Simple words)

10 points possible _____   Write instructions for teacher presenting the lesson.

10 points possible _____   Include the TESOL strategies applicable to teaching
                                this chapter. (Strategies are found in the ESOL
                                matrix in Appendix A) Explain your strategy
                                choices.

15 points possible _____

Create three authentic alternative assessments, one for each language level. Make sure your instrument assesses your objectives.
Beginner level
Intermediate level
Advanced level

Total points out of 100_____

Resources: Journals and Websites

Journals

(By no means a complete list: Hundreds of journals exist for the ESOL teacher.)

Annual Review of Applied Linguistics
Applied Language Learning
Applied Linguistics
Applied Psycholinguistics
College ESL
Cross Currents
Discourse Processes
DSH Abstracts (deafness, speech, and hearing)
ELR Journal (English research)
ELT Journal
English for Specific Purposes (ESP journal)
English Language Teacher
English Teacher Journal
English Teaching Forum
English Today
Essential Teacher
Guidelines
International Journal of American Linguistics
International Review of Applied Linguistics
IRAL (International Review of Applied Linguistics in Language Teaching)
ITL Review of Applied Linguistics
JALT Journal (Japan)
JETT (Journal of English Teaching Techniques)
Journal of Educational Research for Language Minority Students
Journal of Linguistics Journal of Memory and Language
Journal of Multilingual & Multicultural Development
Journal of Psycholinguistic Research
Journal of Research in Reading
Journal of Second Language Writing

Language
Language and Speech
Language in Society
Language Learning
Language Learning Journal
Language Research
Language Testing
Linguistics
Modern Language Journal
Modern Language Quarterly
Modern Language Review
NABE: Bilingual Research Journal
NYSABE Journal
Papers & Reports on Child Language Development
Reading in a Foreign Language
Reading Research Quarterly
Second Language Research
Studies in Second Language Acquisition
Sunshine State TESOL Journal
TESL Reporter
TESOL Journal (formerly)
TESOL Quarterly
TESOL Matters (formerly)
TESOL Newsletters
TESOL Quarterly
TESOL Talk
The Canadian Modern Language Review
The Education Digest
The Language Teacher (Japan)
The Modern Language Journal
World Englishes

Websites

AP = Florida Educator Accomplished Practices:
http://coeserver03.fiu.edu/efolio.feap.html

Using ESOL Standards: www.tesol.org/assoc/k12standards/it/06.html

ESOL Standards Pre-K–Grade 3: www.tesol.org/assoc/k12standards/it/07.html

ESOL Standards Grades 4–8: www.tesol.org/assoc/k12standards/it/08.html

Glossary of TESOL terms: www.tesol.org/assoc/k12standards/it/10.html

TESOL = Florida TESOL standards (Teaching English to Speakers of Other Languages):
www.fldoe.org/aala/perstand.asp

INTASC = Interstate New Teacher Assessment and Support Consortium:
www.ccsso.org/Projects/interstate_newteacher_assessment_and_support_consortium/

Stephen Krashen's webpage:
www.sdkrashen.com/SL_Acquisition_and_Learning/index.html

Jim Cummins's webpage (BICS/CALP):
www.iteachilearn.com/cummins/bicscalp.html

TESOL International: www.tesol.org

www.esl.net

www.ed.gov

www.cis.yale.edu/ynhti/curriculum

www.bilingualeducation.org

www.ed.gov/offices/OBEMLA

www.remember.org

www.ncela.gwu.edu

www-rcf.usc.edu/~cmmr

www.teachingtolerance.org

Massachusetts Department of Education: www.doe.mass.edu/ell

California Department of Education: www.cde.ca.gov/el

Webpage for Making Rubrics: http://rubistar.4teachers.org/index.php

SIOP® Lesson Planning Guide

The SIOP® Lesson Planning Guide was developed by Jana Echevarria, MaryEllen Vogt, Deborah Short, and Chris Montone, through research sponsored by the Center for Research on Education, Diversity, and Excellence (CREDE) with a grant from the U.S. Department of Education, Office of Educational Research and Improvement.

This guide was developed as an aid in planning sheltered lessons. The right column can be used for writing notes or as a checklist to ensure attention to each indicator.

Unit Plan Theme: _____

Preparation

1. Clearly defined *content objectives* for students
2. Clearly defined *language objectives* for students
3. *Content concepts* appropriate for age and educational background level of students
4. *Supplementary materials* used to a high degree, making lesson clear and meaningful (e.g., graphs, models, visuals)
5. *Adaptation of content* (e.g., text, assignment) to all levels of student proficiency
6. *Meaningful activities* that integrate lesson concepts (e.g., surveys, letter writing, simulations, constructing models) with language practice opportunities for reading, writing, listening, and/or speaking

Reproduced with permission from J. Echevarria, M. Vogt, and D. Short (2008). *Making content comprehensible for English learners: The SIOP® model* (3rd ed.). Boston: Allyn & Bacon.

Building Background

7. *Concepts explicitly linked* to students' background experiences
8. *Links explicitly made* between past learning and new concepts
9. *Key vocabulary emphasized* (e.g., introduced, written, repeated, and highlighted for students to see)

Comprehensible Input

10. *Speech* appropriate for students' proficiency level (e.g., slower rate, enunciation, and simple sentence structure for beginners)
11. *Explanation* of academic task clear
12. Uses a variety of *techniques* to make content concepts clear (e.g., modeling, visuals, hands-on activities, gestures, body language)

Strategies

13. Provides ample opportunities for students to use *strategies*
14. Consistent use of *scaffolding* techniques throughout lesson, assisting and supporting student understanding (e.g., think-alouds)
15. Teacher uses a variety of *question types, including those that promote higher order thinking skills* (e.g., literal, analytical, and interpretive questions)

Interaction

16. Frequent opportunities for *interactions* and discussion between teacher/student and among students, which encourage elaborated responses about lesson concepts
17. *Grouping configurations* support language and content objectives of the lesson
18. Consistently provides sufficient *wait time for students' responses*
19. Ample opportunities for students to *clarify key concepts in L1* as needed with aide, peer, or L1 text

Practice and Application

20. Provides *hands-on* materials and/or manipulatives for students to *apply content and language knowledge* in the classroom
21. Provides activities for students to *apply content and language knowledge* in the classroom
22. Uses activities that integrate all *language skills* (e.g., reading, writing, listening, and speaking)

Lesson Delivery

23. *Content objectives* clearly supported by lesson delivery
24. *Language objectives* clearly supported by lesson delivery
25. *Students engaged* approximately 90% to 100% of the period
26. *Pacing* of the lesson appropriate to the students' ability level

Review and Assessment

27. Comprehensive *review* of key vocabulary
28. Comprehensive *review* of key content concepts
29. Regularly provides *feedback* to students on their output (e.g., language, content, work)
30. Conducts *assessment* of student comprehension and learning of all lesson objectives (e.g., spot checking, group response) throughout the lesson

GLOSSARY

Acquisition Versus Learning Hypothesis   Describes language acquisition as a process that does not require conscious grammatical rules or drills. Meaningful interaction in the target language produces natural communication. Learning a language, on the other hand, is a formal process through the use of grammar rules.

Active participation   When the student takes an active role in the classroom participation.

Affective Filter Hypotheses   States that only when learners feel secure and comfortable enough does the language acquisition process work. If learners are bored, angry, frustrated, unmotivated, or stressed out, they cannot be receptive to language input, and so they screen the input. This screen is referred to as the *affective filter*. Teachers need to try to maintain a low affective filter so that learning can take place.

Algorithmic process   The process used in calculating math, such as division or subtraction.

American paradigm   When, in true intercultural competence, one knows the rules of American culture and will avoid making inappropriate social or cultural mistakes.

Approximate (v)   When language learners cannot reproduce the sound perfectly (often because they cannot hear it correctly), they make the sound the best way they can. The sound is not exact, but it is approximate. So the language learner *approximates* the sound that he or she interprets. (People who are deaf often approximate the sounds they cannot hear.)

Basic Interpersonal Communication Skills (BICS)   Often referred to as "playground English" or "survival English." It is the basic language ability required for face-to-face communication on a social level. Dr. Jim Cummins is the researcher who first coined this phrase, based on his research measuring native English speakers' standardized tests compared to English learners' test scores on standardized tests. He found that ELLs can pick up social language pretty quickly and sound like native speakers, which is confusing when they cannot do well academically on standardized tests.

Behaviorist theory   A belief based on work by psychologist B. F. Skinner, who posited that behavior is learned by imitation. This theory was applied to language learning, where the belief was that language is learned by imitation.

Bidet (French, pronounced bee-day)   A bathroom fixture similar in design to a toilet with water faucets, straddled for bathing the genitals and the posterior parts.

Bien educado (Spanish)   Cultured, ladylike, polite, and well mannered.

Body language   Describes gestures and facial expressions that show nonverbal communication.

Bottom up   The individual study of grammatical structures or sentence structures. It focuses on small components of the language (individual sounds, morphemes, or words) in order to interpret the whole message. This phrase is used in reading as well, as opposed to "top down," where you read the whole text and try to make global sense of what you are reading.

Brain-based research   Forwards the idea that adults and children use different parts of their brain to learn a second language.

Brain-based theories   Theories based on the belief that the structures and functions of the brain influence language acquisition and how language is used.

Brown v. the Board of Education of Topeka, Kansas   In 1954, the Supreme Court decision in case of *Brown v. Board of Education of Topeka, Kansas* provided the legal basis for equal educational opportunity. The Court ruled that "in the field of public education, the doctrine of 'separate but equal' has no place. Separate education facilities are inherently unequal. We hold that the plaintiffs and others similarly situated are by reason of the segregation complained of deprived of the equal protection of the laws guaranteed by the Fourteenth Amendment."

Chaemyon (Korean)   Describes how Koreans keep their self-esteem according to the perspectives of others, or living up to the expectations of others. In social situations, there is an expectation of behavior that people must adhere to in order to save face in the culture.

Chronemics   The study of the use of time in nonverbal communication.

Code-switching   Any switching between languages in the course of a conversation. The speaker may start in one language and go back and forth between two languages.

Cognitive Academic Language Proficiency (CALP)   The language ability required for successful academic achievement. Dr. Jim Cummins researched the standardized test scores for native English speakers and compared them to English learners. He found that it can take 5 to 7 years for NNS to catch up to native English speakers in academic achievement. Without academic language, ELLs are at risk of dropping out of high school since they speak English well socially but lack the academic vocabulary to be successful. *See also* BICS.

Cognitive process   The mental activities people's brains are engaging in when they are making intellectual sense of something. Each person's mental process is based on the person's own schema, background, or experience.

Cognitive styles   Individual differences in mentally processing and analyzing information, in knowledge, and in reactions to teaching and learning styles.

Common underlying proficiency (CUP)   Cummins explains his theory by noting how the first language helps learners with skills in the second language. Once a task is learned in the native language, the knowledge will be transferred to the second language. The only problem may be new vocabulary or idioms, but not the concept.

Communicative competence   The ability to communicate correctly in the target language and speaker know-how in using the language appropriately in all social and cultural contexts.

Compadrazgo   In the Hispanic cultures, the idea of godparents or coparents "compadrazgo" carries a more significant meaning than the English "godparent."

Comprehensible content or input   When learners acquire language by being given the appropriate, understandable input. The input should be easy enough that they can understand, but just beyond their level of competence. Krashen included this stage in his Monitor Model Theory and depicted it "I" + "i."

Confucianism   The religion based on the teachings of Confucius that seeks to delineate the nature of a life worth living. It emphasizes the importance of human relationships—those within the family, between friends, and those between governments and their citizens. Confucius' ideas set out the desired ethical character of human beings and how they relate to others. Cultures that live under the beliefs of Confucianism showed this influence in all areas of life, such as government, education and public relationships.

Context clues   Sources of information that help students understand what they don't know by using clues to identify the answers.

Critical framing   When learners evaluate what they have learned by critiquing their own work.

Critical period   A concept proposed by G. H. Lennenberg that language can be acquired only within a certain time frame, usually from early infancy to puberty. Other language researchers have applied this hypothesis to L2 learners as well as Ll.

Cultural cues   Information one receives that give one an idea about meaning in other cultures. With cultural clues, we are better able to negotiate within another culture.

Culture shock   A sense of confusion and frustration with feelings of anxiety that may affect people who come from a different environment or culture without adequate preparation. Manifestations of culture shock can by physical, emotional, or mental.

de facto ESOL teachers   Teachers who are not officially ESOL teachers but have English learners in a classroom and are responsible their academic success. Therefore, the teacher is a "de facto" ESOL teacher.

Deep culture   Cultural norms that are not easily detected unless one is born and raised in that specific culture or spends an extended amount of time in the culture.

Don   A term used with the first name of a man to show respect in Hispanic etiquette, as in *Don José*.

Doña   The feminine equivalent of *Don*, as in *Doña Rosa*.

ELL (English language learner)   Student whose first language is not English and who is in the process of learning English.

Embedded   When an item is built into an idea or concept. For example, context clues are embedded in the text. By reading the text, you can figure out the meaning.

English as a second language (ESL)   An educational approach in which English language learners are instructed in the use of the English language. Their instruction is based on a special curriculum that typically involves little or no use of the native language, focuses on language (as opposed to content), and is usually taught during specific school periods. Students may be in an ESL program or receive ELL support while they are in a mainstream or bilingual class.

ESOL (English for speakers of other languages)   Another, more accurate, term for ESL.

Ethnocentrism   When one feels one's ethnic group or culture is superior to all others.

Febles   Haitian Creole for "feeling weakness."

Feita   Diminutive in Spanish meaning "little ugly girl."

Field-dependent learners   Learners characterized as global, socially sensitive, and interpersonally oriented learners who like to work with others to achieve a common goal.

Field-independent learners   Learners characterized as being analytical self-reliant, and impersonal in orientation. They work well individually.

Five Pillars   One of the principal tenets of Islam, consisting of acceptance of the creed, prays, almsgiving, fasting during Ramadan, and pilgrimage to Makkah (also known as Mecca).

Flaco   Spanish for "emaciated, shrunken, or skinny one."

Foreigner talk   The simplified way of talking native English speakers use with English learners to be sure they are understood.

Formalism   A concept that emphasizes accuracy in speaking rather than fluency. These students will not answer questions in another language for fear of making a mistake.

Formative assessment   A type of evaluative process that helps guide teachers in collecting and analyzing student work to determine that students understand.

Fossilized error   A language error becomes permanent if the student never gets corrective feedback. The error may not affect communication or comprehension.

Generation 1.5   Students who come from other countries and enter the U.S. school system while still learning English, usually in their teens or middle school age. Immigrants who are students educated in the U.S. educational system while they are still in the process of learning English. They share characteristics of both first and second generation immigrants

Gordito* or *Gordita   In Spanish, adding "ito" (for a male) or "ita" (for a female) can soften the meaning of an adjective such as fat (*gordito/gordita*), ugly (*feito/feita*), or old (*viejito/viejita*).

Graphic organizer   A visual guide, graph, chart, or aid that helps prepare a student before, during, or after the lesson. It can provide prior knowledge for the lesson and offer cues to listen or look for to remind students of what they are learning.

Gurus   Teachers of the Holy Scripture, language, and science in Indian culture, regarding education as a holy duty.

Halal   Arabic for "lawful" or "permitted," referring to food that is permissible to consume during Ramadan.

Hands-on activites   Any instructional activites used when students work with objects relevant to the content being studied.

Hangul   Another name for the Korean language. It's alphabet is very different from the Romanic alphabet, which confuses Korean students trying to learn English.

Haptics   Refers to communicating through touch.

Heterogeneously   The grouping together of students who have varying abilities, interests, or ages.

High context   Refers to people of a certain culture who do not communicate verbally but understand each other by a look or a nod of the head.

High involvement with a low considerateness   When people of certain cultures talk and interrupt each other without being bothered by who interrupts them; they all talk at once.

High-stakes testing   The primary method of monitoring and improving school performance, usually gauged by grades students make on standardized tests.

Hijab* or *Chador   A scarf that covers the heads of some Muslim women.

Home culture   The culture one gets from the home and one's environment.

Incongruence   Discord or disharmony when people, cultures, or teacher and students are not in agreement.

Indigenous child   One who is native to the land. In the United States, indigenous children can be American Indian, Alaska Native, First Nations, Inuit, and Métis.

Input Hypothesis   The idea that language is acquired by receiving comprehensible input (one of the theories in Krashen's Monitor Model). That is, we have to receive input that is just beyond our competence but not beyond our understanding. According to Krashen, language is acquired through the learner's efforts to understand or comprehend the L2, rather than through trying to use the L2. Speaking and writing are simply the end products of the learner's attention to input.

Jaw-breaker   Slang term for a word that is hard to pronounce.

Kafiyyeh   What some Muslim men wear as traditional headpieces to demonstrate pride in their cultural identity, usually carries no religious significance.

Kinesics   The study of body language; refers to nonverbal communication, including gestures, facial expressions, and stances.

Kinesthetic objective   An objective that utilizes the intelligence reflected in body movement or active participation.

KWL chart   A graphic organizer in the form of a chart. Teachers elicit information from the students by asking them to complete the following descriptions: *K* stands for what one knows about a subject; *W* stands for what one wants to know about a subject; and *L* is identifying what one has learned about the subject.

L1   The native language of the speaker.

L2   The second language that the speaker is trying to learn.

Language Experience Approach (LEA)   A literacy strategy that allows the students to dictate a story, which allows them to see their verbalization in written from. The student can then utilize his or her own language as reading material.

Language interference   The negative effect of language learners' first language on their production of the language they are learning.

Lau v. Nichols   A legal suit filed by Chinese parents in San Francisco in 1974 that led to a landmark Supreme Court ruling that identical education does not constitute equal education under the Civil Rights, and as a result, school systems must provide remedies that afford equal educational access regardless of native language.

Lavman   Haitian Creole for "enema," used to purify the inner body.

Learning style   An individual's preferred way of learning.

Lexicon   The words of a language, or its vocabulary.

Loas or *Iwas* (Haitian Creole, based on African origin)   A spirit that can be called upon to help families, bring good fortune, and protect from or attack enemies. In return, families leave gifts such as food, drink, or flowers.

Low context   Cultures that are considered low context include those of North America and much of Western Europe. Communication is direct and verbalized so that the meaning of participants is absolutely clear.

Low involvement with high considerateness   Characterizes a culture in which one does not disrupt a person speaking, listens politely, will show interest, and speaks one at time.

Mainstream classroom   Typical classroom with native English speakers. No accommodations are made for ELLs.

Mainstream culture   The majority culture of the mainstream population; in the United States this refers to native English speakers, usually Caucasian.

Maldyok   The Haitian Creole word for "evil eye," which is brought on a result of an envious glance from another.

Masjid   Mosque for midday prayers.

MATESOL   Master of Arts in Teaching English as a Second Language. A master's degree in the study of English as a second language.

Meyer v. Nebraska   Court case in which German Lutherans filed suit against Nebraska. The Supreme Court ruled in June 1923 that forbidding teaching non-English speakers until the eighth grade violated liberty under the 14th amendment.

Modals   Auxiliary verbs used with another word to indicate its mood. Words such as *can, may, might, must, should,* and *would* are modals.

Monitor Hypothesis   Principles of learning language according to Krashen. This hypothesis refers to a supposed error-correcting mechanism in the brain that edits the utterance of language learners and helps a learner to focus on the correct form. The "editing" or repair of the error takes place only when the learner knows the correct rules of the language.

Monochronic   Refers to a culture that prefers to make one sound or complete one action at a time.

Monolingual teacher   A teacher who has knowledge of only his or her native language.

Morphology   The study of how words are formed.

Motherese (or Parentese)   A social environment with truncated speech that is believed to promote an understanding of speech between parent and child.

Mullahs   Islamic clergy who teach religious law and doctrine.

Nativist theory   Noam Chomsky's idea that children are born with the basic capacity to learn language biological patterned in the brain (LAD-language acquisition device).

Natural Order Hypothesis   According to Krashen, language is learned in a predictable sequence.

Negative transfer   The errors that language learners make when mistakenly transferring first language knowledge to the second language.

Nonmainstream culture   Refers to individuals coming from cultures other than the mainstream or dominant culture.

**Nunchi*   In Korean culture, the subtle art of listening and gauging another's mood.

Paralinguistics   The elements outside or beyond speech that effect and modify vocal speech.

Parallel distributed processing (PDP)   Language learning takes place in different parts of the brain.

Parentese   *See* motherese.

Participation structure   Class participation and interaction in the classroom. Each culture has different expectations about when, where, and how to speak in the classroom. Students must learn what expectations are acceptable in a U.S. classroom.

Pe Lebren or Pere Lebrun   In Haiti, refers to a tire being used as a burning barricade or a mode of execution. A tire is placed around the victim's neck and lit on fire, particularly during political unrest.

Personal independence   A trait that is prominent in U.S. culture and encouraged in U.S. students.

Phonology   The study of the sound system of a language.

Plasaj   In Haitian cultures, the most common form of marriage among the lower socioeconomic class; it is a kind of common law marriage.

Pocket door   A door that slides between the walls instead of opening in or out.

Polychromic cacophony   Multiple sounds at once.

Polychronic   When multiple tasks are done simultaneously.

Positive transfer   When language learners successfully transfer knowledge of their first language to their second language. We will not be aware this is taking place because the student does not make an error.

Pragmatic rules   The rules of a culture that determine the underlying meaning of communication or indirect speech.

Pragmatics   How people use words and language within a culture.

Project-based activities   Activities, such as role playing or putting on a play, in which students show knowledge by creating the activity, often through their own research and writing.

Proxemics   The study of personal distances maintained by speakers and their use of personal space both consciously and unconsciously.

Ramadan   The Muslim religious holiday that takes place during the ninth month of the Islamic calendar. Observers fast and do not eat or drink anything from dawn until sunset.

Reliable   When a test is considered reliable, it means that the test consistently measures the same thing every time it is used; therefore, it is a reliable measure.

Sadhus   Holy men of India.

Scaffold   An instructional technique in which the teacher breaks a complex task into smaller manageable tasks, then models how they should be done. Students receive support until they are able to do the task alone. A scaffold helps the student until it is not needed, thus promoting success.

Schema   An outline, diagram, plan, or preliminary draft. When referring to students, it is prior knowledge from the student's individual background. A student's schema will determine how he or she makes sense out of the world.

Semantics   Word and phrase meanings in communication. People give meaning to words that often is not literal, that is, that has an "insider" meaning not obvious to the language learner.

Semitic   A subfamily of the Afro-Asiatic language family that includes Hebrew, Aramaic, Arabic, and Amharic.

Sheltered English or Sheltered Instruction   An instructional approach used to make academic instruction in English understandable to English language learners by using scaffolding and special instructional strategies.

Sheltered Instruction Observation Protocol (SIOP)   A format that incorporates language and academic teaching in a specialized lesson plan. The SIOP plan incorporates language and content objectives.

Silent stage   An early stage in the second language acquisition process during which the learner is silent while listening and internalizing the sounds of the new language and which is part of a natural process that the learner goes through at his or her own speed.

Social interactionist theory   Refers to children who learn language by socially interacting with others.

Special education (or exceptional education)   Programs designed to help students with learning disabilities of exceptional students

Stereotyping   Preconceived ideas about a particular social group or culture that are usually based on physical or verbal appearance.

Summative evaluation   The process of measuring learning achievement after a specified task that utilized specific objectives, materials, and methods.

Surface culture   Cultural differences that can be seen through native dress, food, music, etc.

Syntax   The acceptable pattern of the parts of speech in a language; common grammatical patterns or word order.

Tag question   A form of question followed by a mini-question. The whole sentence is a "tag question," and the mini-question at the end is called a "question tag": *e.g., You like candy, don't you? You didn't eat candy, did you?* English learners have problems forming or answering these types of questions because when the main part of the sentence is negative, the tag is positive. Conversely, when the sentence is positive, the tag part is negative.

Target language   The language that a student is learning as a second or additional language. For English language learners in the United States the target language is English.

Task-oriented   When a person is motivated to finish a project or task.

Thematic approach   The instruction of curriculum around themes. Thematic instruction integrates content such as reading, math, and science within the exploration of a broad subject.

Tirando piropos   The accepted common occurrence in some Hispanic cultures of making flattering remarks to women.

Top down   The studying of language (or in reading a text) as a whole without worrying about the individual components of language. The learner is trying to understand using cues such as intonation, tone of voice, or body language without focusing on specific words and structures.

Total Physical Response (TPR)   An approach to teaching a foreign language through physical actions. James Asher made this a popular method of teaching through commands.

Vaastu Shastra   In India a line of thought based on promoting harmony between physical and metaphysical flows of energy.

Valid   Refers to a test that measures what it is supposed to measure.

Viejito   A Spanish diminutive that means "little old man."

Vodou or Voodoo   A religion that combines African spiritual beliefs with rituals derived from Roman Catholic symbols.

Yut Nori   An ancient traditional Korean board game played during Korean New Year.

REFERENCES

Ableza Native American Arts and Media Institute, San Jose, CA. (1998). *Tips for teachers.* Retrieved January 1, 2004, from www.ableza.org/index.shtml, and www.ableza.org/dodont.html

Adeed, P., & Smith, G. P. (1997). Arab Americans: Concepts and materials. In J. A. Banks (Ed.), *Teaching strategies for ethnic studies.* Boston: Allyn and Bacon.

American-Arab Anti-Discrimination Committee (ADC). (1993a). *Educational outreach and action guide: Working with school systems.* Washington, DC: Author.

American-Arab Anti-Discrimination Committee. (1997). *1996–1997 Report on hate crimes and discrimination against Arab Americans.* Washington, DC: Author.

Anderson, J. A. (1988). Cognitive styles and multicultural populations. *Journal of Teacher Education, 24* (1), 2–9.

Ariza, E. N. (2000). Actions speak louder than words—Or do they? Debunking the myth of apathetic immigrant parents in education. *Contemporary Education, 71* (3), 36–38.

Ariza, E. N. (2002). Cultural considerations: Immigrant parent involvement. *Kappa Delta Pi Record, 38* (3), 134–137.

Ariza, E. N., Morales-Jones, C.,Yahya, N., Zainuddin, H. (2002). *Why TESOL ? Theories and issues in teaching English to speakers of other languages in K–12 classroom* (3rd ed.). Dubuque, IA: Kendall Hunt.

Asher, J. (1972). Children's first language as a model for second language learning. *Modern Language Journal, 56,* 133–139.

Asian American Almanac. (1995). Detroit, MI: Gale Research.

Axtell, J. (1988) *After Columbus: Essays in ethnohistory of colonial North America. New York:* Oxford University Press.

Axtell, R. E. (1998). *Gestures: The do's and taboos of body language around the world.* New York: John Wiley & Sons.

Bachman, L. F. (1990). *Fundamental considerations in language testing.* Reading, MA: Addison-Wesley.

Baik, Y., & Chung, J. Y. (1996, March). Family policy in Korea. *Journal of Family and Economic Issues, 17* (1), 93–112.

Baker, C. (1996). *Foundations of bilingual education and bilingualism.* England: Clevedon Multilingual Mattus.

Banks, J. A. (2001). *Cultural diversity and education* (4th ed.). Boston: Allyn and Bacon.

Banks, J. A., & Banks, C. A. (1993). *Multicultural education: Issues and perspective* (2nd ed.). Boston: Allyn and Bacon.

Baruth, L. G., & Manning, M. L. (1992). *Multicultural education of children and adolescents.* Boston: Allyn and Bacon.

Bennett, C. I. (Ed.). (1990). *Comprehensive multicultural education: Theory and practice.* Boston: Allyn and Bacon.

Bialystock, E. (1978). A theoretical model of second language learning. *Language Learning, 28* (1), 69–83.

Bloom, B.S., et al. (Eds.). (1984). *Taxonomy of educational objectives. Book 1: Cognitive domain.* White Plains, NY: Longman.

Brand, D. (1987, August 31). The new whiz kids. *Time, 130,* 42–51.

Brinton, D. M., Snow, M. A., & Wesch, M. B. (1989). Content-based second language instruction. New York: Newbury House.

Brown v. the Board of Education of Topeka, Kansas, 347 U.S. 483, 74 S. Ct. 686 (1954); 349 U.S. 294, 75 S. Ct. 853 (1955).

Brown, H. D. (1994a). *Principles of language learning and teaching* (3rd ed.). Englewood Cliffs, NJ: Prentice Hall Regents.

Brown, P. L. (1998, December 31). Where the spirits of vodou feel at home. *New York Times,* B1, B18.

Burt, M., Peyton, J. K., & Adams, R. (2003). *Reading and adult English language learners: A review of the research.* Washington, DC: National Center for ESL Literacy Education & Center for Applied Linguistics.

Cadiero-Kaplan, K. (2004). *The literacy curriculum and bilingual education: A critical examination.* New York: Peter Lang.

Canale, M., & Swain, M. (1980). Theoretical bases of communicative language approaches to second language teaching and testing. *Applied Linguistics, 1,* 1–47.

Cantoni-Harvey, G. (1987). *Content-area language instruction: Approaches and strategies.* Reading, MA: Addison-Wesley.

Capps, L. R., & Gage, M. S. (1987). Mathematics spoken here. A case for language and vocabulary in mathematics (pp. 4–6). In Houghton Mifflin (Ed.), *Current issues in mathematics.* Boston: Houghton Mifflin.

Capps, L. R., & Pickreign, J. (1993). Language connections in mathematics: A critical part of mathematics instruction. *Arithmetic Teacher, 41* (1), 8–12.

Carrell, P. (1983). Some issues in studying the role of schemata, or background knowledge, in second language comprehension. *Reading in a Foreign Language, 1,* 81–92.

Chamot, A., & O'Malley, M. (1987). A cognitive academic language learning approach: A bridge to the mainstream. *TESOL Quarterly, 21,* 227–249.

Choi, S. (1991). Children's answers to yes-no questions, a developmental study in French and English [Electronic version]. *Developmental Psychology, 27,* 407–420.

Chomsky, N. (1979). *Language and responsibility.* New York: Pantheon.

Civan, M. B. (1995). *Haitians' history and culture.* Coconut Creek, FL: Educavision.

Coker, D. M. (1988). The Asian students in the classroom. *Education and Society, 1* (3),. 19–20.

Colin, J. M., & Paperwalla, G. (1996). Haitians. In J. G. Lipson, S. L. Dibble, & P. A. Minarik (Eds.), *Culture and nursing care: A pocket guide* (pp. 139–154). San Francisco: UCSF Nursing Press.

Collier, V. P. (1989). How long? A synthesis of research on academic achievement in a second language. *TESOL Quarterly, 23,* 509–532.

Collier, V. P. (1992). A synthesis of studies examining long-term language minority student data on academic achievement. *Bilingual Research Journal, 16* (1–2), 187–212.

Comer, J. P. (1984). Home–school relationships as they affect the academic success of children. *Education and Urban Society, 71,* 323–337.

Coriel, J. (1983). Parallel structures in professional and folk health care: A model applied to rural Haiti. *Culture, Medicine and Psychiatry, 7* (2), 131–151.

Coriel, J., Barnes-Josiah, D. L., & Cayemittes, A. (1996). Arrested pregnancy syndrome in Haiti: Findings from a national survey. *Medical Anthropology Quarterly, 10* (3), 424–436.

Cosgray, R. E. (1995). Haitian Americans. In J. N. Giger & R. E. Davidhizar (Eds.), *Transcultural nursing: Assessment and intervention* (pp. 501–523). St. Louis, MO: Mosby.

Council of Chief State School Officers (CCSSO). (1992). *Recommendations for improving the assessment and monitoring of students with limited English proficiency.* Washington, DC: Author.

Council on American-Islamic Relations (CAIR). (1997). *An educator's guide to Islamic religious practices.* Washington, DC: Author.

Craan, A. G. (1988). Toxicologic aspects of vodou in Haiti. *Biomedical and Environmental Sciences, 1* (4), 372–381.

Crandall, J. A. (1993). Content-centered learning in the United States. *Annual Review of Applied Linguistics, 13,* 111–126.

Crawford, J. (1999) *Bilingual education: History, politics, theory, and practice* (4th ed.). Los Angeles, CA: Bilingual Education Services.

Crawford, J. & Krashen, S. (2007). *English learners in American classrooms: 101 questions, 101 answers.* New York: Scholastic.

CultureGrams. (2001). *CultureGrams 2002 Standard Edition* (2 vols). Chicago: Ferguson Publishing.

Cummins, J. (1981a). Age on arrival and immigrant second language learning in Canada: A reassessment. *Applied Linguistics, 2,* 132–149.

Cummins, J. (1981b). The role of primary language development in promoting educational success for language minority students. In C. F. Leyba (Ed.), *School and language minority students: A theoretical framework* (pp. 3–49). Los Angeles: Evaluation, Dissemination and Assessment Center, CSULA.

Cummins, J. (1982). *Tests, achievement and bilingual students.* Wheaton, MD: National Clearinghouse for Bilingual Education.

Cummins, J. (1984). Wanted: A theoretical framework for relating language proficiency to academic achievement among bilingual students. In C. Rivera (Ed.), *Language proficiency and academic achievement.* Clevedon England: Multilingual Matters.

Cummins, J. (1994). The role of primary language development in promoting educational success for language minority students. In C. F. Leyba (Ed.), *Schooling and language minority students: A theoretical framework* (2nd ed., pp. 3–48). Los Angeles: California State University, National Evaluation, Dissemination and Assessment Center.

Dale, T., & Cuevas, G. (1992). Integrating mathematics and language learning. In P. Richard-Amato & M. Snow (Eds.), *The multicultural classroom*. White Plains, NY: Longman.

Damas, D. (Ed.). (1984). *Handbook of North American Indians—arctic*. Washington, DC: Smithsonian Institution.

DeGeorge, G. P. (1988). Assessment and placement of language minority students: Procedures for mainstreaming. *Equity and Excellence, 23* (40), 44–56.

Delgado-Gaitan, C. (1991). School matters in the Mexican American home: Involving parents in the school: A process for empowerment. *American Journal of Education, 100* (1), 20–46.

dePaula, T., Lagana, K., & Gonzalez-Ramirez, L. (1996). Mexican Americans. In J. Lipson, S. Dibble, & P. Minarik (Eds.), *Culture and nursing care: A pocket guide* (pp. 203–221). San Francisco: UCSF Nursing Press.

DeSantis, L., & Thomas, J. T. (1990). The immigrant Haitian mother: Transcultural nursing perspective on preventive health care for children. *Journal of Transcultural Nursing, 2* (1), 2–15.

Diaz, C. (1989). Hispanic cultures and cognitive styles: Implications for teachers. *Multicultural Leader, 2*(4), 1–4.

Diaz-Rico, L., & Weed, K. (1995). *The cross-cultural lauguage and academic handbook*. Boston: Allyn and Bacon.

Dunn, R., & Dunn, K., (1978). *Teaching students through their individual learning styles: A practical approach*. Reston, VA: Reston Publishing.

Dunn, R., & Griggs, S. (1990). Research on the learning style characteristics of selected racial and ethnic groups. *Reading, Writing, and Learning Disabilities, 6*, 261–280.

Echevarria, J., Vogt, M. E., & Short, D. (2004). *Making content comprehensible for English learners: The SIOP model*. Boston: Allyn and Bacon.

Fillmore, L. W., & Snow, C. E. (2000). *What teachers need to know about language*. Retrieved August 1, 2004, from www.cal.org/resources/teachers/teachers.pdf

Fitz-Gibbon, J., & Garcia, E. (2003, July 15). Many Hispanics eschew racial categories, study finds. *The Journal-News.Com*. Retrieved November 10, 2003, from www.nyjournalnews.com/071503/a0115hispanicrace.html

Frank, M., & Jones, R. (2002). *Harcourt science*. Orlando, FL: Harcourt.

Freeman, Y., Freeman, D., & Mercuri, S. (2002). *Closing the achievement gap: How to reach limited formal schooling and long-term English learners*. Portsmouth, NH: Heinemann.

Garcia, S., & Malkin, D. (1993). Toward defining programs and services for culturally and linguistically diverse learners in special education. *Teaching Exceptional Children, 26* (1), 52–58.

Gardner, H. (1993). *Multiple intelligences: The theory in practice*. New York: Basic Books.

George, P., & Aronson, R. (2003). *How do educators' cultural belief systems affect underserved students' pursuit of postsecondary education?* The Pathways to College Network and Clearinghouse. Retrieved August 2, 2004, from www.pathwaystocollege.net/graphics/pathways_label.gif

Gollnick, D. M., & Chinn, P. (1990). *Multicultural education in a pluralistic society* (3rd ed.). New York: Merrill.

Goodman, A. (1997). *Korean Online. Korean grammar*. I. Retrieved on November 9, 2003, from www.sigmainstitute.com/koreanonline/grammar.shtml

Grant, C. A., & Sleeter, C. E. (1989). *Turning on learning: Five approaches for multicultural teaching plans for race, class, gender, and disability*. Columbus, OH: Merrill.

Hakuta, K., & Pease-Alvarez, C. (1992). Enriching our views of bilingualism and bilingual education. *Educational Researcher, 21*, 4–6.

Hall, E. T. (1959). *The silent language*. Garden City, NY: Anchor Press/Doubleday.

Hall, E. T. (1966). *The hidden dimension*. New York: Doubleday.

Hall, E. T. (1983). *The dance of life*. Garden City, NY: Anchor Press/Doubleday.

Hall, E. T. (1990). *Understanding cultural differences*. Yarmouth, ME: Intercultural Press.

Harklau, L., Losey, K. M, & Siegal, P. (Eds.). (1999). *Generation 1.5 meets college composition: Issues in the teaching of writing to US-educated learners of ESOL*. Mahwah, NJ: Lawrence Erlbaum.

Harris, W. J., & Schultz, P. N. B. (1986). *The special education resource program: Rationale and implementation*. Columbus, OH: Merrill.

Hauptman, L. (1995). *Tribes and tribulations, misconceptions about American Indians and their histories*. Albuquerque: University of New Mexico Press.

Herrera, S. G., Murry, K. G., & Morales Cabral, R. (2007). *Assessment accommodations for classroom teachers of culturally and linguistically diverse students*. Boston: Allyn and Bacon.

Hill, J., & Flynn, K. (2006). *Classroom instruction that works with English language learners*. Alexandria, VA: Association for Supervision and Curriculum Development.

Hoover, J. J., & Collier, C. (1989). Methods and materials for bilingual special education. In L. M. Baca & H. T. Cervantes (Eds.), *The bilingual special education interface* (pp. 231–255). Columbus, OH: Merrill.

Huang, G. (1993). Beyond culture: Communicating with Asian American children and families. *ERIC/CUE Digest Number 94* (ED366673).

Hvitfeldt, C. (1986). Traditional culture, perceptual style, and learning: The classroom behavior of Hmong adults. *Adult Education Quarterly, 36*, 65–77.

Hymes, D. (1972). Models of the interaction of language and social life. In J. J. Gumperz & D. Hymes (Eds.), *Directions in sociolinguistics: The ethnography of communication* (pp. 35–71). New York: Holt, Rinehart, & Winston.

Igoa, C. (1995). *The inner world of the immigrant child.* Mahwah, NJ: Lawrence Erlbaum.

Ishii-Jordan, S., & Peterson, R. (1994). Behavior disorders in culture and community. In R. Peterson & S., Isshi-Jordan (Eds.), *Multicultural issues in the education of students with behavioral disorders* (pp. 251–262). Cambridge, MA: Brookline Press.

Jackson, M. L. (1997). Counseling Arab Americans. In C. C. Lee (Ed.), *Multicultural issues in counseling* (2nd ed., pp. 333–352). Alexandria, VA: American Counseling Association.

Kayser, H. (1998). *Assessment and intervention resource for Hispanic children.* San Diego: Singular.

Kim, J. M. (1998). Korean children's concepts of adult and peer authority and moral reasoning [Electronic version]. *Developmental Psychology, 34* (5), 947–955.

Kim, P. H. (2001, June 8). [Korea business culture] Korea viewed by 7 cultural measures. *Digital Chosun-Ilbo.* Retrieved November 10, 2003, from http://english.chosun.com/w21data/html/news/200106/200106080184.html

Kim, Y. Y. (1985). Intercultural personhood: An integration of Eastern and Western perspectives. In L. A. Samovar & R. E. Porter (Eds.), *Intercultural communication: A reader* (4th ed.). Belmont, CA: Wadsworth.

Kim-Rupnow, W. S. (2001). A collaborative project between NTAC-AAPI and the Center for International Rehabilitation Research Information and Exchange (CIRRIE) at the State University of New York at Buffalo [Electronic version]. *Asian Culture Brief: Korea, 2* (1).

Kleinman, A., & Good, B. J. (1985). *Culture and depression.* Berkeley: University of California Press.

Kohls, R. (2001). *Survival kit for overseas living* (4th ed.). Yarmouth, ME: Intercultural Press.

Korean Overseas Information Service. (1997). *History of Hangul.* Retrieved November 9, 2003, from www.sigmainstitute.com/koreanonline/hangul_history3.shtml.

Krashen, S. D. (1978). The monitor model for second language acquisition. In R. C. Gingras (Ed.), *Second language acquisition and foreign language teaching* (pp. 1–26). Arlington, VA: Center for Applied Linguistics.

Krashen, S. D. (1981). *Second language acquisition and second language learning.* Oxford: Pergamon Press.

Krashen, S. D. (1982). *Principles and practice in second language acquisition.* London: Pergamon Press.

Krashen, S. D. (1999). What the research really says about structured English immersion: A response to Keith Baker. *Phi Delta Kappan, 80*, 705–706.

Krashen, S. D. (2002a) The comprehension hypothesis and its rivals. In *Selected papers from the Eleventh International Symposium on English Teaching/Fourth Pan Asian Conference* (pp. 395–404). Taipei: Crane Publishing Company.

Krashen, S. D. (2002b). *Explorations in language acquisition and use: The Taipei lectures.* Taipei: Crane Publishing Company.

Krashen, S. D., & Terrell, T. D. (1983). *The natural approach: Language acquisition in the classroom.* Hayward, CA: Alemany Press.

Kreeft, J. (1984). Dialogue writing—Bridge from talk to essay writing. *Language Arts, 61*, 141–150.

Lambert, W. E., & Tucker, G. R. (1972). *Bilingual education of children.* Rowley, MA: Newbury House.

Lareau, J. (1987). Social class differences in family–school relationships: The importance of cultural capital. *Sociology of Education, 60*, 73–85.

Lau vs. Nichols, 414, U.S. 563 (1974).

Lee, A. (1989). A socio-cultural framework for the assessment of Chinese children with special needs. *Topics in Language Disorders, 9* (30), 38–44.

Lee, G. L. (2003). Understanding immigrated Korean children's educational needs [Electronic version], *Kappa Delta Pi Record, 39* (4), 168–172.

Lee, J. Y. (1996). Some tips for teaching English to Korean students. Presented at the INTESOL Conference, Indiana University, Purdue University, Indianapolis, November 1, 2003. Retrieved November 8, 2003, from www.intesol.org/lee.html

Lennenberg, E. (1974). *Biologic foundations of language.* New York: Wiley.

Lewis, R. B., & Doorlag, D. J. (1987). *Teaching special students in the mainstream.* Columbus, OH: Merrill.

Loewen, J. (1995). *Lies my teacher told me: Everything your American history text got wrong.* New York: Touchstone, Simon and Schuster.

Logan, J. R., Stowell, J., & Vesselinov, V. (2001, October). *From many shores: Asians in Census 2000.* Albany: State University of New York, Albany, Lewis Mumford Center for Comparative Urban and Regional Research.

Los Angeles Times poll, April 13, 1998.

Mandell, C. J., & Gold, V. (1984). *Teaching handicapped students.* St. Paul, MN: West.

Martin, M. A., Rissmiller, P., & Beal, J. A. (1995). Health-illness beliefs and practices of Haitians with HIV disease living in Boston. *JANAC, 6* (6), 45–53.

Matsuda, M. (1989). Working with Asian parents: Some communication strategies. *Topics in Language Disorders, 9* (3), 45–53.

Mazurek, K., & Winzer, M. (2005). *Schooling around the world: Debates, challenges and practices.* Boston: Allyn and Bacon.

McDade, K. (1995). How we parent: Race and ethnic differences. In C. Jacobson (Ed.), *American families: Issues in race and ethnicity* (pp. 283–300). New York: Garland.

McIntyre, T. (1993). Reflections on the impact of the proposed definition for emotional and behavioral disorders: Who will still fall through the cracks and why. *Behavioral Disorders, 18* (2), 148–160.

McIntyre, T. (1995). *The McIntyre assessment of culture: An instrument for evaluating the influence of culture on behavior and learning.* Columbia, MO: Hawthorne Educational Services.

McLaughlin, B. (1980). Theory and research in second language learning: An emerging paradigm. *Language Learning, 30,* 331–350.

Meyer vs. Nebraska, 262 U.S. 390 (1923).

Moon, I. (2001, August 27). For Korean kids, a long trip to school—Why parents are enrolling kids abroad [Electronic version]. *Business Week,* Retrieved October 14, 2008, from www.business week.com/magazine/content/01_35/b3746069.htm

National Clearinghouse for Bilingual Education (NCBE). (1990). *Two-way language development programs.* ERIC Digest. Washington, DC: ERIC/CLL.

National Council of Teachers of Mathematics (NCTM). (2000). *Principles and standards for school mathematics.* Reston, VA: Author.

National School Public Relations Association. (1993). *Capturing the best of the 1993 NSPRA seminar.* Arlington, VA: Author.

New London Group (NLG). (1996). A pedagogy of multiliteracies: Designing social futures. *Harvard Educational Review, 66* (1), 60–92.

No Child Left Behind Act of 2001. 107th Congress of the United States of America. Retrieved August 7, 2004, from www.ed.gov/policy/elsec/leg/esea02/107-110.pdf

Nunan, D. (1989). *Designing tasks for the communicative classroom.* Cambridge, UK: Cambridge University Press.

Nydell, M. (1987). *Understanding Arabs.* Yarmouth, ME: Intercultural Press.

Oberg, K. (1998). Culture shock and the problem of adjustment in new cultural environments. In G. R. Weaver (Ed.), *Culture, communication and conflict: Readings in intercultural relations* (2nd ed., pp. 185–186). Needham Heights, MA: Simon & Schuster.

Ogbu, J. (1988). Class stratification, racial stratification, and schooling. In L. Weiss (Ed.), *Class, race, and gender in American education* (p. 163). Albany: State University of New York Press.

Oh, Y., Koeske, G. F., & Sales, E. (2002). Acculturation, stress, and depressive symptoms among Korean immigrants in the United States. *Journal of Social Psychology, 142* (4), 511–526.

Olsen, L., & Jaramillo, A. (1999). *Turning the tides of exclusion: A guide for educators and advocates for immigrant students.* Oakland, CA: Coast Litho.

Onishi, N. (2003, September 21). Divorce in South Korea striking a new attitude [Electronic version]. *New York Times.* Retrieved October 14, 2008, from http://query.nytimes.com/gst/fullpage.htm/?res-9900E7DA113AF932A1575ACOA9659CBB63

Pajares, F. M. (1992). Teacher's beliefs and educational research: Cleaning up a messy construct. *Review of Educational Research, 62* (3), 307–322.

Pajewski, A., & Enriquez, L. (1996). *Teaching from a Hispanic perspective: A handbook for non-Hispanic adult educators.* Phoenix: Arizona Adult Literacy and Technology Resource Center. Retrieved on August 4, 2004, http://literacynet.org/lp/hperspectives/

Park, E. J. (1995). Voices of Korean-American students [Electronic version]. *Adolescence, 30* (120), 945–953.

Pease-Alvarez, C. (1993). *Moving in and out of bilingualism: Investigating native language maintenance and shift in Mexican-descent children.* Santa Cruz, CA: National Center for Research on Cultural Diversity and Second Language Learning.

Peregoy, S. F., & Boyle, O. F. (2001). *Reading, writing, and learning in ESOL: A resource book for K–12 teachers.* Longman: New York.

Perez, M., Pinzon, H., & Garza, R. (1997). Latino families: Partners for success in school settings. *Journal for School Health, 67* (5), 182–184.

Philips, S. U. (1983). *The invisible culture: Communication in classroom and community on the Warm Springs Indian Reservation.* White Plains, NY: Longman.

Pierre, G. (1971). *American Indian crisis.* San Antonio, TX: The Naylor Company.

Preston, R. A., Materson, B. J., Yoham, M. A., & Anapol, H. (1996). Hypertension in Haitians: Results of a pilot survey of a public teaching hospital multispecialty clinic. *Journal of Human Hypertension, 10* (11), 743–745.

Purcell-Gates, V. (2001). What we know about readers who struggle. In R. F. Flippo (Ed.), *Reading researchers in search of common ground* (pp. 118–143). Newark, DE: International Reading Association.

Ramirez, M., & Castaneda, A. (1974). *Cultural democracy, bicognitive development, and education.* New York: Academic Press.

Rueda, R. S., & Forness, S. R. (1994). Childhood depression: Ethnic and cultural issues in special education. In R. Peterson & S. Ishii-Jordan (Eds.), *Multicultural issues in the education of students with behavioral disorders* (pp. 40–62). Cambridge, MA: Brookline Press.

Rumbaut, R. G., & Ima, K. (1988, January). *The adaptation of Southeast Asian Refugee youth: A comparative study.* Final Report to the U.S. Department of Health and Human Services, Office of Refugee Resettlement. Washington, DC: U.S. Department of Health and Human Services.

Shen, W., & Mo, W. (1997). Parental involvement: A new challenge to Asian-American parents. In *Perspective of Chinese American education in the 21st century* (pp. 59–64). Houston: Chinese American Educational Research and Development Association.

Short, D. J. (1991). *How to integrate language and content instruction: A training manual* (2nd ed.). Washington, DC: Center for Applied Linguistics.

Siu, S. F. (1992). *Taking no chances: Profile of a Chinese-American family's support for success.* Boston: Wheelock College. (ERIC Document Reproduction Service No. ED 361446).

Skinner, B. F. (1957). *Verbal learning.* New York: Appleton-Century-Crofts.

Spolsky, B. (1989). *Conditions for second language learning: Introduction to a general theory.* Oxford, UK: Oxford University Press.

Tharp, R. (1989). Psychocultural variables and constants: Effects of teaching and learning in schools. *American Psychologist, 44* (2), 349–359.

Tharp, R., & Yamaguchi, L. A. (1994). *Effective instructional conversation in Native American classrooms (Educational Practice Report No. 10).* Santa Cruz, CA: National Center for Research on Cultural Diversity and Second Language Learning.

Thomas, W. P., & Collier, V. (2002). *A national study of school effectiveness for language-minority students' long-term academic achievement.* Santa Cruz, CA: Center of Research, Diversity and Excellence.

Tompkins, G. E. (2001). *Literacy for the 21st century: A balanced approach* (3rd ed.). Englewood Cliffs, NJ: Prentice Hall.

Trueba, H. T., & Cheng, L. (1993). *Myth or reality: Adaptive strategies of Asian Americans in California.* Bristol, PA: Falmer Press.

Utley, C. (1983). *A cross-cultural investigation of field-independence/field-dependence as a psychological variable in Menominee Native American and Euro-American grade school children.* Madison: Wisconsin Center for Education and Research.

Valdez, G. (1996). *Con respeto: Bridging the distances between culturally diverse families and schools.* New York: Teachers College Press.

van Kraayenoord, C., & Paris, S. G. (1996). Story construction from a picture book: An assessment activity for young learners. *Early Childhood Research Quarterly, 11* (1), 41–61.

Vogt, L. A., Jordan, C., & Tharp, R.G. (1987). Explaining school failure: Producing school success: Two cases. *Anthropology and Education Quarterly, 18,* 276–286.

Vygotsky, L. S. (1962). *Thought and language.* Cambridge, MA: MIT Press.

Vygotsky, L.S. (1978). *Mind in society.* Cambridge, MA: Harvard University Press.

Watkins, S. (1992). *Native American history, reference manual.* Beverly Hills, CA: Myles.

Wei, T. (1980). *Vietnamese refugee students: A handbook for school personnel.* Cambridge, MA: Lesley College (EDAC).

Wiggins, G., & McTighe, J. (2005). *Understanding by design* (2nd ed.). Alexandria, VA: Association for Supervision and Curriculum Development.

Willis, S. (1993). Multicultural teaching: Meeting the challenges that arise in practice. *Association for Supervision and Curriculum Development Curriculum Update,* September, 1–3, 6.

Wong, S., & Teuben-Rowe, S. (1997). Honoring students' home languages and cultures in a multilingual classroom [Electronic version]. *Sunshine State TESOL Journal* (Fall 1997), 20–26.

Wong-Filmore, L. (1991). When learning a second language means losing the first. *Early Childhood Research Quarterly, 6,* 323–347.

Woo, J. (1985). *The Chinese-speaking student: A composite profile.* New York: Bilingual Education Multifunctional Support Center at Hunter College.

The World Factbook, CIA homepage, country profiles, Haiti. Central Intelligence Agency, Office of Public Affairs, Washington, DC. Retrieved August 6, 2008. www.cia.gov/cia/publications/factbook/index.html

Zemelman, S., Daniels, H., & Hyde, A. A. (1998). *Best practice: New standards for teaching and learning in America's schools.* Portsmouth, NH: Heinemann.

INDEX